Cary looks at Africa and sees it for what it is: a land of poverty—because of wrong agricultural and mining methods—with deserts increasing, fertility of the arable soil declining, rainfall decreasing, forests disappearing. He sees Africa as a land of ignorance and superstition, with a desperate need for education of its people, especially adults. And he sees the dilemma of the African, whose only way of dealing with the modern world is to "have modern knowledge, a modern apparatus of living."

Cary also looks at the world and tries to see how Africa can achieve with the least suffering its inevitable place. He sees emerging after two world wars a new concept of the purpose of government: No longer is it expected merely to maintain peace and dispense justice, but now also to foster industry and bring civilization.

University of Texas Press

The Case for African Freedom

and other writings on Africa by

Joyce Cary

McGraw-Hill Book Company

New York Toronto London

First McGraw-Hill Paperback Edition, 1964.

CONTENTS

MAPS

PREFACE

Brought together here are two small books by Joyce Cary, *The Case for African Freedom* and *Britain and West Africa*, now published for the first time in this country, and three shorter pieces by Cary on Africa. *The Case for African Freedom* was originally published in England in 1941 as a volume in George Orwell's Searchlight Series, and in 1944 the publisher, Secker & Warburg, brought out a considerably revised and enlarged edition. It is this later version which is printed here, along with the brief introduction which Orwell had supplied to the first edition. *Britain and West Africa* was published in 1946 by Longmans, Green as one of a series of pamphlets on the British Commonwealth, and republished the next year with an added appendix. The text of the 1947 edition is followed here. The shorter pieces, all originally published in American magazines, appeared as follows: "Africa Yesterday" in the *Reporter*, May 15, 1951; "Christmas in Africa" in *Esquire*, December, 1953; and "Catching Up with History" in the *Nation*, October 16, 1954.

INTRODUCTION

Joyce Cary's profoundest reflexions on Africa are contained in his novels; the five pieces included in this volume may be read as a supplement to them. *The Case for African Freedom,* published in 1944 (an expanded version of a pamphlet published in 1941), and *Britain and West Africa,* published in 1946 and republished in 1947, are already historical documents. They speak to us from a vanished world. When in 1944 Cary used the phrase "the African powers" he meant the European powers controlling Africa: today the phrase could mean only the independent African states, over twenty of them, scarcely even dreamed of in 1944. When he wrote the sketch of West African history included in *Britain and West Africa* he began with the Europeans who intruded there, as if West Africa had not existed until Europeans noticed it—a viewpoint no serious historian (nor Cary himself were he still alive) could conceivably adopt today. Then, however, it seemed obvious, even inevitable.

Yet, though the African scene has changed immeasurably, these two pieces still illuminate it. They also have real historical value. Cary, one of the finest British novelists of this century, entered the administrative service in Northern Nigeria as a young man in 1913. He served in West Africa until 1920, when he retired from ill health. He revisited the country briefly during World War II, when he was stranded there on his way to Tanganyika, where he helped to make the film *Man of Two Worlds.* Several of his early novels—*Aissa Saved, The American Visitor, The African Witch,* and *Mister Johnson*—have a Northern Nigerian setting. *Mister Johnson,* the best of them, is one of the most moving and perceptive pictures of the British colonial situation ever made.

In these two pamphlets he expounded his vision (the word "blueprint" he explicitly repudiated) of West African development—a rare example of the creative artist working in a political and economic field. *Britain and West Africa,* the shorter of these works, was written to introduce West Africa to British people. It was first published in 1946; a revised version appeared in 1947. It may seem strange that such an introduction was necessary. Yet all through the period of British imperial expansion and domination people in Britain remained curiously ignorant of their Empire, knowing and caring little about the vast territories, the enormous populations, ruled in their name. Cary's pamphlet was news to most of its readers. He begins with a historical survey of West Africa. It is full of errors: the contemporary historian who reads it feels his fingers itch for a blue pencil. But it has been left unchanged in this reprint, if only to illustrate the poverty, during the colonial period, of West African historiography, upon which Cary (no historian himself) had inevitably to rely, and which he revivified with his own wonderful creative powers.

What must have startled his readers most was the last page. Here, in an era when most people still believed implicitly (as some still do) that Africans are incapable of original creative work, that they are only imitators whose own culture must wither away under the impact of Europe, he prophesied that the European impact would stimulate, not stultify, native talents, and that "a new African civilization, new arts, new religion," would emerge in the future.

The Case for African Freedom first appeared in 1941 in the Searchlight Books series edited by George Orwell, who contributed a short laudatory preface; it was revised and enlarged in 1944 (the revised version is reprinted here). In it Cary sets out a coherent policy for the development of Africa. All British Africa is included, but the discussion applies chiefly to West Africa (though there are also interesting sections on Kenya, and on the Union of South Africa, with prescient comments on the probable results of a policy of racial segregation). He insisted that economic development, the usual panacea, was no solution by itself, and could only be effective if the African peoples were also educated to adjust to an industrial society. He was against handing over political power to African leaders before the adjustment was achieved lest the change of power mean merely a change of masters. Political realist enough to perceive the truth of Nkrumah's famous words, "Seek ye first the political kingdom and all things shall be added unto you," he saw its dangers as a principle for immediate action in countries with large illiterate populations.

Cary saw freedom as something positive—as "freedom to," not "freedom from." Hence his dislike of the theorists (there were many at that time in the United States) who demanded that colonial peoples be immediately freed from their shackles without considering what was to become of them afterward. He knew that an illiterate man in a remote African village could no more make use of such theoretical freedom than a paralysed deaf-mute could make use of his "freedom" to stand for Congress.

By 1944 most informed critics of British colonial policy realized this: a collection of articles published in London in 1945 by the Fabian Society, edited by Arthur Creech-Jones, Colonial Secretary in the 1945 Labour Government, makes many of the points Cary was making. What differentiated Cary from them was the personal experience, which enabled him to see West Africa in terms of concrete situations and to analyse problems to be solved at grass-roots level, and his readiness to face (what many liberal-minded people preferred to ignore) the dangers of an educated African elite exploiting the uneducated—a theme he made use of in his novel, *The African Witch.*

Cary thus expressed the perpetual ambivalence of recent British colonial policy, oscillating between a generous desire to give emergent peoples independence and a paternalistic fear that independence must not be given too quickly lest it be misused. Yet he was no paternalist. As a young man in Northern Nigeria he took part in the "Indirect Rule" so widely used in British West Africa—a system by which African rulers were left to govern their peoples in traditional ways, checked and guided by British officials. At first he deeply admired a system that preserved African culture from the disrupting effects of European ideas, and allowed for slow development without any sudden breach in continuity. The letters he wrote as a young district officer display what today seem the narrow, illiberal prejudices against educated Africans then current among his colleagues in Northern Nigeria. But he came to realize that Indirect Rule also allowed obscurantist despots to entrench themselves under the protection of the colonial government, so that old tyrannies were not only perpetuated but strengthened. By the 1940's he saw that it was outdated, that Africa could no longer be preserved intact as in a vast Red Indian reserve, and that it was holding back the spread of the education and the new ideas which Africans had to have if their freedom was to be a positive reality.

He exposed ruthlessly the arguments (one sometimes hears them still in one form or another) for preserving Africans in their "native simplicity"—at best the sentimental dreams of latter-day Rousseau-ists pining for a fantasy-world more beautiful than their own, at worst the specious hypocrisy of those who see that the illiterate and helpless can be easily exploited.

Cary was interpreting to a largely indifferent British public a profound but scarcely noticed revolution that had taken place in British colonial policy. For generations governments in London had insisted that colonies must support themselves and must pay for development plans out of their own revenue or do without. In 1929 it was tentatively made possible, and during the 1940's it became an accepted principle, for British taxpayers' money to be spent to develop the colonies. During and after World War II government money was poured out from Britain to inaugurate and carry on what Cary wanted—education programmes, and the development of medical services, of industry, and of communications. By the standards of today the amount of this aid may seem small. But in the context of the British postwar economy and of a colonial policy traditionally opposed to imperial subsidies, it was revolutionary. Once money was made available, the schemes he outlined—which seemed impracticably expensive to most of his early readers—could be begun in countries hitherto starved of capital, building the foundations for a genuine African freedom.

For the American public, too, Cary interpreted colonial Africa. In an article called "Africa Yesterday" in the *Reporter* for May 15, 1951, he described, with delightful self-ridicule, the problems of a powerful colonial officer in his attempts to rule while preserving local law and custom. Humorously, yet with deep seriousness, he expressed his political wisdom, emphasizing the essential humanness of good government, because "Systems, ultimately, are men," and revealing from his own experience the pitfalls of a chief of state, since "Power does not so much corrupt the ruler as the whole world in which it is compelled to work."

An enforced Christmas in Borgu (after an overdue leave failed to materialize) is recalled in "Christmas in Africa," published in *Esquire* in December, 1953. Here Cary expresses his deep feelings for the people of that remote, strangely beautiful region, and justifies the need for ruling them paternalistically under certain circumstances. We also see him in a more personal light, displaying the sartorial eccentricity for which some British colonial administrators were noted, sitting in court uniformed to the waist: "what I wore beneath the table fell, I considered, into my private domain."

In his review of the late Richard Wright's *Black Power* in the *Nation*, October 16, 1954, Cary leaves reminiscence for the contemporary political scene. (It is, incidentally, typical of the already mentioned historical ignorance of his generation that he should reiterate in it the phrase "Stone Age": iron has been worked in West Africa for at least a thousand, perhaps two thousand, years). Here he again turns to the theme treated in *The African Witch* of the charismatic African leader. It is still too early for us to judge dispassionately the estimate he gives of Nkrumah —but his is nevertheless a verdict many would today unquestioningly accept.

What shines through these pages (as through everything he wrote) is Cary's own humanity, his hatred of the theorist who sees people as statistics or concepts, his compassionate concern with people as individuals, not as abstractions. In his later novels he uses a Chester Nimmo to illustrate the British political scene (so vividly one wonders how historians can leave him out), or a Gully Jimson to illustrate his theories of art. In *The Case for African Freedom* too he illustrates the general by the particular. Individuals he has known spring to life to exemplify his arguments. Reminiscence for its own sake can be unbearably tedious: who does not shut his ears to the raconteur who begins, "I remember a man in Nigeria who . . ."? But here a master storyteller is in charge, and the people he conjures back from his past make his points for him lucidly and dramatically in the concrete empirical way he always followed.

The empirical British tradition which Cary adorned has its pitfalls. There has been so much talk (it has been said) of the British genius for "muddling through" that every British muddler thinks he is contributing to the national genius. But Cary was no muddler. He saw clearly what he hoped the future would bring Africa and explained it in concrete, not abstract, terms.

The future has proved the wisdom of what he wrote. Fortified by large outlay on education and development the British West African colonies evolved along the lines he envisioned—though at a speed he could scarcely have foreseen and possibly would have regretted. Given responsibility, African leaders used it responsibly, as he said they would. Violent revolution was avoided, as he prophesied it could be. Risks were taken, as he insisted they must be, and the case for African freedom was shown to be justified.

Christopher Fyfe

EDINBURGH UNIVERSITY

The Case for African Freedom

Foreword to the 1941 Edition

The Searchlight Books aim at setting forth a coherent policy, and the earlier books in the series have most of them stated in black and white "what one can do" about the particular problem they were tackling. If Mr. Cary's book is more discursive and more detailed than the others, it is because the problem of Africa is so vast and, in England, so little known that a preliminary survey is needed before any policy can be usefully stated. A workable programme can only be based on a knowledge of the actual situation.

Mr. Cary has had long experience as an administrator among primitive African peoples. The title of his book shows where his sympathies lie, but he is first and foremost a realist. He has no use either for the ignorant settler or businessman who secretly regards the African as a slave, or for the left-wing sentimentalist who imagines that the African peoples can be "set free" by a stroke of the pen and that their troubles will thereupon be ended. He knows that the exploitation of the coloured peoples by the whites has got to be ended, and as quickly as possible, and he also knows that in the age of the bombing plane a primitive agricultural people cannot be genuinely independent. In the case of Africa the problem is enormously complicated by cultural and economic differences. In Africa, human beings are living at every level of civilization between the late Stone Age and the twentieth century. There are areas where racial discrimination is more brutal than anywhere in the world, and there are areas where there is no colour-bar at all. Moreover—a problem which does not exist in Asia—there are large communities of white settlers who have lived in Africa for many generations and cannot be left out of the general picture. It is because he so well understands the complexity of the situation that Mr. Cary is especially fitted to plead for African freedom.

He has an unusually independent mind, and many readers will feel a certain relief in reading a book on a political subject by a man who has thought deeply over the problems of our time, and has been above current political movements and their characteristic jargon.

George Orwell

CONTENTS

AFRICA: PHYSICAL

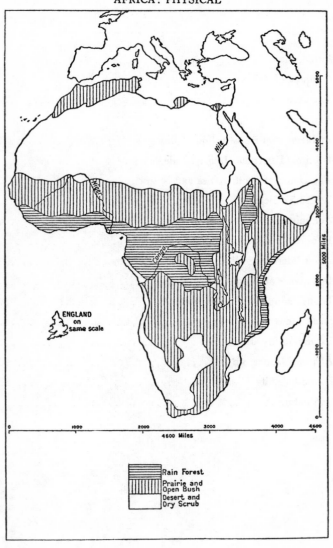

Rain Forest

Prairie and Open Bush

Desert and Dry Scrub

AFRICA: POLITICAL

TO
H. S. W. EDWARDS AND T. F. CARLYLE
OF THE OLD NORTHERN NIGERIAN SERVICE
FROM A GRATEFUL JUNIOR

1:

Introduction

THE ARGUMENT OF THIS BOOK has met with so much support in many different circles that I am glad of the chance, in a new and enlarged edition, to give it further development; and to relate it to the various statements on post-war policy made in the last two years.

But questions and letters, and sometimes even the accord expressed in articles or pamphlets, have shown that that argument is still not entirely clear to all readers, either in its theoretical or practical form.

For instance, to begin with a detail of some importance, economic development, on a wide scale, is now urged from almost every quarter. But many who urge this development, and who write in terms of raw material and local labour, or local industry, forget that economic development is a part of a complex general development; that supply requires a demand; industries need markets; and markets depend on factors which are often more psychological than economic; on habits and customs, taste, and even religious tradition.

When I urged economic development in the first edition, I pointed out how much that development needed a new education, new social services; that is to say, a total development.

Standards of living is a phrase which tends to hide a fundamental truth; that it is not an abstract wage-earner which goes to market, but a real man or woman, with personal needs and tastes. That all political economy depends finally on tastes and needs.

There is now a danger that economic development may become a catchword for escapists; or a slogan for those who care less for people than politics, and cannot be troubled with the problems of African education on the necessary wide scale.

Standards of living cannot be raised in Africa, or anywhere else, without an alteration in the standards of life. Whenever, then, in this book, the phrase "economic development" is used it must be understood to assume, as premise, all those other developments, social and personal, without which it can only be superficial and local.

Secondly, it has been suggested to me, from several quarters, that the use of foreign capital in Africa means exploitation of the African. And I have been asked if it would not be the best means of avoiding the exploitation, to begin with some large devolution of political power to Africans.

Both these suggestions, and others of the same kind, have obviously the same root, in the idea, very deep-rooted in the political thought of recent generations, that there is only one kind of freedom, political and national liberty. This is the source of the notion, isolationist in type, that all employment of African labour, by foreign capital, is exploitation; and also of the belief that freedom can be achieved and developed only in the political quarter.

But the fundamental argument of my book was that social education and economic development by themselves can increase freedom, and that political devolution, except in states already economically developed, usually means a sacrifice of freedom, by the masses, for the benefit of the few. The worst exploitation of native labour, all over the world, in Africa, India, China, has been by native employers; the worst oppressors of the African people have been their own native rulers.

I do not mean that Africans should not take an increasing share in government; but only that political devolution by itself would lead to disaster for the African masses.

I am the more anxious to make this clear because it is the point of the whole book, which seems to me worthless unless it is grasped.

Political science, like psychology, of which it contains so much, is often denied the name of science; because it deals in quantities and qualities which cannot be exactly measured or analysed. This criticism is sound, and a political writer who attempts to make what is half-art and half-metaphysic look like a science is deceiving himself and may deceive others.

But he can, with profit, take from science and logic some hints on method. One is that of definition. He should define for himself and others his standpoint; and he should attempt, if possible, to show how his judgments are formed. He should, as mathematical masters say, show his workings. So I explain now that the control, in the scientific sense, by which I try to measure and adjust all my political thought, is the individual person. In any political question, I ask first, how does this affect the real men on the ground, the people in their private lives?

This plainly is not to confine oneself to economics and education. It is not to cut out such matters as national liberty, racial dignity. But it is to range them all in a certain perspective. And unless a political argument is so arranged, and the principle of arrangement is made perfectly clear, I don't think it worth writing or reading.

For instance, there is at present a direct conflict between two colonial policies, and yet we often find both of them pressed in the same paper. Or if the conflict is noticed at all, it is in those phrases which we hear from discreet people who are anxious to glide past an embarrassing place in conversation.

That method may be necessary in party politics; in a book it is so far from being scientific that it is not honest.

The conflict is between those who desire first of all a general development in Africa; and those who demand first immediate self-government for the colonies. The second group has strong support in the U.S.A.

Each side has of course followers who are not so much interested in African politics, as their own. Many of the first secretly desire to put off the devolution of power to Africans; many of the second secretly or openly desire the destruction of the British Empire.

But there remains in each party a majority of entirely sincere people, wanting what they honestly believe right. The first derives its creed from an ideal sympathy with the African masses, suffering under bad conditions of health and pay; the second, from the ideal of nationalism, which has often handed over those very defenceless poor to local exploiters of the most barbarous type.

The two ideals can therefore be directly opposed. And when the same person puts them forward, he usually contradicts himself. On the other hand, man is not an economic animal. To raise the standard of living among the masses without at the same time enlarging their political responsibilities, may endanger the future of those masses, by producing an unstable polity. Self-government must be a political object; even though it has no direct value in raising standards of life.

A man cannot ride two horses at once. He must ride one and lead the other. So in this case, the horse I ride is the advantage of the masses, the forgotten millions; and self-government is the led horse. In any conflict of ideas, the first sets the pace and the other, though he must follow, follows at that same pace. Readers who think, as many may fairly think, that political devolution should lead the way, can make their own adjustments.

Finally, I might be allowed a personal explanation. It has been suggested, chiefly from official circles, very reasonably and politely, that a man who spent only a few years in the African service, is not qualified to set up as an African expert. But on this point, I am misjudged. I do not write as an African expert who has given his life to African problems, but as a man who, in his African service, made mistakes, who afterwards reflected on that experience and its meaning; who, after ten years of active, thoughtless, and various experience in the world, began, rather late in youth, to ask what it amounted to; to dig up all his foundations, to find out exactly what they were; who discovered then, as you might expect, that some of them were mud, some were hollow caves of air, others sand; and who then slowly and painfully rebuilt them, as far as he could manage the task, as a coherent whole, on which to found a new life and a new mind.

When I was asked in 1931 by the Liberal Committee to write about politics, I at first refused. I had forgotten politics. I was deep in other studies, in philosophy, history, and letters. But when I was offered a free hand to write what I liked, and began to consider politics, I found to my own surprise and, I am afraid, the surprise of the Committee, that the philosophy, since it dealt with realities, led, logically, to a new state theory.

The Committee, to their great honour, but not to my surprise, for a Liberal always expects from Liberals altruism of the finest strain, loyally accepted a work which must have seemed to them bizarre, obscure, and even dangerous to the very ideals of their faith. But perhaps they reflected, wisely, that few would read the book and fewer would understand it.

In the same way, when I was asked three years ago to write about Africa, I said "I have not been in Africa for years, and I am busy with other things"; but the publishers answered, "You have a certain point of view about politics, and in the series we are planning we want statements, as clear as possible, of definite policy. If your views apply to Africa, let us have them."

I make this point with intention, because I myself learnt more about the political conditions in Africa during a recent journey of only three and a half months, to and fro across central Africa, than in nearly double that number of years in the service of one protectorate. Those years of service were invaluable in teaching, practically, what can't be learnt otherwise, the art and limitations of actual government; but it gave me no comparative standards; no notion of what was being done elsewhere; of what might be done; and of what, therefore, I was failing to do.

The measure of general political experience, from which general policy must be conceived, is not years in one job and one place, but many contacts with new minds, new places, new political situations.

So a minister of state may pass with growing success through a dozen offices in his political career, while in each separate office men remain for twenty or thirty years, with complete mastery of their own special department; but outside that department, opinions of little more value than those pronounced every day by men who have no government experience at all.

2:

Conquest of Africa

TROPICAL AFRICA, within the memory of millions not yet old, was a no man's land where anyone with the power could do what he liked. Men mutilated as children for sale into the harems of moslem chiefs are not yet fifty; in any village, the middle-aged fathers can tell stories of the slave raiders, black and white, the recruiter or black-birder as he was called, and the wanton ingenious cruelties of the pagan round-ups.

Africa was the last frontier; and one more lawless and brutal than any yet seen in the world. The first white settlers in South Africa described the natives as vermin and set out to hunt them down as we hunt rats. Even at the outbreak of this war, men could still say in public that the negroes had no rights in Africa.

That they had no sovereign rights, in their own country, was so much a matter of course to Europeans that no one threw any doubt upon it.

Immediately after the great discoveries of Livingstone, Burton, Speke, and Stanley, in the middle of the last century, the European powers began to reach out for control. Between 1876, when Leopold of Belgium called a first conference at Brussels, and 1898, when England and France signed a Convention fixing their West African frontiers, they divided the continent between them. They marked their boundary lines, often in unexplored territory, as tailors mark cloth with chalk; and divided tribes in half, cut off native farmers from their farms, villages from their water, capital towns from their markets, as if rivers, farms, towns had been no more than ink on paper.

Thus in 1939, the owners of Africa, excluding Egypt and the small native republic of Liberia, were six different European nations: France, Britain, Italy, Belgium, Portugal, Spain, and one nation of African whites, the Union of South Africa.

The slave trade came to an end, gradually, towards the end of the last century. Slavery remained in Abyssinia, and slaves were still carried by smugglers into Arabia, but the devastation of the Arab raiders, who massacred whole tribes in order to catch a few thousand young men and girls, had been stopped by the new rulers of the continent.

They found, however, that administration in the new territories, even of the simplest type, proved highly expensive, and to make their conquests pay at least the expenses of occupation, they followed the policy of granting concessions and monopolies to chartered companies. So the British Niger Company had a monopoly of trade of the lower Niger, the German East Africa Company had a concession in what is now Tanganyika; France, Spain, Portugal all granted monopolies. King Leopold of Belgium retained what was practically the whole of the modern Belgian Congo as his personal property.

Trading companies, which acted only as middlemen, buying native produce and importing European goods, did little harm and sometimes much good. But those which tried to make money by exploiting native labour did great evil. In the Congo, natives were forced, under cruel penalties, to collect rubber for export. Elsewhere they were set to work on European plantations; nominally under contract, actually slaves.

The Concession policy is still followed by Belgium and Portugal, and to a less extent, by France. All these countries now have colonial legislation protecting the native. How far it is effective depends chiefly on the man on the spot; but there has certainly been a great improvement in conditions.

This is largely due to economic pressure. It has been discovered that no government can afford to waste native labour.

From the beginning, whatever their policy, the African powers formed different aims. Some, like France and Belgium, desired to associate the new colonies closely with the mother country. Algeria with a million white inhabitants grows more French every year; the natives of French West Africa are taught to value French culture and to regard France as their chief centre of civilization. This is true even of French Morocco, a French protectorate under its own Sultan, where there is also increasing white settlement.

Belgium's policy, since the Belgian Government took over the Congo Free State from Leopold in 1905, has been to increase by every means economic ties with the motherland.

British policy, in tropical colonies, might be summed up, roughly, in the phrase of a former Lieuténant-Governor of Nigeria. "The great merit of British rule is that there is so little of it."

This has had the advantage of producing good relations between the white magistrate and the black subject. It has obvious disadvantages in a world of rapid change, where only highly organized states can hope to meet successfully frequent dangerous crises, both economic and political.

It has also produced, by lack of that foresight or prepared plan which goes with more positive government, some very difficult racial problems; especially in Kenya, on the East Coast. The Kenya uplands have been leased to European settlers, who have made their homes there, and seek, naturally, to control the government. The natives are in reserves; and there is also a large population of Indians, traders and middlemen, who wish to secure their own position against both the British settlers and the natives, and who claim, at any check, the protection of the Indian government.

The Kenya plateau is healthy for Europeans. So is South Africa, where whites have been settled for nearly three centuries. South Africa, including now, as the Union of South Africa, Natal, the Cape Colony, the Transvaal, and the Orange Free State, is a self-governing Dominion. Its parliament has absolute power. It represents two million whites who are natives of South Africa and have no other home-land, and it rules also six million Bantus of various tribes. The policy of the Union is, above all, to maintain white standards and white supremacy. The Union has a colour bar, forbidding natives to own property outside certain native reserves scattered through the white area, to work for any but a white employer, or to undertake certain skilled jobs.

Southern Rhodesia, just north of the Union, with sixty thousand white settlers, also has an independent government. Natives have a vote, but the local assembly wishes to take it from them. There is no legal colour bar but there is practical discrimination against native skilled labour, for instance, on railway work.

The Union is the wealthiest of all the African states. It produces nearly forty per cent. of the world's gold and fifty per cent., by value, of its fine diamonds. Its industrial development began with the discovery of diamonds in 1867.

The economic progress of Africa has been slow. Bad transport, and throughout the tropics, a bad climate, a sparse population, and the barriers of desert, jungle, and swamp have made organization expensive and difficult. The advance of the last twenty years has exceeded that of a century before. This is due, above all, to improved transport, especially motor transport.

But Africa is still chiefly agricultural. Even in Algeria the chief employment is agriculture, in vineyards, and palmgroves for oil. Out of an estimated population for all Africa of a hundred and fifty millions, at least a hundred and forty-three live by the land. Many farmers, of course, practise native crafts and small trades; but the land is their chief support.

Industry itself is mostly small and ill-equipped, the largest is still mining. The South African mines employ over four hundred thousand natives; the copper mines of Northern Rhodesia, fifty thousand; and the gold mines of the Gold Coast, thirty-five thousand. The Katanga copper mines in the Belgian Congo, and the immense diamond fields in the same province, the largest in the world for industrial diamonds, also maintain a large labour force. The Belgian government has followed a policy of stabilizing and educating native labour. Its principle is to use natives in all possible jobs, skilled as well as unskilled. It is therefore training mechanics and foremen for all branches of its industry.

Both Belgian and French rule of the natives is autocratic by British ideas; but their governments will answer your criticism by saying, "This is a modern world and we are equipping our African subjects for modern life, modern standards. Since they are bewildered by that world so strange to them, we treat them as children, in their own interests as well as ours."

Portugal, which had at one time, like the old Congo Free State, a bad reputation for exploitation of natives by forced labour on European concessions, has lately begun to follow the same policy as Belgium and France.

It is often said that the European powers put an end to the slave trade only to bring in a more thorough and despotic exploitation; that even under the slavers, native Africa was free; that under the whites, there is no free native in the continent.

This, like most general political statements, is more false than true. The slave trade in Africa was the cruellest and most destructive ever known. The European exploiter, the rubber collector, the sub-contractor on a construction line, even at his worst, has never equalled the Arab slaver and his gang of perverts.

European conquest, with all its faults, has brought incomparably more good than harm to Africa.

It must never be forgotten that even in the worst days, for instance, of the white invasion of the South, and the hunting down of the bushmen, the missions were taking their schools and hospitals, and a religion, which at its crudest was infinitely better than any native creed, to the tribes.

Europe should not forget this debt. Without the record of the missions, still continuing, it would have little to be proud of in its African adventure. It could say that many administrators have done good and self-sacrificing work. It could claim that it had rescued scores of millions from some of the most bloody and stupid tyrants ever seen on earth. But it would have to admit that the administrators acted less from government altruism than their own; and that the establishment of justice and peace, almost its sole large achievement, were the by-products of an occupation directed by motives very little concerned with the good of the African masses.

And it has replaced native tyrannies by a rule which, at its mildest and most reasonable, is still despotic. The new masters of Africa are all-powerful. Their organization, their material power, make them irresistible, and the African peoples are more entirely in their hands than any since the Red Indian tribes were expropriated by the U.S.A. or the Tasmanians were exterminated by the British.

The difference is that the Red Indians and the Tasmanian blacks were small minorities; the Africans are a huge and growing majority. There are in all Africa five million whites. They are outnumbered thirty to one. In the tropics, they are outnumbered thousands to one; they are simply a few high officials, or missionaries. It is quite common there, even in districts nominally administered for forty years, to meet natives who have never seen a white man.

So we have a continent with a population of one colour, owned and administered by a very small number of immigrants with a quite different colour and appearance.

This situation, since it is established, to many people appears normal. It is, in fact, very odd. It is as though in England the mayors, the magistrates, the doctors, the lawyers, the officers of the army, were black. It is not only odd; it is dangerous; and the danger increases rapidly with an educated class among the natives. The enormous power of the sovereign race, if it leads to self-complacency, does not make the danger less.

3:

The Case for Freedom

SOMEWHERE DOWN THE NIGER VALLEY, twenty years ago, a horse boy was arrested by the local Emir, and sent to my camp for talking sedition. He had been telling the local pagans, wild islanders, that a black king was coming, with a great iron ship full of black soldiers, to drive all the whites out of Africa. The Emir suggested that he ought to be flogged and deported.

My political agent, Musa, an old Hausa from the north, said that the village markets were full of this talk and asked if there were any truth in it. I told him that it was nonsense. But he looked unconvinced and said doubtfully, "A steamship, they say, sir, a white man's ship, but with black officers and a black crew."

"How could that be, Musa? It's only village talk."

Musa was a professional diplomat and agent, of a kind no longer known in Europe, without a nation of his own. He offered his gifts, as negotiator and adviser on local affairs, as gauger of local feeling, to the highest bidder. He had belonged to two Emir's courts before he came to me. He seemed to be as far removed from racial prejudice or nationalist feeling as any dog-fancier who is called in to manage an international show. He was a cosmopolitan, cool, well-mannered, extremely shrewd, and rather lazy-minded. His feelings were shallow. But the notion of a ship with black officers and crew, coming across the ocean moved him to some deep and private excitement. He was unwilling to believe that such a ship did not exist.

The horse boy denied the story and I advised the Emir to let him go. It was not for many years afterwards that I heard of the Black Star Steamship Company and its founder, Marcus Garvey, provisional President of Africa.

I don't suppose any of my colleagues heard of him sooner, if at all. Marcus Garvey was a negro who held a congress in New York and drew up a Declaration of Rights for the negro peoples of the world. He also founded the Steamship Company, to be under negro control, and to trade with Africa.

Garvey's representatives were deported from Liberia, and chased out of the Belgian Congo. The Governor of Sierra Leone congratulated President King of Liberia on "showing the door to spurious patriots from across the Atlantic, men who sought to make Liberia a focus for racial animosity."

The ship company failed, and there were bitter quarrels among the directors. The whole episode, at least in the white newspapers, cut a comic figure. Yet Garvey's manifesto went all through Africa. I cannot be sure, of course, that the story which came to my remote district, four days' journey from a telegraph office and eight from a railway, was about Garvey and his ship. I thought it nonsense, asked for no particulars, and I don't remember its date. I was like the other whites. I knew nothing of what was going on in the native mind. Seeing primitive people in their isolated villages, I assumed that their ideas of the world were primitive, that they were isolated also in mind.

But they were not. In a continent still illiterate, where all news goes by mouth and every man is a gatherer, news of any incident affecting the relations of black and white, a strike in South Africa, war with Abyssinia, spreads through the whole country in a few weeks. It is the most exciting of news; above all, if it tells of a black victory.

To Musa, I suppose, with his education, his cynical pessimism, the black steamship appeared like a startling triumph. He thought nothing of manifestos or the rights of peoples, but he was clever enough to set great value on economic power, and the control of expensive machinery. He had not expected to hear of black men owning and driving ocean-going ships, and he was deeply moved. He felt his colour.

This is a root fact of African politics: colour, race.

Garvey's Declaration told of the workings of the colour bar:

"Nowhere in the world with few exceptions are black men accorded equal treatment with white men but are discriminated against for no other reason than their race and colour.

"Against such inhuman and un-Christian and uncivilized treatment we protest and invoke the condemnation of all mankind.

"We believe in the freedom of Africa for the negro people of the world; we demand Africa for the Africans."

Garvey was a Jamaican, and, as Africans pointed out, he did not represent Africa. But only officials completely cut off by office work from political reality could fail to know that his declaration represented two things far more powerful than votes: a racial grievance and the moral sense of humanity. These spring from entirely different roots but they are two of the most powerful political forces in the world. They never cease their growth and pressure.

It was not votes that abolished the slave trade. It was a few enthusiasts, despised and politically impotent, Quakers, poets, appealing only to moral force, who began that agitation, which, in the end, cost the British parliament twenty million pounds, and the U.S.A. a civil war and nearly a million dead.

The British government was wise, even at a time of national poverty, after the Napoleonic war, to spend some millions on freeing the slaves. It saved itself from far greater expense and incalculable misfortune.

Garvey's movement effected nothing at that time, but it would be folly for any European government, with African dependencies, to forget it, or to forget the realities of its position in Africa. It may be one of the better colonizing powers, honestly seeking the welfare of its subjects. But it stands before the world as a defendant. It has to answer a charge. "What are you doing in Africa? What are you getting out of it? What does the African gain by your rule? Have you a colour bar?"

This is the moral question. It may be said that though public opinion always acts upon a moral impulse, it takes often a long time to gather momentum. Official contempt of Garvey's movement, and a great many others of the same kind, is based upon the secret reflection, "Things will last for my time." But will they?

Officials in India, thirty years ago, despised the Indian Congress. They said: "It is self-elected. It represents nobody but itself. It is a rabble of disgruntled clerks who have failed in their examinations. We give India the best government it ever had, the most just, incorruptible, altruistic; and the masses know it. They dread above all things the rule of caste and the Indian exploiter. Congress rule would mean disaster for India; a return of all the evils of corruption, jobbery, family influence, and religious wars, from which we saved it."

All this was perfectly true. But Congress is already so great a power in India that the Viceroy cannot ignore it.

It does not represent the people; but it represents a racial grievance.

Racial feeling, simply as a natural prejudice, has no moral ground. On the contrary, it has produced enormous evils. It is the favourite weapon of the Nazi and the Fascist. But it has very deep roots in human nature.

The Imperial government can make a good answer to the racial propaganda. It can say: "Any racial discrimination that has existed in India was temporary. We aim at Indian self-government, but we can't hand over power until Indians have learnt by gradual experience to use it. Our job meanwhile is justice between individuals without regard to race."

This is a good answer. Any government in the world that can say: "We are preparing the people for self-government, but meanwhile we have to take responsibility for order and justice," has a strong case.

But the power of the Indian Congress rests in difference of race, colour, and religion, and it could easily prove too strong for any national and moral argument based merely on social justice. Even in India, racial grievance alone could outbalance all the good work of the Imperial government and destroy it. The ignorant masses, the untouchables, the outcastes would not know the disaster prepared for them, until it had arrived. They would not recognize it then. They would be too busy keeping themselves alive.

In many parts of Africa racial feeling enforces a strong moral case. The natives feel not only the bitterness of race discrimination but a sense of moral outrage. They say to the whites: "You call yourselves Christian people and you treat us like animals. When you first came to our country, you hunted us like vermin. Now you have taken us captive, you keep us as beasts of burden, pack horses, plough mules."

African governments have sometimes tried to ignore the moral charge; none of them has been able to forget the danger of a race war.

The case for African freedom is that it is the only answer to the first, and the only escape from the second.

Freedom is an abused word. It has been called "The smoke screen of an escapist." A statesman said, "When a man begins to talk about liberty I lock up the spoons."

It is especially important to know what we mean by freedom when we are dealing with Africa. For half the opposition to any suggestion for native freedom is based on a misunderstanding.

The old definition of freedom is absence of restraint. That means, complete freedom is only possible without any government, or any laws at all. It means that Robinson Crusoe was the freest man that ever lived.

People who know Africa and think of freedom under this term, naturally say, "If you simply remove white government, you will get chaos and misery for the African."

Obviously it is no good writing a book about African freedom without knowing what we mean by the word.

This is not the place for a philosophical argument, but roughly it may be said that modern philosophy does not like negative definitions. For instance, the definition of space as an absence of matter, a vacuum, produced all sorts of trouble for physics, and is now rejected.

In the same way the old definition of liberty produced, even for a great man like John Stuart Mill, insoluble difficulties. The chief of these bears directly on the African problem. It was this. If liberty is absence of restraint, and if liberty is a good thing, then all government, which imposes restraint, is bad. Even the criminal law is an evil.

Space is now regarded, by modern physicists, not as an absence of matter, but as a field of power.

If we describe liberty, not as an absence of government, but as a kind of power, the power to do what you like, we get rid of Mill's difficulty. For a government can increase a man's power to do what he likes. If any government, for instance, had offered Robinson Crusoe a free ticket to London and a settled income, he would not have hesitated long to exchange his abstract liberty for a real one.

Real freedom then can be greatly increased by social organization; for instance, by transport which increases a man's power to travel, if he has a taste that way; by education, to put it in his power to learn; by labour legislation which secures his income and gives him bargaining power, or political power.

It is in fact no paradox that a modern Englishman or American, in a very complex society, has much more freedom to indulge his tastes and realize his talents than had his ancestor of a hundred years ago, in a simple society with few laws but no organized education, no protection from the exploiter, and miserable pay.

In short, the power to do what you like is not much good to you on a desert island. You need the means to use it, and the means can only be provided by a complex social organization.

Of course, not all modern societies aim at freedom. Highly complex states, like Nazi Germany, were designed not to give the individual power of self-realization, but to make the ruler strong. Our argument says only that freedom is not incompatible with government, even with modern government; that such a government can be designed actually to increase freedom to every individual.

C.E.M.A., for instance, which brings music and plays to remote villages, at government expense, is actually, in the most literal sense of the word, increasing freedom. It has enabled thousands of people who were born with the love of good music, or dramatic sense, to enjoy it for the first time. Whereas they have said before, "I should like to hear a real orchestra, but I've never been able to find the time and money to go to town," now they have the power to listen to an orchestra or see a play, in their own neighborhood, at small cost. Government action has given them a new freedom which formerly they did not possess.

I don't pretend that I understood this when I went to Nigeria. I remember an old chief complaining to me, "Yes, you say we mustn't catch slaves, but all our land is a slave."

This was on the Dahomey frontier, then primitive enough. A great trade road passed close to it from the cattle lands of Northern Nigeria to the Southern provinces, thickly populated and well off, but full of tsetse fly, so that cattle could not be bred there. Traders and merchants passing up and down this road through the wilder districts were always in trouble. Highway robbers murdered them, the local pagans robbed them, and the old chief suddenly clapped a guard on the road where it crossed the frontier and stopped most of the outgoing trade.

I told him that he was wrong; Nigerian chiefs had real power and the proof of it was that he had misused it and nearly caused an international incident.

He answered, "How did I know it was wrong to catch the foreign merchants—they were buying all the oil and my people had none. You say I am a chief but now I am a fool and a slave. I don't understand anything."

He was too proud and too well-bred to sulk. But his grievance was deep and spoilt our relations. It seemed to spoil also his own self-confidence. He became more and more irresponsible and dangerous until, some time later, he had to be deposed.

I did not understand the force of this old man's bitter complaint. I thought it was enough to say, "I give you freedom to act, carry on." I did not realize his feelings when he discovered that what he thought was a reasonable act, was to me stupid and wrong. In fact his complaint, that he felt like a slave, was not a piece of petulance, as I supposed, but one of those sayings in which a very simple man of honest feelings penetrates in one stroke to the heart of the matter.

He meant that it was not much good telling an old man to take his freedom, if he could not understand the new order. He merely tumbled into humiliation.

You cannot give liberty to people by a wave of the hand, as you throw open a cage. If you attempted it you would find that your victims, like cage birds turned loose, would only injure or poison themselves. They would be lucky if, more or less damaged, they found at last another cage, however small, to creep into.

The whole conception of producing freedom by a sudden political act belongs to a school of thought which never did face the root problem of liberty; which did actually believe, or try to believe, that Robinson Crusoe had more liberty than an ordinary British or American citizen. To make a man free you have to create a whole social order of a special kind: the democratic.

The growth of freedom in Europe, of education, of wealth, of social and political organization, has been a long and slow process, with frequent interruptions by political dictators. These interruptions have become shorter, as real freedom increased. The power of education, which means nowadays economic power, in the people, has become so formidable that even the dictators while they fight against liberty, try to pretend that they are serving it. They use socialist slogans and talk of liberation.

But in Africa, there has been no growth. African peoples know no

other government but dictatorship, direct or indirect, and it is quite easy
for the African dictators to think and even to speak in public of the
natives as helpless serfs or slaves.

This, as I have said, does not make the position in Africa any less
dangerous; it makes it only more difficult.

4:

African Poverty

POLITICAL LIBERTY, and even education, is no good to a starving man. It
would have seemed very odd, perhaps, to the political scientist of the
last century, who wanted to discuss freedom for Africa, to say, "We had
better begin with the standard of living." But it is a fact that if, before
the war, we had wanted to make a scale of social freedom in the world,
we could have begun by asking for statistics about the standard of living.
The list would have shown the U.S.A., Britain, France, Sweden, Holland
about equal at the top, and Africa at the bottom.

The war, of course, has made a temporary alteration in this scale; but
after the war, it is safe to say that standards of living will again be a
fair guide. The reason is a double one. A high average standard means
both that a people has been able to secure fair conditions from the government, and that they have power to defend them. A very poor people,
a real proletariat, on the other hand, can neither obtain economic power,
nor keep what they have got. They have no resources; their unions, if
they have any unions, are poor; they are very soon starved out.

I don't mean that political liberty can be ignored. It is the crown and
indispensable guardian of real freedom. But it comes at the end, instead
of at the beginning, of a people's emancipation.

The first steps therefore towards African freedom are economic. These
are the more urgent because African economy is not merely primitive;
it is ruinous.

Many people still think of Africa as a rich country, needing development. In fact it is a very poor one, going rapidly downhill. Its enormous deserts are increasing, the fertility of its arable soil is declining; its rainfall is growing less every year, so that the great Lake Rudolf in Kenya has fallen at the rate of a foot a year for twenty-five years, and the sands left bare around its shores are now being blown over the neighboring farms; its forests are being destroyed at the rate of thousands of square miles in a year, and the greater part of any valuable timber which they once contained has been already cut down and carried off. Its whole economy is on the edge of collapse.

It might be said: "Africa is an old continent—European penetration began more than a century ago. If African economy is unstable why did it not collapse long ago?" The answer is, first, that all over the world economic change is accelerating, so that five years now count for fifty in the last century; and a thousand before the last; secondly, that this change has had more sudden radical and dangerous effects in Africa, still primitive in mind, than anywhere else.

The tractor in England is transforming the farm but it is handled by men who have practised high cultivation for generations; who, by education, are enabled to study new results of research into soil fertility and who themselves contribute to that research. English farmers discussing the new multiple ploughs, the new tractors and their effect on different soils, in different states of the weather, are rural scientists equipped not only with traditional knowledge but the power of comparing and balancing their judgments.

In Africa, where the tractor has enabled the primitive farmers to extend their fields by a hundred times, to pass straight from cultivation with the hoe to the gang plough tearing up square miles of bush in a few days, there is no tradition, no record of the past, no notion of what will happen to the soil under the new treatment or how long it will take to recover. African soil is for the most part poor and thin; once it is laid bare, it quickly degenerates. The African climate is the most destructive in the world. Long dry seasons turn an exposed top spit to dust; storms of rain wash it away so fast that some first observers mistook the enormous gullies not five or six years old for geological faults. Those who read the book, *The Grapes of Wrath,* have some notion of what can happen to a country that loses its soil cover. But Texan erosion is nothing to the wreck of Africa. In Texas we have the slow degeneration of a few hundred square miles by drought; in Africa the rapid destruction of thousands by every natural force: parching dry heat, cracking cold; whirlwind, gale, and flood. In Texas the green prairie became the wheat mine; in fifty years it was the dust bowl. In Africa, the forest is succeeded so quickly by desert that the mud walls of the hunters' compound remain to shelter the traveller from a level storm when there is no tree in sight larger than a currant bush. What is high jungle this year and a farm the next, will be, under the tropics, a gullied waste of brick earth in four more seasons.

I am not reproaching any capitalist or exploiter, any government, for this destruction. It is due to no man's fault; to ignorance, to the pressure of life upon poor men, to the climate, to the limitations of governments which had to pay their way.

The negro's own method of agriculture is a chief cause of deforestation. For certain main crops, for yams, for maize, rich feeders, he seeks virgin ground and manures it with wood ash. Every year he burns down a little of the forest and clears the ground for his seed. Every year, therefore, there is a little less high forest, a little more scrub, and a consequent drop in the rainfall.

This was realized twenty years ago, and if you ask why nothing had been done to prevent it, or nothing effective, the answer is not that rulers are malevolent but that they have not had the power, the knowledge, or the money to do the effective thing.

I remember making angry speeches to a village which had destroyed a patch of high forest, marked for reserve. I told the people that without the trees their country would become a desert. Afterwards, when I was strolling through his farm with a young farmer, to see his crops, he said to me suddenly, "There is already less rain here—even I can remember more."

"Then why on earth do you destroy the trees?"

He began to smile, that smile of careless resignation which always angered me then, as a young and stupid officer. But before I could begin to make the usual speech which begins, "You people are hopeless," he suddenly became serious and said, "But, master, how can I stop it—if I do not burn, someone else will and I will get the old worn-out land, and no ash. We all know that the country is going dry—we speak of it often but what can we do?"

I could not tell him what to do, for I saw all at once that my indignation was escape. I was dodging the real problem; how to feed growing populations on a land too poor and small for them. It is easy to say, "This forest shall be a reserve," but it isn't easy for the heads of families living next that forest to watch their children starve while they know that by burning down a few trees they could grow rich crops.

Yet when, in a former year, on the steamer going back to Lagos, I was asked by a firm of oil-nut merchants if I could guarantee a minimum tonnage of shea butter delivered on the Niger bank in exchange for a collecting station, I had to say no. I promised a road and even a sub-station at the chief market. I could give an assurance that plenty of butter would come in the dry season, the women would bring it, but I could not promise any minimum amount in one season.

Their representative said to me, "You officials talk of developing the country; isn't it true that in your district, bigger than Wales, twelve thousand square miles of wild bush, the shea nuts fall from the trees and rot on the ground because nobody takes the trouble to pick them up?"

"Perfectly true, but to guarantee you a minimum tonnage and a constant supply means to take the people from their farms."

"They won't need pressing when they begin to see our money."

"No, and that's one of our troubles. We can't forget what happened to the rubber collectors. They left their farms to gather root rubber and to make money; then the market for root rubber collapsed and the collectors starved. Lucky for Nigeria that there weren't many of them dependent only on the rubber."

"I can't spend money on a river station and a clerk and river transport unless I can be sure of a minimum supply. Shea butter will always be wanted. It will always fetch a good price."

But I could not take the risk, and the shea nuts continued, for the most part, to rot on the ground; wealth which could have doubled the income of my poor farmers.

I confess this failure because it is typical both of the problems everywhere in Africa, and of the nature of the difficulties which face a responsible officer, a responsible government. It is no good crying out that the bureaucrat is shortsighted, that he has no enterprise. From the governor of a colony to the humble junior magistrate in charge of poverty-stricken tribes on the utmost frontier, each is responsible for human lives, and even more perhaps in the case of the bush officer, for actual people of whom he may know many by name, and who know him and come to him for help and advice. It is one thing to plan vast schemes of development on paper and say, "I take the risk," and another to visit some starving disease-ridden village which is ruined by your own fault.

My dilemma in Borgu was typical of all Africa, a conflict between immediate profit and dangerous insecurity in the future. This is not the only African problem but it has been the most pressing for the last twenty years. For many districts in Africa have been dependent on European markets. The Gold Coast, a British colony on the West with a progressive people, one of the most advanced in Africa, produces chiefly from small farms about half the world's cocoa; large parts of Southern Nigeria depend on the oil palm; great areas of Uganda and the Eastern Sudan on cotton, Nyasaland on tobacco. The Chagas who farm the slopes of the greatest mountain in Africa, Kilimanjaro, in Kenya, and who have devised for themselves an elaborate and efficient irrigation system, have taken in late years to growing coffee for export, and many of them, like small farmers in all these cash crop areas, have given up the old native plan of living off their farms. They sell their crops for cash, and buy a large proportion of their food.

They buy other things too; imports into the Gold Coast, especially from the United Kingdom are, per head, among the highest in tropical Africa. But they have ceased to be self-sufficient. They are involved in world economy, and the slumps of 1921 and 1930 ruined millions of Africans who had never heard of the balance of exchange. Also they brought all colonial development to a stop.

The whole native economy of South Africa depends on the mines, chiefly on gold. No one can conceive what would happen to the Swazis, the Bechuanas, or the Basutos without their wages from the Cape mines. But the mines are wasting and gold has ceased to be currency. The last English sovereign was coined in 1926. Bullion is used only to back a currency. It is dug out of the ground of Africa and buried again in some bank vault. It is useless, in quantity, except as an international standard and though such a standard has great value in an anarchic world of nationalist soap-boxers, it might appear any day that enough for that purpose was already mined. How much gold is needed to adjust exchanges? Possibly much less than exists at this moment. As the nations learn to control or even to abolish slumps, a very few million of gold bars, permanently bolted into their cases, and incessantly travelling the world, would suffice to keep exchanges steady. Then the mines will be closed, all but one or two of the richest, and whole tribes will be destitute. It may be said, "Africa is no worse off than any other part of a world whose economic whole is still cut up by artificial boundaries into jealous and spiteful parishes, each ready to commit suicide if its corpse will poison the next man's water." But, in fact, Africa is much worse off, because of its ignorance and poverty. A slump in any European state produces at once resources of organization and capital. Nothing has been more surprising than the resilience of the modern European economy; I do not call it capitalist or socialist because it is neither, it is a hybrid of both and as a mixture something quite different from both its parents. But the African economy is almost everywhere stiff and brittle. It has nothing behind it; no stored capital, no ingenuity, not even hope. It is not, as in peace-time Europe, the temporary form of a rapidly expanding real wealth; but the thin skin over a superannuated organism, already sick and declining towards its end. Each European slump leaves behind it a better machinery to deal with slumps, a closer organization of industry, union, and state bent upon the more even production and distribution of that wealth poured out every year, in increasing volume, by modern machines, and modern scientific advance, itself increasing by compound interest. An African slump is like a paralytic stroke to a half-ruined frame. The doctors bring drugs; anything to prolong the invalid's life. After a time, he revives. But he totters forward on the same path as before, only a little more decrepit, a little nearer to dissolution. He is not better fitted to meet the next crisis, but worse; weaker in spirit and resource. He goes back to the same farm, already losing fertility, to grow the same crops which have slumped before; or in East Africa, among the pastoral tribes, he begins again to add to the vast herds of half-starved scrub cattle, which are eating new deserts in Kenya and Tanganyika, even faster than the Sahara in the North-West.

Neither can this sick man cure himself even when he wills it. On the Gold Coast it was decided to begin banana growing, so that the farms should not be dependent only on cocoa. But it was found that the soil had already lost so much fertility by repeated cropping that bananas could not be grown within economic range of a port.

5:
Problems of Reconstruction: Political

WHAT THEN IS TO HAPPEN in Africa? Either a great collapse, famine, and bloodshed, a world outcry against the incompetence and blindness of the African suzerains; or reorganization. With the possible exception of the Nile delta, there is no part of Africa which does not need it. I am not saying that the same measures will apply to cash crop areas of Kiliman-jaro or the Gold Coast, to the nomadic herdsmen of East Africa, the farmers of the Congo or the parasitic kraals of the South, living on re-mittance from the Rand mines; but only that all these need quick medi-cine.

Reorganization in Europe means often the mere rearrangement of functions in some working concern: a factory or a government. But in Africa it must mean something so much larger and deeper that the word should be rather reconstruction. It requires, therefore, far more than any European plan, a very definite idea of what kind of result is wanted.

As I have said, the European modern economy in such organized states as Scandinavia, Holland, Belgium, and Britain, with all its faults, has shown an unexpected resilience to crisis and surprising powers of growth and adaptation. That adaptation has taken place, in Britain, amidst loud cries of "We are done for—we are ruined—we are betrayed," but be-hind the noise of daily gossip or the political campaign, we know very well that standards of living, education, housing, even of literature and music, have improved steadily throughout the last century. The cries which we still hear, from honest men, are cries of impatience. They see how much has been done with very small effort, very little imagination, and they realize what would be possible, even in their own lifetime, with very little more.

But if we say that what we want to give Africa, eventually, is a full modern economy, we shall raise violent opposition on both flanks: from those who believe that the African is not fit for civilization, and from those who are convinced that civilization is not fit for him.

The first are all those who think that the African can never rise to full responsibility. They argue that he is a light-hearted but also light-headed sub-man, a born helot and parasite. Take him out of his tribe and he goes to the devil. Give him money to spend and he drinks himself to death. Teach him to read and write and he becomes an irresponsible demagogue. Put him into trousers and you have a conceited and ill-bred bumpkin who, to prove his worth as a man, pushes everyone else off the pavement. You have turned a savage into a brute.

The second and more dangerous school of critics argues: "The African is happy in his tribal life. He escapes there from all the diseases of the European soul: its loneliness, its personal ambition, its personal responsibility, its perpetual struggle and anxiety which fills the asylums with lunatics. He has dignity and peace; honest work and leisure to enjoy. He is essentially more civilized than ourselves. For his life is passed in the communal friendship and mutual help of which idealists dream. You speak of freedom for Africa. You say that freedom is a man's power to do what he likes in a world that suits him; that gives him the means of self-achievement. He needs a certain kind of society and the society needs him because it is made of him. But the tribal African lives in just such a world already. True, he cannot drive a motor, play golf, or listen to a band in the park. He cannot earn wages in a factory or buy a radio set. But he doesn't want to do these things. He is, by your definition, free. Let him alone, for God's sake, to be free in his own way."

We need not argue with the racialist. If there is difference in race it is not so great as the difference between individuals. Who could not pick in any European state, thousands of men, stupider, more unfit for responsibility, than the average negro? Who has not found among African minds as ingenious or responsible as those of the average European statesman or official? Whether Africa will ever produce a great philosopher, artist, or musician no one can tell, but it is certain that the average standard of ability is quite sufficient to receive and keep the amount of education which now enables Europe to drive its machines and conduct its political affairs. It does not take a special genius to drive a lorry or to vote; common sense is more valuable than higher mathematics to the trades union secretary or the factory foreman. Common sense itself is the product of tradition and experience.

I have heard a don and a coal-miner, chance-met in the train, discuss the same political problem, and it was the miner who talked the better sense. In millions of African villages, the headmen struggle with the daily problem of government, the difficult management of people, in which they need and show quite as much political sense as the white bureaucrat or magistrate. As for ingenuity, I was once asked to build a bridge across a dry river bed, forty feet deep, of bush timber, without nail, bolt, or wire. I had made a specialty of such bridges over small streams, designed like an R.E. trestle bridge, with forked poles in place of lashed scantlings. My bridge builder was a little pagan called Tasuki, about four feet high, and six stone weight, with a face and chin and beard very like the famous Kruger. He was ragged and dirty, usually in pain from a complication of diseases including syphilis, and always laughing. I could not supervise the beginning of the big bridge, but I sent for pulleys and tackle to raise the road bearers, whole tree-trunks, into the great upright forks. When I arrived, the pulleys had not come but the first trestle was up. Tasuki had invented all by himself and for this one job, the compound lever, the multiple pulley and several new devices never seen before and probably never used again. His pulley was a double fork well oiled with ground nut oil. He had fixed one end of a tie-tie rope to a branch, looped the bight around the tree trunk in the river bed, passed the free end through the fork, once more round the trunk, once more over the fork, and so to his gang. Sixteen men raised a palm trunk butt ten feet, propped it up and began on the other end. In an hour, the second transom was forty feet high in its forks. Tasuki had never seen a multiple pulley in his life, but he perfectly understood why the gang had to pull in twenty feet of tie-tie to raise the log five feet. He explained it to me in order to apologize for the slowness of the work. "Four ropes pull stronger, four times stronger, but, of course, they have to go farther, four times farther."

But every African traveller knows instances of such cleverness, and any one of them, too, can testify to the African's character; to his courage, honesty, loyalty. With different names and places these stories could be told of any European peasantry.

We need not think only of an African peasantry and its intelligence. There is already a large class of educated Africans. All the different government services, indeed, depend on such a class, and I have heard it said by an official that he would rather work with Africans than Europeans, "because they enter into things."

I knew what he meant. My own experience was the same—of a keenness which made you feel that the work was being enjoyed for its own sake.

I remember a young clerk who sat up all night to copy a report in time for the mail. I did not ask him to work for twenty hours on end, at the dullest possible job; I had given up all hope of catching the mail and said that the report would have to await the next.

No doubt when he appeared in the morning, with bloodshot eyes and a triumphant smile, to show me his copy, he was taking pleasure in giving me a surprise. But I know from other instances that he had also the strongest sense of duty; a zeal which sometimes got him into danger, as when he tried to stop a fight in the town, single-handed, and was nearly killed.

But I think the official, like myself, was thinking more of the personal relation than the general loyalty, and that in Africa, even in the government service, personal relations count for more than in Europe. The educated African, it seems to me, does not lose by education a characteristic of his race, which, according to your view, is either good or bad; he is still strongly moved by personal sympathies. If he knows that you like him and that you appreciate his help, he is the best colleague you could find; he enters into things with an eagerness, a freshness of mind, that makes him a perpetual source of encouragement even in dull routine work; but if he should find himself kept at arm's length, he shows often boredom and a kind of resigned indifference which may look like apathy.

I think this may be one reason for the frequent complaints in all parts of Africa, especially from Africans themselves, against the African clerk, in minor posts of what may be called impersonal public services: railway booking offices, post offices, the customs. Their contacts are too slight and frequent to excite any personal sympathy, and so they are tempted to be careless and arrogant.

This is worth noticing because of the old belief that Africans cannot be employed in administration without making themselves and the administration detested.

Obviously, this is wrong. For vast areas of Africa have always been administered by Africans, under chiefs or European magistrates, without special difficulty.

But I think there is substance in the charge that the small clerk in the post office or the railway does often show his boredom in rudeness, and this is the natural defect of a racial temperament which prefers a friendly to a formal relation. The cure is obviously in special instruction and a new tradition. I used to wonder why London bus conductors, with their very hard work, were so much more genial than country ones. I was told that it is a matter of tradition. But the general point, that the African is capable of equal education and responsibility with Europeans, is beyond argument to anyone who deals with realities, that is, who has known real Africans. The Mahomedan judge, subtle and learned, the great chief with his political shrewdness, the hospital assistant, the village headman, the lorry driver, the sergeant-major; put any of them into a white skin and they would take their place, in the same rank of European society, on equal terms. They would appear like the rest, the lawyer among lawyers, the chief among statesmen, the government clerk among officials; the sergeant-major among that natural aristocracy of the soldiers of career —the non-commissioned officers.

Racial differences may be deep but no race exists, except perhaps a few remnants of the primitive bushmen, which is not capable of that degree of education and responsibility necessary to carry on the modern state.

The second criticism, that to give Africa a modern economy instead of tribalism is to go back instead of forward, is more dangerous because it appeals to some deep instinct in the educated man. It receives support therefore from the most unexpected quarters, among scholars, idealists, progressives, as well as from the antiquarian nationalist. De Valera and Gandhi, Hitler and the Christian anarchist, all have this in common, that they think the world has gone backwards from a golden age in the past, when manners and morals were simpler, nobler, when Adam delved and Eve span. They would like to see the end of what is called modern progress, modern mechanics, modern thought, modern art. Thus among those who talk most bitterly of the exploitation of Africa one finds such opposing types as the sentimental nationalist, the liberal anarchist, the antiquarians whose interest is in ancient custom, and the idealist who has never seen Africa but hates modern civilization for its ugliness and confusion.

Above all these and adding the greatest weight to their argument are officials of high standing and long African experience, who say, "I knew such and such a tribe when they were bare-arsed pagans, the finest chaps I ever met, honest as the day, straight as their backs, clean as their own rain-washed skins. And look at them now since they got stores and ploughs and mission schools, trousers and clap. The lousiest, laziest, most worthless lot of mean bums that ever disfigured the dung-heap they live in."

Let me confess that I, too, thought like this when I first joined the Service, saw the idle wasters in the towns and then, on the remote frontiers, met the wild pagan. I, too, preferred the naked savage to the mission boy, with his scraps of second-rate knowledge, his attempts to copy the white man. I found out, too, in a very short time that most of the criminal class and all the most contemptible blackguards, the mean swindlers, the dealers in women and children, the small exploiters of the poor, came from the towns and the European schools. I, too, said, "European civilization, so called, is the ruin of these people—it is a crime to break up their tribal organization and to change these dignified self-respecting clansmen, farmers, hunters, patriarchs, with their traditional way of life, their ancient customary law, into the wretched scum known as free labour, so much desired by the planter and the mining promoters."

When I saw, with my own eyes, the Tulas of the Gombe hills, a tribe completely isolated till that year, come into our town to sell their produce and handle their first money and then go back laden with rubbish from the company store, I could not decide whether to be more pleased with the political triumph of my resident, who had brought a dangerous people into concord without a shot fired except a few dozen arrows at himself, or disgusted to find that ten minutes in a company store could change a warrior fit for the Parthenon pediment into a nigger minstrel.

But since then I have been struck by this point: that in deploring the loss of the tribal standards and tribal dignity by the native, I never asked myself what the native himself wanted; I never said: "Why is it that the Tulas are so delighted with the stores and the things that they can buy there? Why do they flock to earn sixpence a day about the station, or volunteer for the tin mines and the railway gang?"

It struck me that the tribal native is often extremely bored with tribal life. He finds the same attraction as Europeans in change and discovery; above all, in new freedom, even that small amount to be bought for a wage of sixpence a day.

"But this is our fault," the idealist answers. "I admit we have gone far to ruin Africa. But why should we finish the bad work? You have not explained that. And you have not answered my question about freedom. By your definition, the tribal African was free within the social organization of the tribe. It served him and he found his enjoyment in it. Why then do we allow it to be destroyed? The case for African freedom has been stated when you describe your happy guileless Tulas. Keep them so. Keep the cash economy away from them and they will stay free."

This is a good argument which must be answered. For if we close the old impassable breach between the free man and organized society, we are faced at once by the new and profound question, "If a man is free when he does what he likes, why not teach him to like what you want him to do?"

This is the tribal scheme or, at least, what is supposed to be its scheme. This is the plan of authority everywhere, especially in the modern world, where, although freedom has barely been examined in its real character, it is well understood by dictators. All of them are trying to teach the mass of men to like the totalitarian state, the modern tribe; to enjoy serving it, to achieve themselves in its glory.

The answers are two. The first, on the psychological ground, is simply that you can't fit men into a totalitarian scheme without breaking them. Men are not putty, to be moulded. They are born with characters which grow one way, and not another. Education can only perfect what is already there; and cannot add or take away. It cannot make a born fool into a wise man; or a tone-deaf child into a musician. It can only add knowledge to intelligence; skill to genius.

The second, on the practical ground, is that when it has been tried, it has failed. The dictators have not made their subjects enjoy the tribal state. The proof is that it needs the biggest and most ruthless police force the world has ever seen to prevent them from breaking out of it. The authoritarian state, in the modern world of wireless, of quick communications, can be maintained in no other way, and then only for a short time. For the result of forcing young minds into a few selected moulds is to destroy all the best of them. So that the tribal state, in Europe, soon becomes a foolstate and either breaks up for lack of ability to manage its own affairs, or is destroyed in conflict with the free.

In Africa, it remained for countless centuries in the Stone Age, until some Arab slaver arrived with a few guns, and wiped it out in an afternoon; or some European brought to its neighbourhood a civilization whose very casts-off were so fascinating that it had to have them at any cost.

Unless therefore the tribes could be cut off completely from all contact with European ideas, returned to their Stone Age as the monkeys are shut up in artificial wildparks at the Zoo, they cannot be preserved even in the Stone Age. But it is impossible to cut them off. The cash economy and the idea of freedom have penetrated everywhere.

African tribes do not wait to be destroyed by European influences; they disband. The foreigner does not need to attack the tribal idea; at the first rising of the other idea of liberty, even in the crudest shape, it begins to grow pale and weak. The tribal form is still preserved all over Africa from the Nigerian pagan to the Masai and the Basuto, Zulu and Mashona. It exists, apparently still effective, side by side with the great numbers of detribalized natives in every large town. But even where its form has been kept, its reality is profoundly changed. A chief whose young men, as in South Africa, go to work in the mines; or whose people, as in the Gold Coast, bank their money and listen to the radio, is not a tribal chief in the old sense. He is not the living soul of the clan but a political representative who is supported because his power or influence may be useful in securing or defending some privilege from the white overlord, or the white enemy. The members of his tribe no longer feel, "I am part of him and he is part of me—we are one being," but such reasons, "He is respected by the white man, he is useful to me."

The clansmen had given place to the individual; and the tribe is no longer a primitive organic person, but an organization for mutual benefit, like a friendly society. But to deal with a tribal people is quite different from dealing with people organized in tribal groups. In the first case, we go to the chiefs alone; in the second, to the individual as well as the chief. In Africa, already, we dare not forget the individual.

The tribe cannot be preserved. As feudalism disappeared out of Europe because lords and serfs both wanted to be free of its obligations, so tribalism is dying out of Africa. The question of tribalism, whether to preserve it or destroy it, need not be argued. It has answered for itself.

The tribes are breaking up from within. But they are also being broken from without by these changes of order which are neither economic nor racial, but zoologic and ethnographic. It has often been remarked that Nature has its own balance, and that to change the balance has unexpected results. The man who brought the rabbit to Australia or the grey squirrel to England, changed such a balance. The Black Death of the fourteenth century altered the social proportion of whole nations and gave labour a new power and status.

In Ireland the new hygiene of the eighteenth century halved the infantile death-rate and sent the population leaping. The result of better doctoring, and especially better midwifery, combined with the development of estates, was the famines of the 'forties, the great emigration and a century of anti-British feeling in America.

The result of peace, industrial development, and better hygiene, in India, has been to increase the population by 100 millions in fifty years. Thus India is approaching the same catastrophe as Ireland; and the British government, if it remains in supreme power, will be blamed for it, unjustly, but reasonably. For a perpetual government, one not answerable to the people, assumes the terrible responsibility of foreseeing and forestalling these evils, with which often no possible government, in the same political circumstances, could deal.

That is to say, evils against which a democratic national government would be equally helpless. For nations, like men, by self-indulgence, by folly, by self-deception, by mere bad luck may entangle themselves in a course of fate from which there is no escape. They are dragged helplessly into ruin and misery.

In the old Africa, tribal warfare, infantile death-rate, and local famine kept the balance between population and subsistence. In the new Africa, modern science has already upset the balance. This, at present, is not so plainly seen in the people as among the cattle. The government vets are beginning to control cattle disease. The result is that herds of cattle, especially in the East, increase continually. These great herds, wherever they go, leave the pastures eaten to the bone and yet they starve. They are ruining the country.

But with such tribes as the Masai, whose vast reserves cover thousands of miles in Kenya and Tanganyika, cattle have a religious significance, as well as being the mark of prestige. Cattle are also the necessary price of a wife. So that the herds are never weeded and the owner never wishes to sell. Here is tribal custom and religion in conflict with necessity. The herdsmen, left to themselves, having created a desert, will starve in it together with their cattle: or they must change their customs, and what is even more deeply rooted, their social and religious feelings. The cure suggested fifteen years ago, was a secondary industry: tanning pits and beef factories. The herdsmen must be induced by taxation on beasts above a certain age, by propaganda and education, or compelled to sell at least their poorer cattle for cash. At the same time, their grazing lands could be defined and parcelled out, so that the bush and grass had time to grow. It was said: "By this means you will gradually bring the people to settle and give them other standards of rank besides mere numbers of cattle. Like other pastoral tribes long settled, they will take up permanent quarters, build houses, extend their farming and their crafts."

The Masai are famous lion hunters. They drive lions, as in India tigers are driven. But when the lion, surrounded, breaks out of the grass, the nearest hunter does not shoot him from a tree platform, he crouches down behind his shield, and takes its charge on his spear. The lion may be killed; the hunter is nearly always mauled.

The Masai, a brave, proud, handsome race, are admired by all travellers. Nobody likes the idea of such a people settled, tamed, and commercialized. But the Masai, even if they modify their religious customs, and learn to sell their cattle, even if they must be educated to do so, need not be spoilt, and they will certainly be spoilt if they are allowed to destroy their grazing lands.

It is a mistake to make sharp abstract distinctions and say of a primitive people: "Either it remains primitive and keeps its virtue, or it acquires new ideas and goes to the devil."

We in Britain have been acquiring new ideas for a thousand years. All this time there has been a chorus of past-lovers crying out: "We are degenerating—the good old days are gone for ever. All this pleasure, this new taste for amusement, this horrible modern art, so-called, and disgusting licence of convention, all this innovation is the ruin of us." But we are not ruined yet. Nor do I see any marks of decline in the new generation; taller, heavier, more intelligent, and quite as enterprising as any in the past. New ideas would not necessarily do any harm to the Masai.

Neither is it just to compare the nomad with the townsman and say, "Here is a splendid savage—and here is a rabbit."

Two great wars have taught England how well the townsman fights, how tough are his nerves and deep his stamina. I did not notice in the Cameroons that my pagans were better men than the city-bred Hausa, or the Yoruba from Ibadan, largest native town in Africa.

How far, it is asked, can industry be developed in Africa; how far ought it to be developed?

The weight of the attack against the negro capacity for education has been in the thought, "If we admit that the African can be a skilled worker, a foreman, a manager, we will have to allow also that Africa is capable of full industrial development, on its own account"; we will have to say: "It must be accepted that Africa is destined to become a citizen of the world, in equality with Europe, the Americas, Russia."

The suggestion may seem laughable, especially to those who know anything about Africa. It is obvious that such a development will take a very long time. But to see that it is possible is important because it alters the whole approach to the African problem.

Too many who agree that the African economy is dying out and must be rebuilt, still keep in their minds, perhaps unacknowledged, the idea of palliative industries; like those set up in Ireland during the famine, or in the British distressed areas. They imagine, that is, an Africa essentially unchanged, a native peasantry living under traditional rule by small husbandry; with a few industries established here and there to provide surplus labour with work, and the governments with tax. People who think or feel this are in practice enemies of all real progress in Africa. For they begin with the notion, "Let us make as little disturbance as possible —let us change only what has to be changed."

But if we agree now that the African is capable of world citizenship, and that he can achieve, in time, a full modern economy, then we begin with the different idea—"Let us get rid of every obstacle to development as soon as we can. For great changes are needed in a very short time."

Great changes will happen in any case: good or bad. Time is short to make them good.

Enormous as the difference is now, between African standards of living and those of Western Europe, it is going to increase faster in the next years. This war, like the last, will give an immense drive to the organization of the modern state, for production and distribution of wealth. In fifty years, perhaps in twenty, great cities of to-day, London, Paris, New York, will seem as far from us in history as the Alsatia of Fielding or the Seven Dials of Dickens. No one will understand then how we tolerated such dirt, misery, ignorance, muddle; such a waste of childhood. And at the same time, no one will be satisfied with the present. Nothing fails like success. It is only mediocrity which lies down in self-satisfaction; and whatever we may think of the world now, its violence, rawness, and confusion, it is not mediocre. The Silver Age of the Renaissance is dead. We live the roaring 'forties. Our very despairs are those crude reactions provoked by impossible demands, supernatural hope. In twenty years, England has made more social progress than in a hundred before, but no one thinks anything of it, and this is quite right; for what has been done, compared with what might have been done, is contemptible. I put "might" instead of "could" because "might" lives in the ideal world and "could" has to deal with living people and actual parliaments, wars, panics, slumps, cranks, and careerists.

But "could" learns every day by its own success, from its own new schools and factories, playing fields, and six-penny books. The impetus in Europe has an irresistible force. But it is the native impetus. It is a wave that springs from its own sea. In Africa there is no such drive of accumulating weight over the long sweep of progress, from its own element. Thus the advance of Europe came to primitive Africa in waves of flood, drowning all its landmarks, and carrying all its natives off their feet. They became lost, bewildered, hopeless, and finally despairing. Like the Agwarra natives I saw once during an unexpected Niger flood, the second in a month, sitting on the roofs of their houses in a cold dawn, shivering and miserable, not knowing what to do next, they can only shout jokes at each other and laugh at their own predicament. Like the same natives, too, when they become confused or daunted by the unexpected, they are difficult to rescue. Some of these Agwarra men, when we came with boats, suddenly lost their tempers and refused to be taken off, shouting, "We're done for—we'd rather drown. Everything is finished." They were full of spiteful rage against the mysterious fate which had sent them two floods when floods had never been known before; that is, since fate is nobody or anything, they were angry with everything and everybody.

All African travellers have seen the same change of expression in some laughing farmer, accused by his chief of robbing field stores; or some amused wife when her angry husband declares that she has been going with the soldiers. All at once they grow furious. The farmer shouts that his store is empty. The crop was bad. The rains failed. There is a curse on the land and may he be flogged or killed. He runs forward, tears off his shirt and throws himself on his face. "Flog me now—kill me—that's what I want—yes, I want it."

It is true that he wants it. To be flogged is something that a man can feel and understand; it is release. The African's feelings are strong, and need release or they explode. The woman suddenly begins to scream at the top of her voice that her husband is syphilitic, that he beats her, that her children die, that the child she has with her is not his and she's glad of it. Yes, she's been among the soldiers and she'll go again. She'll follow the soldiers next time—she never wants to see this land of savages again, and she too, asks to be punished.

It is not so common for women as men to make this demand. I used to think that the reason was in a sexual difference, that the men were more enraged by the sense of their helplessness, the women more resigned and passive. Now I think it was because African women are less affected than the men by social and economic change. Like the greater number of European women, they do not feel themselves responsible for events outside their own households, and do not try to grasp them. But women, more even than men, are passionate and revengeful in despair. Since they are conscious, especially in Africa, of minding their own business and working very hard at it, they are especially critical of those whom they suppose responsible for public business. Women's risings in Africa, such as the Abba riots of ten years ago, have always been marked by extraordinary ferocity and resolution. No one dare expect that if and when the African finds himself, as he thinks, the fool of the world, starving, diseased, enslaved, among nations infinitely more prosperous than any yet known, that the women will not cry out, too, "Flog us—kill us," or as an alternative rise and flay, kill, torture the rich whites. The mood of suicidal despair is also the utmost spite of the rebel.

A critic says, "I agree with every word—I would put it even more strongly, but what can be done while Africa is split up between seven different powers, with different systems of government, each with different ideas of the destiny of the African? What can be done while in Kenya a league of white planters demands controls, and in the Union of South Africa the parliament of whites has decreed a colour bar and proposed segregation of natives in closed areas. What is the good of talking about any improvement while the African, in Africa, is treated like a slave, a racial inferior; and his country is divided between rulers who cannot agree on the most fundamental principles of social reform?"

It is a tragedy that so many who have felt the strongest sympathy for the African people have been at the same time political idealists or abstractionists, and so ineffective. If someone should say, "The British kitchen is a muddle but it cannot be replanned while the church is split into competing sects," we should think him foolish. But politics is like plumbing. It is necessary and important but not the first thing in life. Above all, it is a practical job, with defined aims. It deals with facts and seeks positive results. The facts in Africa are a great diversity of peoples and climates as well as of governments. To remove the latter complication, if it were possible, would not solve the former. Africa, no more than any other continent, is a racial whole. The difference in race and culture between the Arab, the nomad Fulah, the Copt, the negro, Hamite, Bantu, the variety of local traditions, are at least as great as those of Europe or Asia. There is no more reason why Scandinavia and Italy should join together in a common exclusive polity than that the fair-skinned semite of North Africa, reserved and jealous, should make one cause with the negro or the Southern Bantu.

A final point, which must never be forgotten in our enquiry, is that world federation, though perhaps, as a political act, still far in the future, is always, as a process, advancing. It never ceases its work. And we see everywhere political consequences of the real fact that the world is an economic unity, in which each part increasingly depends on a world-complex of trade relations and exchange. This drawing together, at first private, began some hundreds of years ago with the invention of bills of exchange; and the international banking credit which brought together for the first time in continuous relation Asia, India, and Europe. In the last century, the Postal Union, the international Red Cross, the Peace Convention, the Hague Court; in this, the League, a great number of international conferences and agreements, extending even to an agreed time-table for expositions and games, the allotting of wave-lengths and the exchange of weather reports, have shown that the pressure of fact is driving the national politicians, however jealous and unwilling, in the same direction. Dependence has increased so much that even in war-time bitter enemies are obliged to maintain relations. Japan and Russia negotiate over fishing rights, Russia and Germany make trade agreements.

To the original fact of commercial dependence, growing each year with the development of industry, of markets and the exchange of raw materials, is added now the fact of vulnerability. The plane makes every nation open to danger, even from distant enemies. No one can therefore be indifferent, as formerly, to the nationalist war-maker or the nationalist parasite. The world finds itself now in the same situation as the Germany of the eighteenth century, cut into political fragments, each with a jealous ruler and a people stuffed with local prejudice and parish conceit, yet dimly aware of common interests and common dangers. The old Empire was already powerless, federation was not suggested or thought of; yet letters and books of the time show in the most diverse minds the first idea of it and a feeling of impatience with restrictive boundaries and artificial distribution.

The reason of this was an increasing commerce, the improvement of roads, which enabled Marlborough to march to the banks of the Danube in twenty days and fight there a decisive battle. It is true that Germany did not begin to draw together, by political act, until Napoleon had marched all over it, and beaten every part in detail; that even then the act was not completed for another sixty years. But that is quick work for nationalist statesmen of the last century. Allowing one year of this for three of that, we shall be lucky, if the world has established any real and effective central authority to secure peace and order, standards of labour, currency, and personal freedom in the next generation. It may not begin to take form for a century; and then only as a consequence of far greater confusion and disorder than we see to-day. But the important fact for us now, in considering the diversity of Africa, is that such a federated system is in process of development, growing, like all sound political fabric, from the bottom, and proceeding from the simple and limited to the more complex and ambitious.

Thus there is an actual history, as well as those factors making for racial and nationalist strife, others which turn away from conflict[1] towards co-operation, peace and world organization. And the second set of motives appear, in the long run, to be stronger than the first. For in the first, racial and national conflicts are self-destructive. Races that fight and continue to fight, eliminate each other. The second are necessary and co-operative. People that co-operate in production, grow richer, more powerful. We can reasonably expect, therefore, that in time, fifty or a hundred years, long to us, but short to world history barely started on its course of millions of years, the world will consist not primarily of national units, but of people. Each man will still belong to his nation, and feel, if he choose, the strongest local patriotism, but like the different nations of the British Commonwealth, he will recognize also common citizenship, a common obligation, to the greater federation. An Englishman

[1] Some of these functions were examined in the pamphlet, *Process of Real Freedom,* Michael Joseph; 9d.

or Scotsman, or Australian or Canadian feels now not less but more proud of his own country, more devotedly attached to her traditions, because they belong not only to her but to the history of the Commonwealth. Italian music, French painting have not been less valued by Italians and French because they belong also to the world.

When all peoples are dependent on a world authority, local divisions will have little political importance. And though that event may still be at a distance from us, it is in the making and needs to be taken into account even in our present reckoning. In Africa, especially, it would be waste of time and effort to seek exclusive political unity; or to regard the continent as one. Certain problems belong to the whole land mass, but only as that belongs to the land mass of Europe and Asia. Transport, health, and the control of pests even now extend beyond the limits of Africa.

Mutual convenience and profit already, before the war, were linking the different transport systems; international commissions were designing joint action for the quarantine of disease carriers, for research into public health, for the destruction of locusts. Neighbouring regions, with similar climates and economy, co-operated in trade agreements, and this co-operation is increasing fast on account of the war. It appears likely that French, Belgian, and British North African colonies will be closely linked together by commercial treaties. But even here there must remain very great differences in the conditions and policy between countries so diverse in race, culture, and climate as Morocco, the Guinea coast, Nigeria, Dahomey, and the Congo. If we add to these Egypt, an ancient kingdom, Abyssinia, a primitive empire, East Africa, Kenya with its white planters, the Portuguese colonies and Zanzibar, the Union of South Africa with its white government, and the regions of native labour dependent on the gold mines, we can see at once that world federation may come before African federation, in any real or useful sense.

But this is not going to prevent economic reconstruction. Though—like Africa—Europe, Asia, and India are one land mass, no one talks about Euroasianindia for the Euroasianindians or imagines that the problems of Europe will never be solved until Asian intruders like the Finns, Magyars, and Turks are turned out. Why then should anyone suppose that white settlements in Africa cannot exist side by side with the native, or think that there is any greater difficulty in adjusting relations between regions of Africa, occupied by different races, than obtains already between the different nations of any continent?

Diversity of governments and races in Africa is not the basic problem, which is economic and social. Make all its peoples richer and more secure, give them better health and education, and the political aspect will change in accord with social reality.

This does not mean that local politics can be left out of account where they have direct impact on the local economy; but only that the form of government in the different regions of Africa is not so important as its purpose. It is a commonplace to say that many republics are actually dictatorships, that the Scandinavian kingdoms are more democratic than Venezuela or Bolivia, and that the British Empire is more like a union of republics than the Russian U.S.S.

The real character of a government can be judged only by its results; and by its purpose.

6:
Political: Direct and Indirect Rule

IT IS PRECISELY on its results, and its purpose, that British colonial government has been criticized. Its results are said to be economic neglect and stagnation; its purposes, whether it rules directly by white magistrates, or indirectly through native chiefs, the perpetuation of its own authority.

The first of these charges has been encouraged, I am afraid, by my own book. But I did not charge the British government with neglect of economic development; I only suggested that it was needed. This is a very different matter.

I am glad of the greater space allowed me in this edition, because it allows me to explain a complex situation, affecting all governments as well as our own; and to do some justice to a great generation of public servants.

The purpose laid down from the beginning, through all the forms of

British colonial government, direct and indirect, has actually been, at least in theory, to prepare the dependent peoples for self-government. and many officials, brought up in the old tradition, still think that this is their chief duty. They write and speak as if they wish to be judged by their success in teaching the African to run his own institutions. And they are puzzled and even angered by any criticism which ignores this success and asks, "What is the standard of living among your people and what does the average man in Africa think of these institutions which you have preserved?"

A profound change has taken place, not only in colonial policy, but in world opinion, without anybody, apparently, except a few students, giving it any close attention. It certainly has not been published with enough emphasis. Many, I daresay, have realized that the colonial office and the British parliament, in offering a development fund, as a free gift, to the colonies, has set out upon a new policy. But they have not realized that this policy departs from the whole conception or set of conceptions which, until the last few years, have informed and controlled the relations of the imperial government and the colonies. A secretary of state, even fifteen years ago, asked to explain his position, could still say, "My job is to see that the colonial peoples have justice, peace, liberty in all civic rights, in their religions, their language, their business or trade; protection from exploitation and oppression. I must also make sure as far as I can, that they get full value for their labour and their taxes. That they are not over-taxed for the benefit of an official bureaucracy which, in their primitive condition, they can't afford. That if we give them a railway system, new roads, or markets, it is done without bringing upon them a burden of debt charges which will mortgage their future."

That is to say, the conception was rooted first in legal security against violence, then in the old idea of liberty as an absence of restraint upon lawful action, and finally in self-development within local resources.

This was the foundation of British political thought, especially liberal thought, in the nineteenth century. Britain itself was ruled on the same principles, which still obtain in many parts of the constitution, for instance, in local government, where, to a large extent, local resources still measure or limit the power and freedom of the local authority.

This old ideal of liberty, local and national, was a great one. It has inspired generations of devoted service; and it was the chief inspiration, until very lately, of the Colonial service. It is still the fundamental conception of American politics. It reveals itself always in jealousy of a state power and state organization; in respect for local conditions and local prejudice, in hatred of everything, good and bad, which may be called imperialism, and so also of foreign alliances, which might limit the free exploitation of national power. It is, at its best, the chief defence of individual rights against all oppressors; it is, at its worst, egotistic, anarchist, isolationist, and pacifist. It says, that is, "Man is the centre of the universe," but it passes too easily from that premise to the statement, "Therefore man owes no duty to any other man, or to the state, and can even refuse to defend that state which gives him freedom."

A modern thinker would agree with the first argument, that man is a unique centre of free power; but he would not agree that the state is his natural enemy; or that there is no reciprocity in the ties between state and men; or to put it in another way, between one man and his fellow-citizens. The modern theory of liberty is in short founded not on an abstract idea, but upon a reality, freedom, which produces in its turn a new theory of the state, its powers, its functions, and its necessary limitations.

But this new conception has not yet been given complete form by any writer. It is in the early stages of all world-changing conceptions. It floats through millions of minds, not as a conception, but as an assumption, which is not even perceived to bear any reference to freedom. It commands, all over the world, political action of the most vigorous kind, in Russia, China, India, in Britain itself, in the U.S.A., where it is the mainspring of the New Deal, without anyone asking whether this world movement has any deeper roots than those of a political party and its slogans. It is not seen to be a natural development of the same force which created the original idea of liberty; the first democratic and representative constitution, to defend each man's political freedom; the first representative union, to protect his economic freedom and power; the first state education acts, to increase his freedom, his power of mind; the first health and unemployment insurance, to give him personal and domestic security.

Mankind in short is still driving towards the same goal, the realization of its own personal powers, its own unique freedom; and the only change is that the drive is growing more urgent, more irresistible. The masses, all over the world, whose wills give impetus to this tremendous surge of power, are indifferent to theory, unless it gets in their way. They proceed not upon theories but on facts; not on what they think but what they feel; upon appetites and desires; the fear of poverty, of insecurity, hatred of the immediate oppressor; an eager longing to make the best of life for themselves and those they love. And the new assumption, not yet even a theory, is that it is the duty of the government to serve their desires.

Anyone who reads the letters to the newspapers, especially country papers, will have seen that assumption expressed, often with a simplicity which is almost comic. Someone, who lives in a remote country hamlet, and signs himself Worker, writes five hundred words, to say that the people are not going to stand any more nonsense from any government; that if there is not, in future, full employment for everybody, at the highest wages, and guarantees against every possible calamity, there will be a revolution. No suggestion is made of how the government is to achieve the millennium; it is demanded as a right.

But just as the study of neurotics has illuminated for medicine some obscure but powerful functions of the normal mind; so we see in such naive and extreme demands the nature of the driving force which underlies modern political development.

Man no longer feels that the state is his enemy; he regards it as his slave. His notions of what the state can do for him is even dangerously optimistic. And this notion is rapidly penetrating to the remotest quarters of the earth. It is the new creed of mankind.

But since it has arisen from below, and it is not yet described or formulated, it has thrown many of the old theorists and critics of politics into confusion. Especially administrators, brought up under the old principles which are now part of their very natures, cannot understand why, all at once, they are bitterly attacked for policies which, even ten years ago, were praised as the highest achievements of state-craft.

Thus the men to whose devoted work we owe the old constitutions of the colonial empire, such as indirect rule, are now abused or derided for their very triumphs. And the abuse is very unjust. For what has happened is not that the life work of great government servants like Lord Lugard has become worthless; but that the point of view from which all government is judged has suddenly changed. Critics no longer ask of government, "Have you protected the religious liberty and respected the native institutions, as far as possible, of your dependent peoples?" but "What have you done to raise the standards of living, of health and education in the colonies?"

But as we see, the very conception of liberty, of colonial policy, which obtained in the last generation, and almost up to the present war, made it impossible for colonial governors to do very much for standards of living or education. The government provided no development fund; the local government was not only poor; it was founded on the idea of letting native institutions, so far as possible, go their own way. And to raise standards of living or educate on a large scale means great interference with chiefs, often with religious ideas.

Much bitterness therefore has been caused by a change of popular feeling which has not been perceived by either side; to be as deep and important in its origins as the former ideals of policy which it actually contradicts. The work of the pioneers in Africa is not wasted; it has laid the foundations of law, of mutual respect between government and people, upon which the next structure can be solidly based. But it cannot be expected that the structure will be liked by those who imagined quite a different kind of building; or rather, not a building at all, but a growth; the development, more or less slow, of local institutions and local languages from their own seed.

The annoyance, and often the injustice of recent attacks on our colonial administration for not developing local resources, has been increased by a piece of bad luck. Government policy changed decisively in the middle of the war. It has not been fully developed until the last year. But now when governors and directors of departments have at last money to spend, they cannot get materials.

I was talking a few months ago to a district commissioner in Tanganyika, a keen and active man of the new school, who said, "These people are shouting for education, and at last I've got a grant for twelve new schools but every stick of timber and barrel of cement has gone to the army." Now that colonial officials can get the grants they have been demanding for years, they cannot make use of them.

But this defect is temporary. It will pass away with the war. Another may have deeper sources.

It is said that indirect rule, now the most popular system of colonial government, by itself prevents development.

Indirect rule in late years has been very strongly criticized. And much of that criticism has missed fire by its bad aim. It has been disregarded by officials who perceive that it is ill-informed and amateurish.

In all political talk, the amateur is distinguished from the professional by his abstraction. He speaks of notions like Democracy, Fascism, Imperialism, Germany, Russia; and he despises the professionals who discuss what exactly passed between so and so and such an one at such a conference; or why Minister X will always do his best to ruin the schemes of Minister Y.

Indirect rule is a big phrase, in the papers, and in speeches. But as every district officer knows, it is often very hard to make any distinction between indirect rule and direct rule. All governments, of one race by another, use native subordinates. The Romans did so two thousand years ago. If these subordinates are village heads, district chiefs, the situation, at first sight, could be classed either as direct or indirect rule. The only question is, how much authority is delegated to the chief; how much is required by the definition indirect? And both these questions have very different answers, depending not only on theory, but local conditions.

Nigeria, regarded as the chief region of indirect rule, has scores of tribes in every stage of development, naked cannibal pagans on Bauchi plateau, the great Mahomedan kingdoms of the north, highly organized even before the British invasion and ruled by Emirs or Sultans in the oriental tradition, ceremonious, magnificent, and autocratic; and the ancient negro empires of the southern forests, like Benin, or Yorubaland, densely populated, juju-ridden, and yet eager for education.

The white Resident in such an area, or in the northern Emirate, is an adviser, a diplomatic agent. He co-operates with the native ruler, whose power is real. In some smaller Emirates, primitive and remote, like those on the western frontier, or among the wilder tribes, he is, in practice, anything from the power behind the throne to an absolute dictator.

As an acting district officer, in almost the humblest rank of the service, I was in charge of two Emirates, stretching over a region bigger than Wales. There was no telegraph. A letter to Provincial H.Q. took three days or a week, according to the state of the roads and the Niger floods. I could not expect an answer in less than a week. My orders were to do what I thought necessary and take the consequences if I did wrong. In practice I was a dictator, more absolute than Hitler, who must reckon, at least, with public opinion, and the heads of great departments.

At the same time, the senior Residents of the service, at Sokoto and Kano, were obliged to play politics between a powerful native Emir and a watchful home government.

This point is of vital importance, because direct and indirect rule, in practice, are only to be distinguished at the extreme ends of the scale. That is to say, in the great native kingdoms or Emirates at the upper end, and the smallest unorganized tribes, or detribalized settlements at the other. In the first, the white magistrate does actually rule indirectly, he is not in direct contact with the people; in the second, he is as direct a ruler as an English magistrate and town councillor, and the native subordinates are merely clerks or constables.

This is the practical distinction; and it remains whether or no the second official is acting in a region of indirect rule. But there is also a theoretical difference which may be important.

Indirect rule, as designed for Nigeria, and afterwards extended almost throughout the African colonies, was intended not only to govern through natives of the different regions, but through native institutions. And these institutions were to be maintained, as far as possible, in their local prestige. For Africans, an unromantic people, prestige belongs only to power. So of two magistrates even in the most primitive districts: the first, though giving direct orders to humble village chiefs, may still be on the watch to pick out a leader among them, may be trying, so to speak, to grow a native government even where none existed before; the second, in a region of direct rule, may set himself only to get each job done as well as possible. Over a term of years they will produce quite different results.

Thus again for a final distinction, we must ask what is the purpose of a government, what is the main idea. The answer, by the supporters of indirect rule, is, to set on its legs a native government capable some day of taking over the whole administration.

Critics of that government, as it has worked in the great native states, answer that it has merely succeeded in fixing on the African masses tyrannical and obstructive governments which are incapable of real progress.

It will be seen at once that this last fault might easily arise from the first ideal, to set up independent native government.

In short, we have here another development from that change of public opinion which I wrote of before; from the ideal of self-government to that of better standards of living for the people, ideals which often fight against each other. And following my own rule, laid down in the preface, I suggest that though the ideal of self-government is necessary and good, the latter and more modern object, to protect the masses, to free them from ignorance, misery, and dependence should come first.

Indirect rule, therefore, as a theory, is good in so far as it prepares the native Africans for self-government, in his own way; but it is bad if it hinders that progress in education and industry which Africans need.

Has indirect rule, not as theory, but as practice, hindered that progress?

To answer that question we must remember that indirect rule in practice shows a marked difference of character, only in the greater native kingdoms.

Tanganyika is under indirect rule. But Tanganyika is a land of small chiefs, and small tribes, so that district officers are in close touch with the mass of the people. Neither have they any excuse to treat chiefs as local autocrats and independent sovereigns. It is obvious to both parties that if any progress is to be made, the central government must press it forward. The chiefs have not and never had either the drive or the power.

In fact, criticism has been aimed chiefly at Northern Nigeria and Uganda, where ancient native states have been maintained in authority. After forty years of trial, it is being asked whether these states show the progress that might be expected, and whether their political constitution is fitted to obtain it.

The question is unfair in one respect, because, as I say, government policy and public opinion, almost up to the war, did not look for economic progress. But I think that the second question is justified, to this extent. The indirect system, in these great states, is open to special dangers, which may easily turn it into a drag on real progress, and a very serious enemy to political reform.

I write as one who was, for many years, an enthusiast for indirect rule, of which I had practical experience in my service. But like other young officials, I had not then seen the results of any other system. I was, in fact, extremely ignorant of the whole work of government, and very ready to believe all that I was told. I had been taught nothing of political economy; I did not know how to carry out a field survey; and my long and elaborate notes on native custom were completely useless from a scientific point of view; that is to say, from any point of view except my own amusement. My sole useful discovery, in the native land system of a remote tribe, was rendered useless by an equal ignorance at headquarters. Neither of us knew that it was a discovery, and probably, in fact, it had been discovered and forgotten three or four times already by other juniors. I had perhaps one reasonable excuse, as well as those of the romantic, for accepting indirect rule as the perfect system of colonial government. I read in the Political Memoranda that it was not intended to stereotype native autocracy, and that political officers were not to regard themselves only as maintainers of the native institutions, but also as critics and improvers. I can't quote the actual words of the memoranda, which were confidential.

And I saw that the system produced not only good relations between the suzerain power and the African subject, but a smoothly working government machine. In fact, it was almost absurdly easy to run even large and primitive districts, with no more trouble than hard work; and no greater anxiety than occasional outbursts of brigandage, famine, small-pox, inter-village riots, elephant poaching, or extortion by chiefs.

Twice there had been a rising in my district, one just before I got there, when a great many of the administration had been murdered; but the rising had not been against the British officer. It had been aimed at a corrupt chief and his advisers. The people, having killed fifty or sixty of them, ran as fast as they could, not to avoid the nearest district officer, but to find one to tell him all about their troubles and to claim his protection.

So the very rebellion, under direct rule, seemed to prove its value, especially to the white magistrate, who found himself as popular with his subjects as any king of Yvetot. The chiefs did the dirty work, collected taxes, caught criminals, and received all the odium which must attach to any government; the more efficient and active, as a rule, the more odious.

But now I begin to wonder if the very ease and success and popularity of indirect rule may not be its ruin. Prolonged success is no less dangerous to governments than to man. There ought to be a skull on every colonial servant's table, as there was a slave in every Roman Emperor's triumph. And written on the forehead of the skull there should be, "I was a popular success."

Every success is the temptation to be idle and dishonest; easy popularity is the temptation to do or say nothing unpopular, to follow the stream.

Indirect rule was in the popular stream for a long time, and it had that fatal quality which has ruined so many popular actors and film stars: it attracted the sentimental and romantic. The tourist mind is not uncommon among officials; I had it myself, that love of the picturesque which invites the traveller to delight in anything unfamiliar and racy of the soil; in national government, native costume, native dances; national religious ceremony, even national dirt and poverty, so long as it is different from that which he can see at home.

A dozen forces co-operate from different angles to make the indirect ruler feel satisfied with himself and his principles. I may be wrong, but I have a feeling that it is partly, at least, the very forces of easy success, sentimental admiration and popularity, which has gradually brought about some of those very evils which the pioneers of indirect rule foresaw. They have tended not only to stereotype native autocracy but to make it an end in itself.

Sir Donald Cameron, a pupil of Lord Lugard in Northern Nigeria, who as governor of Tanganyika, introduced indirect rule in that country, writes that when he returned to Nigeria in 1931, he was surprised by just such a change. When he had gone away, he left three Nigerian chiefs with autocratic powers; when he came back, he found seventeen.

But apart from this natural tendency to fix a native system, already antiquated, it is grounded in a false and now discredited conception of the government function. It was intended to secure native liberty; not to enlarge native freedom, or to raise standards of living.

Indirect rule had very great advantages which ought not to be thrown away; simply because it has been misused. But it also has immense dangers. There is now some reason to believe that, at least temporarily, the dangers have overwhelmed the advantages; that especially in the areas where powerful native rulers are well established, it may be an obstacle to every kind of real progress.

It is disquieting to see that in Northern Nigeria, with 11 million people, the children in government schools of approved standard are less than 30,000. In Nyasaland, with $3\frac{1}{2}$ million, there are 300,000.

In another twenty years, no doubt, the truth will make itself plain. But in the meanwhile another generation of Africans will have been wasted. And in twenty years, any country that has stagnated in self-complacency may find itself suddenly overwhelmed by the movements of a world yet more resolute for freedom, more impatient of sentimental nationalism, than that of to-day.

It might be wise, before that time, to hold a special enquiry into the working of indirect rule in the bigger native states. Such an enquiry would have to ask first, if indirect rule had failed on account of a departure from its first principles, as laid down by the founders, or by inherent defects revealed only in the working.

And it might also ask if, in the new world, one inherent defect of the system is its lack of direction. For it has, according to modern views, no object or purpose at all. Its very essence originally was to permit the development of something already on the ground. The political officer could interfere to avoid some injustice; to avert, for instance, the mutilation of criminals and the flogging of women; but he was always to support the prestige of the chief and the integrity of native rule.

To a modern view, this is not a policy at all; it has no definite aim. It does not set before itself any real object. And perhaps it is not a coincidence that junior officials often make this very complaint. I can't give names or even hints of my authority, but I have reason to know that many junior officials, on both sides of Africa, have felt very strongly the aimlessness of their administration.

One told me, some years ago, that he would have left the service if it had not been for the war; and that many of his colleagues proposed to do so after the war.

It is proverbial, in the service, that young officials feel cramped and limited. They suffer usually a great disappointment in their first years, and the reason is partly unavoidable. It is due to the nature of all governments, which promise so much in theory, and in practice work slowly and with many unexpected failures.

The other reasons, avoidable reasons, for this disillusionment of the young and keen men who are the type of every colonial service, will be dealt with in their place, under the chapter on government organization; but this one, the lack of definite object in some areas of indirect rule, still remains probably more important than it seems at first sight.

On the other hand, some of the attacks on indirect rule which describe it as a complete failure, and as local fascism, go much too far. Many of course are inspired by the same kind of political thinking which condemns any government, African or European, which does not use democratic forms.

Indirect rule must be judged, like all governments, by its purpose and its results. One must ask of it, does it promote advancement of the African in education, and standards of life? Does it prepare him for a share of responsibility in his own government?

Whatever answers could be made to-day, in Nigeria and Uganda, I don't see why both kinds of progress should not be obtained, under indirect rule, provided that its special dangers of *laissez-faire,* romantic appeal, and lack of direction, are acknowledged and avoided.

The new government policy of development opens a way to a new positive activity, under every system of control.

So long as the district officer, and especially his junior, know what they are aiming at, and approve that aim, they will not complain, as they do now, of obstruction and lack of imagination at headquarters.

This is the important point, that the government, whatever it calls itself, should know what it really wants and that it should be anxious, in all sincerity, to prepare the African to take his part as the full citizen of a *modern* state, in a *modern* world.

If this is well understood, and it is also allowed that the means to that end is through the creation of a modern economy, industrial and agricultural, modern social services and a full system of education, then the form of the government, at any given moment, does not matter very much.

7:

The Union of South Africa and Kenya

SEGREGATION IN the Union of South Africa, by which the country is divided into black and white areas, has been defended on these very grounds. Its supporters, both white nationalists and the white labour unions, have pointed out that white culture, white economy, is at a different stage from that of the negro, and that, in competition, the lower tends to destroy the higher. Negro unskilled labour undersells the white; negro standards of living pull down the general level. They say: "A wholly negro area from which whites are excluded can be developed without those special difficulties which belong to a mixed area. Industry and social services can be designed for a particular tribe at a particular stage of civilization." The policy of reserving native lands in the second area of white domination, Kenya, has the same defence.

But it is admitted that a great many supporters of the Union segregation policy have no intention of allowing the native standard of living to rise. They see in any improvement a threat to their cheap labour supply and they mean to keep the Kaffir poor. They would like also to gain control of the whole continent up to the equator, of the Rhodesias, Bechuanaland, Tanganyika, Kenya, in order, as they say, to secure white supremacy.

Already there is a threat of the colour bar in Northern Rhodesia, where the white labour unions are organizing. They would like to exclude skilled African labour from the copper mines, just as it is excluded from the Rand.

A colour bar in the mines would soon extend to all crafts in Rhodesia. If the Union achieved its ambition of dominating the continent south of the line, race discrimination would be spread over half Africa. This is one of the greatest dangers Africa now faces.

A civil war in Africa between black and white would be not only ferocious and destructive beyond any modern conflict, but it would have no settlement. It would leave behind the same problem as before, in a far worse form. Both segregation and assimilation, even now, in a country of two million white and six million negroes, offer great difficulties, but race war would make them almost insoluble. That is to say, it would end only in armistice and leave each side to prepare for other wars of extermination.

South Africans are wont to answer: "Race war is out of the question. The negroes have no real cohesion or arms, the tribal native is still in the hands of the commissioners working through the chiefs, the detribalized native is a bad union man and his unions are not prepared for extreme action. Some of them even support the republican group in the Union and wish to break away from the Empire." This is true, but it doesn't allow for the two basic facts: the permanent challenge of race discrimination, wherever it exists, and the excitability of the negro.

Native religious movements in South Africa, however they begin, nearly always end in a violent attack on the whites. The reason is simply that a prophet who lives by playing on the emotions of his followers, and must therefore find continually new themes for passions and new evils for denunciation, is bound sooner or later to use the biggest theme, the most exciting grievance of all—white domination.

But religious excitement does not last, and African religious movements do not often find leaders strong or resolute enough to produce great effects. They are primitive in type, emotional, anarchist, destructive; they do not contain within themselves the first elements of cohesion or organization.

Serious revolutionary action, in Africa, is more likely to begin with the strike, where economic wrong is a continuous pressure and leadership requires only obstinate will or resolution in hatred.

One such strike could develop into a series of strikes, each more violent and bitter, until all the native associations, industrial, religious, tribal, united on the one ground of white domination, make cause together. Religious fanaticism is not likely to lead, but it is very ready to support, such a general strike.

Strikes have already taken place in all parts of Africa. In West and East, they followed almost the usual course of industrial disputes in a democratic country; there was plenty of violent language and very little violence, much negotiation and a settlement by agreement.

In South Africa, where strikes are forbidden, they have always tended to violence and bloodshed.

Labour organization has been made difficult for the natives in the Union, but this does not alter the fundamental solidarity of colour, or the fact that the idea of the strike, as a weapon, is now fixed in all negro heads. The agitator, both foreign and native, has been at work for generations. The chief native union which succeeded the first communist agitation during the last war, the Industrial and Commercial (I.C.U.) took the place in South Africa of the American I.W.W. and put forward the same policy of one big union and the communist slogan: "From each according to his abilities, to each according to his needs." Its one big union is a revolutionary policy. It should be noted, too, that the difficulties put in the way of native craft organization, by government, encourages this very plan of one big union.

A general strike of native labour in South Africa would instantly take the shape of race war. It would range whites on one side, blacks on the other. The essentials of war would also be present, for unlike the European general strike, an industrial battle between the colours would represent a true difference of interest.

Such a danger is already the secret fear of the South African whites. For even those who do not acknowledge it feel the uncertainty of their position, outnumbered three to one by subject races who have every reason to hate them. Any trouble with the Union natives produces a cry for repression. After a small riot in Vereeniging, in 1937, when a crowd of natives, resenting the liquor laws which imposed total prohibition upon them, attacked the police, there were at once demands for troops; it was suggested that aeroplanes should fly over the town, to overawe the natives, and the government was pressed to make still more ferocious laws against them.

Fear, acknowledged and unacknowledged, explains a great deal of the repressive legislation of the South, and even the contempt often expressed by white South African citizens for their native servitors. Because of this fear, any party promising to keep the negro down, is sure of votes. Any proposal even to lower the colour bar could not hope to be accepted by a Union parliament. The attempt was made in 1918, during a gold slump, to admit native labour to certain skilled jobs. The result was a strike by the white union in which two hundred and thirty men were killed.

Since then the tendency has been to stiffen the colour bar, and to demand the extension of the Union law and Union control over the neighbouring areas, such as the two Rhodesias. In exactly the same way, the governments of the slave states of the U.S.A. sought to fix slavery on new states adjoining their borders and to exert their slave rights, legal in the South only, over the North. Their object was to defend their position in the old slave states, but their policy led directly to the civil war.

So powerful are the influences, democratic and economic, compelling any government of an area in which races are discriminated, to take this course, that many believe it already too late for any South African parliament or statesman to change the direction of Union policy. A student of American history can see now that, even in the eighteen-forties, when the question arose whether the new state of Texas was to be slave or free, no Southern leader, however influential, could have turned aside from a path leading directly to war. If anyone had attempted it he would have been driven from power. For slavery had already worked itself into the life of the South until the whole socio-economic structure rested upon it. That is to say, its abolition would have meant ruin to thousands of white families.

Those who point out the new measures for native relief in the Union, new grants for schools, a medical service, as evidence of a better feeling between the races, forget that the colour bar itself remains; that it has been even strengthened, and that against all other political facts of the situation, it is the sky to an umbrella. It is something that cannot be forgotten or overlooked for a day, that is brought to mind a hundred times a day in millions of personal contacts. It breeds hatred on one side, fear and anger on the other, faster than thought.

That is why it is doubtful whether the Union leaders in South Africa, any more than the Confederate Union of the States, can save themselves. They are committed to a position, race-discrimination, from which they cannot escape by any action of their own. Also, like the confederate statesmen, they find themselves obliged to make always more extreme demands from the central authority; and to threaten secession.

The authority, in this case, is the British Parliament, which has never attempted to exert a federal power comparable to that of the U.S.A. Senate and Supreme Court. It has no representative from the Dominions and Colonies, and it therefore feels itself unable to use even such sovereignty as remains to it. Its own democratic feeling prevents it from acting as the protector of dependent peoples. It is terrified of the very cry "Oppressor of small nations," and so it has proved itself unable to stand up to any demand, good or bad, of the local South African nationalist. Its only weapon is appeasement, which has not even moral force. For it has meant, in practice, the surrender of the poor to the rich, the weak to the strong, the outcaste to the Brahmin, the ignorant and helpless proletariat to the party boss.

The only hope, perhaps, of rescuing South Africa from a policy which must lead to its own misery and ruin and which will enlarge the numbers of its natural enemies from six to forty millions, is in the creation, after this war, of a new League or Federal Institute, with ultimate control over all African native dependencies, and power to grant mandates to local governments. When I wrote this passage in the first edition, I had in my mind a new and more powerful League, in which the U.S.A. would, this time, take its share of responsibility, and which would have extended powers of supervision in Africa. I was perhaps moved by a formal regard for the old League, of which I was a warm supporter. I am not ashamed of that optimism, and I cannot agree that the old League was a failure. The failure was chiefly in the governments and peoples who might have supported it. Democratic pacifism, government pusillanimity broke the power of the old League, and may easily break a new one, or any institution formed to take its place.

I leave the passage because without it the argument cannot be followed, but it is not imagination, I think, to say that in the last two years there has been a change in the temper of public opinion; that peoples and governments have grown at once more vigorous in idea and more impatient of fine shades. Like soldiers on campaign, they aim at big results and do not feel or show much consideration for special interests which stand in the way.

Recent elections in the U.S.A., and speeches by the statesmen of all parties, point to a central authority different in idea and practice, even if not in name, from the old League.

There will almost certainly be such an institution, under some imposing name, if only to satisfy public opinion. But whatever form it may take, and whatever its declared policies, it is likely to be concerned less with the protection of dependent peoples than military defence, finance, world trade, and economic pacts.

This, in a long view, would be not at all a bad thing. For, in the long run, the only cure for African problems, and indeed the same kinds of racial problems elsewhere, is economic development on the largest possible scale.

But such a development, in Africa, without some defence against the spread of the colour bar, might even increase the tension of racial conflict in the South. The rise of powerful and wealthy African communities, anywhere in Africa, must always be a danger to a white domination, founded on race privilege.

It is true that there is a change of spirit in South Africa itself, due largely to the statesmanship of General Smuts, who has, in several speeches, refused to discriminate between white and black in South Africa. He has claimed to speak for 10 million South Africans.

This is a wiser and safer mode of thought than that expressed by the word trusteeship.

A trustee is appointed to take care of a dependent ward; but the essence of his charge is its limitations. It is limited in responsibility and in time. A trustee is not bound to spend his own means on his ward; and his responsibility ceases when the ward comes of age.

But nations and peoples do not come of age on a fixed date. And many who talk of trusteeship for the African do not in fact contemplate any end to that duty, which is also power.

The word is already growing suspect to the African, who is quick to see through political chicane, and like other dependants, even the children in one's own nurseries, often thinks to detect fraud and hypocrisy in what is only a lack of imagination.

Segregation in South Africa is admitted to be a failure; thus the view which seemed to lie behind General Smut's claim, that equal citizenship for all is the goal of South African politics, would be the solution of a very difficult and dangerous problem. The question is: Can any South African government, even under the wisest leadership, carry the nation with it towards that goal?

In Kenya, the native trust lands are to be administered "for the benefit of the local inhabitants." But it is not certain how government interprets this phrase. Kenya faces the problem of the Union on a smaller scale; a conflict of interests between black and white.

It was the policy of the colonial office, forty years ago, to encourage white settlement on the plateau, and the many British families who went to Kenya, then British East Africa, and invested capital, often all their capital, in the country, were in no sense grabbers or intruders. They were induced, by promises of support from home and by offers of land, to develop great areas which had no native population and were described by the government of the day as vacant.

These settlers and their descendants form a white community quite different from that of the Union. It has the qualities and some of the feelings of the pioneer colonial with the tradition of English country life. At the same time it has a strong sense of local patriotism. Kenya whites are deeply attached to their country and think of it as their permanent home.

Their labour is native; they say that they need it cheap. They were promised cheap labour in the first place, and without it they could not compete in world markets.

The natives' reserves, the trust lands, represent nearly their own former territories. Some are crowded; it seems that most of the arable ground, especially the alluvial plains near Lake Victoria, always carried a large population. But again, without changing the boundaries of tribal areas, we have changed the whole balance of primitive economic development. Tribes which increase fast can no longer migrate to fresh land. Thus, though we have stopped the wars of extermination which often took place between a migrating tribe and the natives in possession, we have created, as in India, a new problem, of how to feed an increasing population on limited resources.

Racial bitterness in Kenya is small compared with that in the Union. The settlers, on the whole, are good-natured masters; there is no colour bar, and the tribes on the reserves do not yet feel discrimination. But there is already competition. The native farmer threatens to undersell the white planter and attempts are made in various ways to prevent his growing the same export crops. This is not a colour bar like that of the white trade unions in South Africa; but it springs from the same cause and has the same object. The cause is the difference of standards between the two races; the object is to maintain white standards.

It is stupid to pretend that there is any easy way to avoid this conflict; it would be stupider to throw away the higher standard for the lower. The problem is therefore fundamentally the same as that of the Union: to keep white standards, and to raise the native standards.

The word trusteeship is also much used in Kenya, and it has been justified where settlers pay good wages and take care of their labour. But even the best of settlers are apt to imagine that there is no alternative to a perpetual trusteeship. The very relation of landlord and tenant, employer and employee, especially where there is goodwill on both sides, tends to make the landlord and the employer say, "We are quite happy and contented here. I know how to look after my chaps better than they do themselves, and they know it. They come to me in all their troubles. Why change things? Why invite discontent?"

And many settlers are devoted to their workers. There was a case not long ago when certain Africans were accused of murder, and condemned to death by the High Court. Their master was sure that they were innocent. He said: "They didn't understand your courts and legal arguments. They got muddled and gave it all up, as Africans do. They said we're done for anyhow, what's the good of arguing."

This man, whose name should be honoured, spent months of time and hundreds of pounds in fighting for his dependants; and in the end he won his appeal, and saved four innocent lives.

Anyone who knew Ireland in the old days can understand how close can be affection between landlords and tenants, so close that it defies political and even religious bigotry.

And those too, who remember those days, can understand how difficult it is for a good landlord who spends not only his money but his life on the welfare of his little kingdom, to realize that any other social or economic arrangement is good, or even possible. Yet it was precisely the best of the Irish landlords, who had lived on their lands and spent their capital on improvements, who were ruined or murdered.

This was unjust, but injustice belongs to all human affairs. What we call luck in private life, is injustice in political affairs, and in government.

The reason for the Irish disaster was the folly of government in not gauging the force and depth of a nationalist agitation based on religious differences and historical legend. In Africa and India the differences of race and colour are far deeper.

That is to say, no trusteeship, however benevolent, can cure the wounded self-respect of a race, or even a people, condemned to perpetual dependence.

Kenya settlers, it is said, have strengthened their local position during the war; and hope to increase their numbers after the war. If this policy is carried out at the expense of further discrimination against the Africans, native to Kenya, it will lead to increasing racial bitterness. And from that, in the long run, the settlers and their children must suffer. The only hope for peace in Kenya is the vigorous development of African economy, with the declared intention of equality, political and economic, between the races. Even this will probably not avoid nationalist agitation, but it is the only possible means of preventing a difficult position from going gradually from bad to worse.

An objection advanced against all raising of native standards in Kenya is that the higher wages and incomes would mean the end of cheap labour. This is true, but necessary. The cheapness of labour is a symptom of that racial difference which is dangerous, and which would have to be removed. But English farmers a hundred years ago, even twenty years ago, declared that they could not afford to pay any but starvation wages. Cheap labour has disappeared in England without the ruin foretold by farmers and industrialists.

The tractor with a skilled man in charge on the farm, improved machinery in the factory, have taken the place of cheap workers and produced for everybody a greater return. Mechanization must come to Africa if it is to make a living for itself, and it should come first to the European farm. Whether the large private farm in Africa will be able to compete, on equal terms, with the small African smallholder, when he understands and practises co-operation, is a question not yet decided. The whole craft of farming is now under reconstruction.

In many parts of Africa the large concession under European management is being abandoned or modified in favour of the peasant owner in some form of co-operative society. Even the Belgians who more than the French stand for a centralized control are beginning to wonder if peasant ownership, with good advice and expert assistance, is not the better method of increasing turnover.

My own view, for what it is worth, is that some products will be found better for the large farm—perhaps a state farm; others for the small owner. And that in each case the best system is a combination of peasant ownership and the state farm. Each worker on the state farm to possess also his own smallholding in a separate co-operative society able to provide machine cultivation, seeds, advice, and marketing.

Smallholding in Africa does not mean the crushing labour and wretched returns of the same acreage in England.

But these are details of organization which must vary in every district. The chief point which I want to make is that in Kenya, as elsewhere, the only hope for a solution of the racial problem is in economic improvement, education on the widest scale.

A man who can earn a fair wage, or even an adequate wage; who has some savings in the bank; some prospects for his family; who can hope to improve his land and his lot; who, above all, feels that he has been given some chance of self-improvement, does not seek to destroy the economy in which his life is cast. He resists even the political agitators who appeal to his racial prejudices. It was not the farmers in Ireland who made the rebellion; it was the middle-class students, romantic and irresponsible, and the town proletariat, the disinherited of the Dublin slums.

The Union problem is, practically, far worse than Kenya's, because the reserves are very small. Lord Hailey, in his report of 1939, asks "whether the reserves can offer those opportunities of social development which some advocates of the policy of segregation seem to have envisaged?"

There is, in fact, evidence to show that they are already hopelessly overcrowded. The Native Affairs Department, in 1937, described their condition as "appalling."

An attempt has been made since then to enlarge the reserves, but it is said that they are still much too small. In the end it will probably be found necessary to take a much larger plan of relief; to treat existing reserves as congested and to move a great part of their population to some other district.

To prepare such a new area for settlement would mean anywhere in

South Africa, where already there is a shortage of good land, a bold and expensive policy of reconditioning, dam building, possibly irrigation; but it is safe to say that the money, if it solved the reserve problem, would be well spent.

This does not mean that the supply of labour so necessary to the Rand mines or the Cape farms would be suddenly cut off. So long as natives, attracted by wages, seek employment for themselves, and so long as care is taken, by direct inspection and control, that they are not ill-used, swindled, or starved, there is, of course, no more reason against their accepting it than against the yearly passage of harvesters, in peace-time, from Ireland to Scotland or Poland to Germany. Labour will follow wages while it finds them attractive.

But the attempt to keep any people ignorant or poor *in order* that they should find low wages attractive, is evil and dangerous.

It is however very doubtful if the South African reserves can be made adequate. Irrigation in South Africa is expensive and often disappointing. It may make bad land worse by dissolving and bringing to the surface salt deposits which lie beneath.

And even if good reserves were settled, standards of living could not improve while Africans remained small farmers of poor land. If the population increases further, as it is bound to do, standards will even fall.

This brings, us in our enquiry, to a point of great importance, not only for Africa. Agriculture with the hoe, the spade, cannot by itself produce, anywhere in the world, a standard of living fit for human beings. It cannot pay for adequate services of health, education, transport, even diet. In those few lucky places where special cash crops, cocoa or coffee, can be grown at high profit, a peasant family may make an income of ten or even twenty pounds a year; but these are good incomes only by the present standards of Africans. They are too low for the state services which men need.

Agriculture, to give an adequate return for labour, needs the machine tool. Smallholders can and should co-operate to share the expense of machine cultivation, of proper manuring and bulk marketing.

But to say that agriculture must be mechanized is another way of saying that it cannot afford to waste hand labour. It must produce the same income, or a larger income, with less hands. The farm that produces, for five people's labour, twenty pounds a year, must produce the twenty pounds with two or three people's labour; or if it keeps the whole family at work, then it must produce thirty or forty pounds. There is no other way of raising the family income.

We notice, in practice, that both processes, all over the world, are now at work. Farms produce larger incomes with less labour. In every country the numbers of rural workers decline as their incomes rise. They produce more per head, and so share a larger income. The modern farm worker, at over two pounds a week, with the use of tractors, multiple ploughs, disc-harrows, drills, reapers and binders, combined harvesters, produces much more than five times as much as his ancestor of 1840, who drew eight shillings a week.

But the men displaced from the farm must find other work, either on new farms, or in industry, and as the higher production of farms soon brings to market all the food that it can absorb, industry is in fact absolutely necessary to the economic development of every people.

Thus, an area without industry is faced by this problem: either agriculture must remain at the lowest level and the people sink gradually into destitution, or agriculture must be improved and large numbers of young farmers be thrown out of work. An improving standard of living for the farmers must mean surplus labour for which there can be no employment except in industry.

Therefore industry is necessary to all African native districts, whether reserved or under mandate; even in the Union, where the colour bar rejects the skilled craftsman. This means, over the greater part of Africa, to establish the new economy among a people who have not even the idea of trade, where the old native fairs are as dead as the village crafts which sent them goods.

Africa is a special problem just because its native economy is breaking down. In Europe, Asia, India, craft-skill and trade were the slow development of centuries. Primitive crafts changed; they did not disappear. The hand-weavers saw a gradual improvement in the loom from Anglo-Saxon times, until, in the eighteenth century, it became a power loom. At no time did it pass beyond the worker's reach of skill and comprehension. The primitive potter learned to use the wheel; his furnace and materials were gradually improved. Even in late years, the village carrier with his van has bought a motor and become a lorry-driver. But he is still a carrier.

Such a development was possible because the workers trained in the earlier form of the craft could always adapt themselves to a small change, and at the same time, markets, middlemen, transport, the supply of raw material and the demand for finished goods, or for services, underwent a parallel evolution.

Civilization is not like a tree, branching from one-stem; but like a forest, in which every kind of growth, all kinds of life, maintain themselves in mutual dependence. The nature of the forest may change, as high bush kills the scrub, or one specimen of tree thrusts out another; but the process is slow and there is always a forest, full of life.

In Africa, a primitive civilization has come to an end, suddenly, as if burnt out, not only because the workers cannot jump twenty centuries of development in a few years, but because, if they did so, there would be no market for their products, none to sell them and no elaborate transport system to distribute them.

If one says "improve agriculture," the answer is, "ploughs are already destroying the soil quicker than the hoe"; if one says, "make roads," the answer is, "there is no trade"; if one says, "clean up the village," the answer is, "the people are too poor and too stupefied by disease and famine to keep them clean, or even to understand why they should be kept clean"; if one says, "educate them," the answer is, "where are the teachers coming from, or the money to pay them, and what will the educated African do for a living? There is no demand for clerks or even for carpenters."

8:
Where To Begin?

THE QUESTION where to begin in Africa has already defeated some of the most sympathetic. The young official, whatever his ideals and his hopes, who finds himself among a primitive people, apathetic, obstinate, cheerful, and undemanding, is very apt to give up the struggle and to say that the African problem is hopeless. Practical men, men who know Africa, often feel this more strongly than they care to say. What they say is, "One step at a time," or "Slow is safe."

But the one-step method, the slow approach, has already failed. The best answer to the question, where to begin, seems to be "everywhere at once." It has often been noticed that African army recruits make a quick and surprising improvement, not only in health but apparently also in general intelligence and responsibility. Dull, drop-jawed loafers, who seem to be half-imbecile, change with extraordinary quickness into brisk youngsters who pick up English and signalling and even simple arithmetic in a few weeks.

The reason for this transformation, of course, is that African recruits get not only clothes, good food and quarters, and instruction, but doctoring. They are freed from the inevitable worms; often of fever too. At the same time, they are removed at one blow from the tribal influence. They move freely among the markets of strange towns, with money in their pockets, enjoying an independence which to us is normal, to them is so strange that we can scarcely imagine it.

This does not mean that any native, taken from his tribe and put on a wage, necessarily makes progress in civilization. Too much freedom may be as bad as too little. In South Africa thousands of such detribalized natives quickly went to the devil. The soldier and the young policeman are learning discipline at the same time as they practise a new freedom. They remain under discipline and are taught to be responsible for their health, cleanliness, and conduct.

The point is not that the African soldier's or policeman's education has special merit. I doubt if it is good for anybody but the volunteer. I am suggesting only that it has quick results because it attacks several points at once. So in the most primitive agricultural community, without trade, without markets, or even roads, I think the best results are got by a wide attack, by seeking to improve crops, to find some exportable product; by opening roads for the traders, and markets where they can barter or buy and sell; by health and education services, all working together and assisting each other. I know that health and education are usually put at the end of reform schemes. Even when they begin to appear in government reports, they are not seen by the bush native. A hospital at a central station, two or three dispensers at native capitals, may make a figure in statistics and even cost a lot of money, but they have no effect whatever on the villages. In the same way, schools, however excellent their work in itself, have no influence upon the masses unless they reach a large proportion of them. There are few places in Africa where the proportion of natives, receiving even the most elementary teaching, touches ten per cent., and in most districts it is less than one in a thousand.

The usual answer to this criticism is that complete services in either health or education would cost more money than any African government can afford; and that both together could not be thought of.

Popular education without health services is almost useless. How can children, of whom every one is suffering from some kind of parasitic worm and most from four or five at once, of whom sixty or seventy per cent. have some form of chronic disease, congenital syphilis, yaws, hernias, fevers, give any nervous energy to learning? Those who do not die, that is, about fifty per cent. under the age of ten, need all their powers remaining from that desperate struggle with dysentery, fever, smallpox, pneumonia, measles, and 'flu, bad food, contaminated water, and the filth of a native village, to battle with their disabilities.

Many people still imagine Africa as a primitive land where the narrowness of life is made up to the natives by magnificent health, a beautiful body, an animal contentment. They think of the Zulus, the lion-hunting Masai, the Nilotic giant, naked among his vast skies, the desert Arab, fighting thirst and sandstorm, the Hausa, adventuring as far as Tripoli and Mecca, as hardy and enviable savages still living in the golden age of a happy and simple world, lost to the depraved and degenerate modern.

This belief, which lurks in the bottom of so many religious creeds, which inspires the anarchist, the pacifist, the Nazi, the Fascist, is pure nonsense. Psychologists may tell us from what secret root it springs; but ethnologists and pathologists, that is, scientists who look for facts and not for slogans or wish fulfilment, pile up every year a mountain of new evidence on the exactly opposite side. It is discovered that the most ancient races were shortlived and full of disease. Their lives, as Hobbes wrote long ago, were brutish and miserable. So, too, are the great proportion of lives in native Africa. Those splendid men in the tourist photographs are the rare specimens of the tribe, in the prime of life, and most of them, even then, have had some form of venereal disease.

The feeble stamina of the French Senegalese troops, picked men, startled the European doctors; the health of the mass of conscripts, from which they were picked, shocked all France and revealed to her for the first time that her African colonies were not, as she had supposed, a welling fountain of man-power, but a rubbish heap of castaways.

The tropical belt of Africa has a higher proportion of lepers than anywhere in the world; tuberculosis attacks ninety per cent. of the more highly populated regions; sleeping sickness, bubonic plague, yellow fever, malaria, and blackwater fever are endemic in great areas; typhus, typhoid, and paratyphoid are prevalent everywhere, and smallpox kills or blinds its thousands every year. Whenever an exact investigation is carried out, the whole native population has been found infected with some variety of worm. Yaws, of which the symptoms are those of syphilis, true syphilis, and gonorrhea infect in many places from sixty to ninety per cent. The proportion is especially high among women.

Africa is not only a very poor country, of which the quarter is savannah or desert, but a museum of disease and frustration. The smiles which greet visitors to a poor village, the uncomplaining cheerfulness of servants and porters, are not the evidence of a general well-being, but of good nature. In this, primitive people are like children, that they do not bear resentment, they do not remember bitterness. A child does not merely forgive, like the Christian; he forgets. He is too busy living to remember injustice, even cruelty. He will love those who ill-treat him because the love springs from his own spirit and is always renewed. The savage is too busy in the struggle for life, for health, for a fragment of happiness and security, to ask himself why others are better off and why he is left on one side by the march of the nations.

But unlike children, they feel responsibility; they have families; they are obliged to use foresight. The African does not rebel from spite or envy, but desperation.

Health services without education are equally wasteful. Latrines will be allowed to fall in unless the village understand their value, unless they want to keep them in order. But the desire for cleanliness does not spring from health propaganda. It is the product of a total change of mind. Education is as necessary to health as health to education.

It is useless to ask impossibilities of any government. No one can afford the millions needed to provide vast thinly populated areas of savannah or mountain with a first-class medical service and schools, while tackling at the same time the urgent problems of erosion and deforestation which threaten the very lives of the people.

But much more could be done with very little or even no more money than governments spend now.

At once some professional experts will say: "I know what he wants

to do—let down the standards—hire a lot of half-trained native assistants to do the worst possible job in the worst possible way."

It is quite true that in medicine or sanitation, a native assistant, with
a few months' training, sent out into the villages at thirty shillings or
two pounds a month, makes plenty of mistakes. The doctor at the native
hospital, who finds that a strangulated hernia has been treated with a
purge or advanced tuberculosis with a cough lozenge, rages and calls
it murder. One can understand his anger and his demand that this sort
of thing must stop—away with the native dispensers.

Doctors like teachers are right to insist on high standards. Both have
done magnificent work in Africa under the greatest difficulty and discouragement. But the professional man by his very training is apt to be
cut off from politics, which deals with an entirely different kind of problem. Professional men have to do always with a limited object, whether
it is in man or metal, a broken leg or bridge. It is an old joke against the
specialist that he forgets sometimes even the human nature of his patient
and talks about him as a case or even a disease. "I saw a very fine tumour
the other day—quite exceptional. I'll give you a photograph if the prints
turn out well." Or he tells some poor wretch that his only chance is a
visit to Davos or permanent residence in Arizona.

"But I can't afford it, doctor. I have a large family."

"Oh, that's not my business. I was asked for a medical opinion."

The doctor is right, like the engineer, to give the best opinion, regard-
less of any financial or human consideration. But engineers and scientists
are notoriously bad political advisers. For in politics there is no special
and limited question to answer, and the centre of the problem, whether
economic, educational, religious, is always humanity in its real nature.

The African problem of health cannot be separated from the economic,
educational, racial complex in which it is a factor. Bad nutrition, for instance, is agreed to be the cause of the low stamina of the African, but
malnutrition arises partly from poverty, partly from ignorance.

Therefore I cannot help feeling that the political officer, taking into
account all these aspects of the situation, and especially the character of a
primitive people, should rather urge a wide attack, however, amateurish,
than a limited service of high quality. I think a native dispenser in each
district or group of villages, a native forestry assistant, even if he can't
write his own name, and a score of native elementary teachers, though
they never heard of algebra, are of much more value to progress than a

first-class hospital two hundred miles away, a European doctor of science attached to the Governor-General, and a model school, equipped with desks and European notebooks, in each capital town.

I don't mean that the doctor of science, the hospital, the planned schools with their expert masters are not desirable, or that any large area can do without the professional expert and his equipment; but only that, where there is the question of another hospital, forestry officer, or model school, and the mass of the people are still without advice or help of any kind, it is far better to spend the money on native assistants. The ideal should be: a skeleton medical service of the first class, with hospital or hospitals; a good training school for native teachers; a central agricultural and forestry institution, teaching native assistants, and an agricultural adviser or dispenser or teacher within the reach of every native. The emphasis is on the last point. Better to cut down expense at the centre than forgo the humble workers who, however limited their knowledge, bring it actually to the people.

The dispenser may make disastrous mistakes, but for every sick native who can see a doctor, a thousand come to him. The government doctor may rage to see patients mishandled, but he does not see the masses who suffer and die wretchedly for want of any help whatever, or the scores who are saved by the simple remedies of the dispenser; an antiseptic dressing, a few doses of quinine. Above all, the dispenser, simply because he is close to the people and practises under their eyes, teaches them. They learn without knowing it, new ideas form in their minds while they still have no words to put them into speech. Those who have tried to teach the tribal native are often brought to despair. I can sympathize with them. I don't know anything more disheartening than the blankness of face and mind, the wooden *non possumus,* with which a crowd of villagers can listen to an appeal from the visiting doctor or vet or forestry officer, except the alacrity with which they disregard it. Having begun with the idea that they cannot understand anything the white man says, they go on to the opinion that it may be good, but it is not good for them. This is worth saying because it has strengthened very much the opposition of the professional expert to the village assistant. He says: "Your dispensers' villages are as dirty as ever, your forestry assistants accomplished nothing."

But this is not true: it only seems to be true. It seemed once true to me, I admit, when I tried to clean up some of the villages in a primitive district. A keen district chief offered every help and we went around the villages together, with latrine diggers and a spell-binder. We told them how worms came from dirt, and especially the guinea-worm from dirty water. This is a worm whose larva, swallowed in water, matures in the leg muscles so that the victim soon has a leg like a bolster from hip to ankle. The worm, very long and thin, makes a hole through the flesh behind the ankle bone, and whenever the wretched sufferer puts his leg into a pool to cool his pain, it lays its eggs in the water.

Guinea-worm, for some months of every year, cripples tens of thousands in tropical Africa. The egg is large. A piece of muslin will filter it from the dirtiest water. It is therefore a crime for police or soldiers to catch guinea-worm; and they rarely do. I don't remember a case in any of my own detachments.

But it breaks out every year in the villages, and especially in that district. The chief and I agreed on a demonstration. We brought the people in each village together, and caused a sufferer to put his foot into water, before them, to show how the eggs were laid. Then we put the water through a piece of loin cloth, such as any villager possessed, and explained that the eggs were caught in the cloth.

This experiment was carried out about nine o'clock in the morning before the sun was high. The same evening I saw villagers in the pool below the rest-house drinking water from their hands.

I told the district head that the only way to stop guinea-worm was to dig wells into which no one could put his feet. We dug the wells, as many as we could afford, but the next year showed the usual epidemic of guinea-worm. Farmers drank from any ditch about their fields.

Meanwhile I found everywhere our bottle-neck latrines, holes ten feet deep, meant to last for years, neglected or fallen in. I wrote in my report that nothing could be done for village sanitation without a regular staff making frequent rounds.

But I was wrong. Even a year later there was a court case in which a woman, making a general defence against her husband, accused him of catching guinea-worm by drinking dirty water; and when I toured again with the district head he showed me new latrines dug by natives themselves, and at least one new well.

The villages, of course, seemed just as dirty as ever, built upon their old midden heaps, and surrounded by the new. It was only in a few scattered compounds that single family heads had dug themselves latrines, and begun to filter their water. I don't claim that all of these were converts. Many, I dare say, wanted to curry favour with the chief or cut a dash among their neighbours. But these, too, serve progress. The snob, the careerist have their value; they are part of the minority who, not only in Africa, provide the condition of improvement; a readiness to accept new ideas, good or bad, and to try them. At least they are adventurous, open-minded. But some of them, I know, could explain why dirt bred worms, for they could give the explanation. They had really grasped the idea. I think every official would agree that there are at least a few in every village, perhaps more than we think, capable of the same logical development from cause to effect; and some at least, though no doubt fewer, ready to act upon it. It is these last, the ones who not only think but act, who have such great value in any community, above all in primitive Africa, where we have to ask: "How and when shall we get things moving?"

9:

Administration

MANY WILL SAY, and have said, the wide attack may be a right beginning for Africa; but what about the government? For that comes before the beginning. No one can begin a task until he has assembled and sharpened his tools.

It is of course true that nothing much will be done in Africa except through the government; and that this, both local and central, has been, especially of late, strongly criticized.

Typical judgments are: first of the imperial government—by a governor: "It never makes up its mind; or if it does make up its mind, it changes it again next day. It also changes its colonial secretary every other week."

By a senior medical officer: "It starves our service and doesn't defend us when we are accused of neglecting the people."

By a Kenya settler: "It is too much affected by home politics. It doesn't really bother about the colonies unless it is frightened of losing votes at home. It is idealist and impractical. It doesn't know anything about the real conditions here or anywhere else."

By a South African: "It is too centralized."

By a Tanganyika settler: "It is out of date, autocratic, and stupid. But it is going to get some big shocks after the war."

By a high African official: "It doesn't tell us what its real policy is." (And he asked me if it had a policy.)

By the authors of several recent books and articles in England and the U.S.A., summarized: "The imperial government is hopelessly unimaginative and out of date. It jogs along at the pace of 1800. It does nothing for the development of the empire and it leaves almost the entire actual work of administration to governors, who, themselves old bureaucrats, have neither the drive, the knowledge, nor the means necessary to set going any really comprehensive plan of economic progress. What is wanted is a central development authority, for the empire, with large capital and the most comprehensive powers."

This last suggestion, in its various forms, some of them in the U.S.A. very extreme forms, has strong support in England, whereas the South African view, that the imperial government is already too much centralized, a view which seems also to be that of General Smuts, represents, I think, the common opinion among settlers in the colonies and South Africans in the dominion. They are directly opposed to a centralized policy. They want devolution.

It should be noticed that the setting up of regional councils for East, West, and South Africa does not necessarily satisfy either party. For such councils can either be instruments of the central power, or centres of delegated power. And in fact one hears them discussed, by officials, in both lights. One party assumes that they will assist in co-ordinating imperial policy, from the centre, and in consolidating the imperial power; the other that they will protect local interests from interference by the British parliament, relieve the colonial secretary of local responsibilities and develop by natural stages into three African dominions, independent and self-regarding, for East, West, and South; the latter being incorporated into the Union of South Africa.

At present all councils are of course advisory; as the central development committees, in London, are also advisory. The government uses them but has not delegated to them any permanent or definite functions. That government therefore is still the secretary of state, answerable to parliament; with his permanent staff in Whitehall; to whom the various governors report direct and from whom they receive orders on their general policy, sometimes in much detail.

And as the S. of S. is served by a permanent secretary and his staff of civil servants, so each governor has his chief secretary and a secretariat staff, who collate for him the reports and requirements of all the separate departments: Education, Medical, Public Works, etc., and convey to them his orders.

The heads of all these departments are of course in close touch with the chief secretary, and the governors can call them into conference when he chooses.

The local system has the same merits and defects as those charged to the central government, and I give some typical criticisms.

By a junior officer: "It's no good sending in any suggestion to the secretariat; it simply plugs up another pigeon-hole."

By a district officer: "The secretariat doesn't know what I'm talking about because it's never been over the ground."

By the officer of a technical department (I cannot give the details because they might point to the officer and colony concerned): "My scheme was actually working and making money, so of course the secretariat squashed it. I don't know what was the trouble—probably big business with a hook up in Downing Street."

By another colonial officer: "The trouble with the secretariat is that it doesn't know anything and thinks it knows everything. I send in a worked-out scheme, and some pip squeak just out from Oxford by the last boat pulls it to pieces."

By a member of the secretariat: "The trouble with the bushman is that he only sees his own district, and has no idea of the general policy handed down to us from the C.O. or H.E. (the governor)."

By a chief secretary: "Technical departments give most of the trouble. They won't even try to fit in. They send in a scheme to cost half a million, and if you say that the estimates only allow ten thousand, they turn sulky and won't do anything at all."

By another chief secretary: "Of course as a bush officer you think us at the secretariat a lot of paper spoilers. Well, the bush officer is the backbone of the service, but I don't know if a backbone, all by itself——" and he left the rest, politely, to my imagination.

By a late governor: "A lot depends on the chief secretary. Some of them are not much better than clerks, experts on 'Previous Papers.' And some governors like them to be clerks. On the other hand you get the C.S. who fights his governor. After all, a C.S. is usually acting governor for a fairly large proportion of his service, and if he's got ideas, he likes to carry them out. I remember when a governor and his C.S. weren't on speaking terms, each of them had his own policy. H.E. of course gave orders, and the secretariat had to put his office in motion, but I doubt if the sausage that came out was made of the same meat that went in."

By a chief secretary: "Men get out of touch. After the war, I should like to fly my officers home every nine months for six weeks' leave."

By a provincial resident (before the present war): "Between ourselves, all this C.S. understands is files, estimates, and bridge. But all H.E. wanted was a bridge partner and a yes-man. And he got him."

By another resident: "I did my turn at the secretariat and I learnt a lot. Every bush officer ought to see the wheels go round."

By a junior member of a secretariat (some years ago, but still typical): "Dicky (the chief secretary) is undoubtedly a brain. I think first class. But of course he does get a bit silent with some of the intelligent tourists who want to tell him about the true significance of the customs of the Wee Wee tribe, in rain making, when he's just had two hours of H.E. on what they did in Borrioboola in 1905, and there's still sixteen hours of papers before bedtime. And that's a pity because the tourists go home and tell their M.P.'s that he's nothing but a bloody bureaucrat without any real human interests."

We may say of all these criticisms, fair samples of many similar, that they have truth in them, or point to truth. The first truth which arises from all of them is that government is largely a matter of persons. It always has been and it always will be. A good governor, a good chief secretary will do good work in spite of defects in the office set-up. Bad ones, or good ones who can't agree, will do badly with the best possible office. But the choice of governors is again a matter of persons. It depends on the colonial secretary. No reform of organization can change the root fact that it is a mere instrument in the hands of actual people.

Secondly, we notice that these critics, like those who find fault with the imperial government, fall into two classes: those who want more centralization, in this case, in their own secretariats, and those who want more devolution, in this case, to the bush officer.

Again both sides have reason. In such a case one looks for a confusion of thought, or of definition, and I think there is a confusion here. I suggest that modern government has two separate functions, and those who think only of one function are not talking about the same thing as those who see only the other.

These functions might be described as the strategical and the tactical: the forming of policy and its execution.

All governments no doubt have had these two functions, but the economic extension of modern bureaucracy, like that of mechanization in the army, has set them further apart. A primitive ruler was scarcely aware of forming policy. He carried on a tradition, he dealt with emergencies according to precedent. Like a tribal general almost his whole art was tactics. A modern government does, or should, form the most extensive and novel schemes for entirely new developments, over many future years.

This function is growing every day. It was only a few years ago that we first heard of a five-year plan; now such plans are put forward every day. And the peoples are so accustomed to this new manner of government that they would consider a government without a plan, more or less far-reaching, and quite distinct from the old political programme with its vague promises (retrenchment and reform) as no government at all. They would throw it out.

Thus, the modern government needs a policy-forming staff, a general staff to gather information, to lay down a general policy, to co-ordinate action and to allocate resources. It needs the separate administration, each with its own staff, not only to carry out the general policy, but to adapt that policy to local conditions.

The general staff requires the highest degree of centralization. It must be organized to secure and bring to focus every scrap of information on a given subject; to handle this mass of information, and to form therefrom as far as possible sound decisions on the general situation.

The local administrations need the highest degree of freedom in the execution of policy.

That is to say, delegation of executive power is just as necessary as centralization of the policy-forming power. An army needs not only a first-class staff with the knowledge and imagination to design a great campaign; it needs, just as much, field officers, subalterns, and finally private soldiers with courage, knowledge, and energy, above all with initiative to devise for themselves, and carry out on their own responsibility the details of that general plan, each of which is itself, on its smaller scale, an independent campaign, requiring its own invention and expert knowledge.

The difference that remains and is vital, is in the kind of skill required. The general staff deals with figures, papers, maps; the subaltern deals with men, events, mud, rivers, and mountains. The first needs great powers of concentration and foresight; the second, a genius for improvisation and quick decision.

Any suggestion, of which there are many, to set up a central imperial development board, or even, as from some writers in the U.S.A., an Anglo-American federal council, which overlooks this vital distinction, is dangerous and retrogressive. Not only central, but local administration wants more scope, more independence, in its own sphere.

Lord Hailey points out that this central development board, proposed in some quarters, would tend to over-rule the governors. If this were so, if any central body were to over-rule a governor in his own sphere of decision, it would be a backward step.

All centralized organization has the same quality, mechanical stiffness. The larger it is, the more rigid. This is inevitable. A subaltern on patrol with half a dozen men, can improvise their shelter and feeding; can change his plans or their route in a moment. To feed and move an army requires another army of clerks, assisted by a huge apparatus of rules, codes, and tables; and once the army is on the move, it cannot be stopped or even diverted, in less than many hours or days of similar effort. And any mistake in the office work may mean complete disaster to the troops. All these faults urged against bureaucracy, its inhumanity, its slowness to change, to initiate, are due to that discipline required by large operations.

That is to say, it is the virtue of a centralized bureaucracy, its precision, which is the prime defect of an executive, which must be flexible and adaptive.

Modern government, if it is to escape confusion on the one hand and deadlock on the other, must combine precise staff work at the centre, first-class strategical planning, with enterprise in the field, imaginative tactics.

Modern armies of all the great powers have accomplished the feat; why not the government.

Thus both attacks on the present administration are justified. It is at once too centralized in one function, the administrative; and too casual and disorganized in another. Local administrations are hampered for lack of scope; and the imperial government, while trying to do much that belongs to local administration, fails to do what belongs to itself: to devise those large plans, that general policy, that central idea, which, in the separate colonies, provides the aim or object of all their activities.

This, of course, is putting into a very simple form, a highly complex process. The whole matter would require a book by itself.

First of all, the balance or division between general policy and local administration continually shifts. And certain subjects tend to pass out of local control; others have already passed. These are air transport, continental communications and hygiene, and large scale finance. In these departments, the central authority must plan for the whole empire in co-operation with other governments. But this should not limit but increase local powers. A poor colony, like Tanganyika, for instance, should no longer suffer from bad roads because it cannot afford better. Its administration will have more initiative, not less, in developing its resources, when its external communications are part of a continental and international grid, and it can draw its funds from a central pool, without being compelled to burden itself with debt charges.

This is a good example of what I mean by the advantage of more centralization on one hand and more devolution on the other; larger imperial policies at the centre, greater scope for local authorities at the circumference. And we can see also, more clearly, the definitions of function. Why the imperial authority requires to be at the centre of things. Why it needs not only the most precise and up-to-date knowledge of the whole political and economic situation, imperial and general, of world politics, world markets, world trends; but the imagination to foresee world developments and to devise those far-reaching schemes of constructive policy, which can alone prevent the colonial empire from falling out of touch, politically and economically, with the general advance.

Again, its appropriate structure may be compared with that of a supreme war council. It requires a commander of true imaginative genius, a staff of specialists, each expert in his own branch, and it needs to be in close touch with the other departments of state, with world industry, world finance, and the representatives of foreign powers.

Its head must also take account of parliament and of public opinion. Here the analogy with army command breaks down. Many would like to see this check or spur removed. Some of those who suggest regional councils, really desire to use them as a screen or buffer between local authority and the British parliament.

It is too soon to know how far a new world opinion, in the future, could replace the direct pressure of parliament on a secretary of state and through him upon local authorities, but history seems to show that there is no good substitute for parliament.

That is to say, I think that regional councils should continue advisory, just as the central development committees, in all their variety, should remain as consultants. The final word on policy must come from the colonial secretary, responsible to parliament, and the actual power of administration must remain with local authorities.

To put it more clearly, central development boards must be the servants, not the masters, of the secretary of state, and regional councils are needed not to supersede governors, but to assist them.

On the other hand, I think it is established that development should be a special function both at the centre and circumference.

Some have proposed that the new information officers, now acting in each colony chiefly as propagandists, should form the nucleus of a development service. They deal with information, both as collectors and distributors. They could therefore act as clearing offices for industrial information.

But I do not agree with this suggestion. I think the information officers have separate functions, far too important to be merged or confused with those of any other department; and in fact that that service itself needs to be extended.

The development branch certainly needs all the information it can get, and it would get much from the information service; but its own function, both advisory and executive, is quite distinct from that of an information service. It wants special information, aimed at a special purpose, and it should have its executive officers in every colony. Just as the secretary of state seeks advice from a medical board or medical expert at home and forms a policy to be carried out by the governor through the director of medical services in each colony; or *vice versa*, the D.M.S. in each colony informs and advises the governor, through the secretariat, on the condition and needs of the people; so the central advisory committee should have, in each colony, its technical head.

This suggestion is open to attack. It will be asked: What is a technical development officer? Where can anyone learn the technique of development in a thousand different industries? But what is a technical secretariat officer, and where does one learn the technique of a thousand different government functions? The advisory board at home does not consist of experts on every possible branch of industry. It consults or recommends experts. The local development officer cannot be expected to judge the value of all suggestions sent to him; even of many trade openings he will hear only from the board at home. His function will be, on the one hand, to collect and classify all available information, and report to the central board; to seek expert advice and, if necessary, to engage experts and technicians for each job; on the other, to push forward local development.

It may be said that his office will encroach upon other departments, the Public Works, Transport, and Medical. But all departments overlap. Each requires the co-operation of the rest; and it is the duty of the secretariat and finally the governor, to co-ordinate their work and their demands.

Why I think a development officer is necessary, is precisely because development belongs, at present, to all departments, and therefore to none. In practice, suggestions for new industries go simply to the secretariat, in an ordinary political report, and if they reach the secretary himself, have at the very beginning, to compete for his time and reflection, against urgent problems from regular departments whose representatives sit in their offices a few yards from his door, meet him every day at the club, or at exercise, and are in a position to say at any moment, "What about my new hospitals, what about my bridges, what about my lorries, what about those schools, what about this disputed succession? We'll have a big row unless something is done before the end of the week."

There is no development officer to say, "What about this proposal for a fish-curing industry at so and so?" And if the secretary himself suggests it, he will hear from the different departments that there is no labour to build the factory, no funds for a new road, no lorries to carry the fish, and that the river villages are too unhealthy for any increase in their labour population.

And he is often not in a position to answer from his files. "All these objections were made against the canning factory at such a place, but it's doing very well."

Another protest will be, "If your development service is under the secretariat, nothing will be done." I quoted the complaint of a junior. Over the course of years I have heard hundreds of the same kind.

I have good reason to know that this feeling is deep and strong enough to be a danger to the whole policy. There is, in fact, at this time, so deep a sense of discouragement among junior officers in the service, so much pessimism about colonial government in its present form, that it would be stupid to write about organization without dealing with it. Organization is, in the first place, actual men, and if the men are discouraged, organization is useless. When the men, as men, form, as I believe, the best service that any nation could hope for, then it is stupid to waste their keenness and their brains for lack of a little imagination.

What is most discouraging to the junior, the man at the bottom, in any service anywhere, is the feeling that he is regarded as a fool; whose opinion, on any matter whatever, is bound to be worthless.

I speak again from experience. I was lucky in my first seniors. I was asked for my opinion, even in matters on which, as I said, I had no right to form one. So it was the greater surprise to me when, later, facts which I alone could give, and advice of which I alone could judge the value, were ignored.

I should have been perfectly content if headquarters had said: "We have received your report and notice your suggestions. But we cannot act upon them because——" and given some reason.

Government is a complex and rough business. A junior should not and does not expect to be handled with kid gloves. I have been damned in heaps by every kind of superior officer, from a Montenegrin corporal and a British sergeant to a resident, with excellent effect, so long as I knew where and why I was wrong. What hurts a junior is to know that he is predamned by men who do not even take the trouble to know what he has to say for himself. And I don't hesitate to say that the result is highly damaging to service efficiency; not chiefly because of any waste of good suggestions; nine-tenths of a junior's suggestions are naturally useless; but because discouragement of this kind, the feeling that all initiative, all independent thought is out of place, is the first step in a degeneration which produces often after ten or fifteen years that very type which is the ruin of every bureaucracy and which juniors detest: the office deadhead—the man who performs routine functions in an office, during certain hours, and cares for nothing else except his pay, his meals, his hobby, and his pension.

We all know plenty of such men, often charming people: witty, well read, delightful companions out of the office, and full of interest in the world, but profoundly cynical about government, about human nature, and utterly convinced that nothing can be done to make the one better or the other richer in resource.

But they are the victims of a system, which picks young men for their intelligence, and then treats them like machines.

A few months ago, on an army transport, as we were entering a certain tropical port, I saw a notice put up that all ranks were to wear slacks and jackets, or battledress. Shorts and short-sleeved shirts were forbidden. The temperature was about ninety in the shade.

Sergeants were shouting the same order among the troops on the lower deck, and adding that any man who broke the order would be crimed. And a little group of men near me, as I stood at the rail, were grousing bitterly about spit and polish.

No one had thought it worth while to explain to the troops that the object of the order was not to make them look smart; but to protect their legs and arms from mosquitoes; or that there had been several hundred cases of fever in the previous convoy, after touching at this port. And no one seemed to consider the cumulative effect on thousands of men of this small piece of official obscurantism.

It is not only lack of imagination which causes such folly; it is also a love of tyranny, which often disguises itself as a respect for discipline.

Discipline and mutual understanding are not enemies. They support and strengthen each other. This, I'm told, is understood in the modern army; the incident of the notice was not a fair test.

But I don't think it is understood in other services, which do not, in fact, impose discipline, how important it is for their whole future efficiency that cadets and juniors should not be given to understand, on first joining, that nobody is interested in their ideas.

A bureaucracy is not a machine. That fatal simile has done infinite harm. No organization of men is anything like a machine, and attempts to make it seem or work like one are ruinous to its whole purpose and value. An athlete is not put on the rack to loosen his muscles. He is encouraged to develop them for himself. The British colonial service is a picked corps; the flower of the country's quality in brains and the energy which goes with brains. It deserves better management.

This is not the place to discuss a general reorganization of the service, which is a matter for experts. But in so far as we are dealing with plans for African development, which must be carried out through the services, we have to ask what has held them up in the past. The first and chief, lack of money, is partly removed; the second, lack of information, should be removed by a development service; but there remains that lack of imagination and drive which certainly has existed in the past, and is said still to exist in some departments.

The junior officer's notion, which I, as a junior officer, shared, that a secretariat exists only to waste paper and get in the way of any real work, is of course absurd. A secretariat, as the central co-ordinating office of the governor, must handle a big correspondence.

But I think there is some truth in the idea that chief secretaries are often overworked at the desk, to the damage of their other functions. They are drowned by mere volume of papers. And some at least of their overwork is due to lack of delegation. An ex-governor said to me, "Technical chiefs are rather apt to put everything on the secretariat. They won't take responsibility for the details of a scheme," and he suggested that they weren't paid enough. "You could not get a first-class man at home for what we pay them."

The same remark was made to me before, years ago, by a technical chief. I think it is sound. It is absurd to grudge a great department, spending many thousands or even millions of pounds, the few hundred which would enable it to compete with business firms for first-class brains and qualifications. It need not offer the very high salaries which business finds it wise to pay, government service has counter attractions for men of goodwill, men who like to feel that their work has direct value to humanity, which can be a set-off against a lower standard of pay. But it can't afford to pay so little that a man of high qualifications, after many years' service, finds himself cramped—and what is worse, his family cramped—for means in comparison with those who have devoted smaller abilities only to making money.

Technical chiefs should be paid on a scale equal to high responsibility. Then they should be expected to take responsibility.

To complain of bureaucrats that they tend to become unenterprising and paper bound as they grow older, is futile if we turn them into slaves of the desk. Big business knows that very well. It distinguishes clearly between the functions of director and manager, but not so closely between the men. It does not turn a manager into a clerk, because it knows that he must, in practice, have power, and must therefore have time and means to study conditions and reflect on policy.

Chief secretaries should not be regarded as superior clerks, but more as assistant governors learning the governor's job. And they should be relieved, as much as possible, from routine paper work. They should certainly have time to tour. Governors should not be too closely confined to their own colonies. They too should be expected to tour; not only in their own colonies, but among their neighbours. Already governors do meet in regional conferences, like that of the East African governors. But they ought to go much further. They ought to be regarded more as assistant secretaries of state and ministers of the crown, than local officials. They should be closely and personally in touch with the ministry at home by frequent visits, and like ministers, they should have the widest possible knowledge, by a personal acquaintance, with all that part of the empire in which the problems resemble their own. It is now the practice for a colonial secretary to make wide tours in the colonial empire. The colonial secretary is at least as busy in Downing Street as any governor in his office. There is no reason why a governor should not, on appointment, or soon after, tour that part of the empire which can throw light on the situation in his own colony.

But not only chief secretaries and governors need to be kept in touch.

The chief secretary who said that he hoped, after the war, to fly his officers home every nine months, for six weeks' leave, made an excellent suggestion; but it might be improved by giving all officers, at regular intervals, special leave, by air, to study conditions in some other district or colony, or to take a course at home.

Good doctors, keen army officers, take refresher courses to keep themselves in touch. A holiday at home spent in playing golf, fishing, or shooting does not necessarily put an official, of any age, in possession of the current feeling of his time.

I write current feeling as the shortest convenient term for that experience which distinguishes a man of affairs, at the centre of things, from one who, with equal or more intelligence, has spent many years in exile. A very important experience because it is from that feeling, based on experience, and not from argument, based on reading or prejudice, that one man, accustomed to big politics, will say of a proposal, "There's nothing very alarming in that. Why not try it." While another, who has known only the politics of a small dependency, is horrified as by something not only revolutionary and dangerous, but out of nature.

These proposals for a new development department to work with the central committee, and with the other existing departments, including the newly established information service, and a little more scope for the local administrations, may not seem very important, after some of the revolutionary schemes lately put forward. But from experience, I still think that what matters in all government is not the structure so much as the ruling idea, and the men who carry it out.

If the idea, still a new idea, of creating as soon as possible a modern civilization, is firmly grasped and loyally pursued, then bureaucratic forms matter little more than the forms of local authority already discussed; no more but no less.

10:
Information Officers
and Public Relations

INFORMATION OFFICES already exist in all the African colonies. They are new, their duties and their own idea of their functions vary from colony to colony. They were set up at first largely to distribute war news and propaganda, and to send home, through the secretariats, information and suggestions about propaganda. The propaganda is largely the work of the ministry of information, which distributes it to the officers.

But to these duties a great many more have already joined themselves. For instance, travellers are sent to the information office for enquiries, and some offices take charge of all visitors. They act as hosts and guides to strangers. One office, the best that I saw, was not only arranging hospitality for many different groups of passers-by, from young Turks on their way to a training station to a film party seeking local talent, but providing them, as far as possible, with what they wanted—amusement, facts, sight-seeing, introductions.

That is to say, what had been designed as an information office, to give out propaganda, was beginning to grow, merely by the initiative of keen and active officials on the spot, into a public relations office. A very important change. For the vital difference between an information office and a public relations office is that the first merely gives out facts; it is a crude instrument in the hands of authority; while the latter not only gives out but gathers. It is not a tool but a sense, a nerve-end.

Its duty is to deal with something very difficult to know except by constant and expert attention; the state of public feeling; not only to advise on information, but its form.

It is sometimes said that the function of a public relations officer is to create consent. This seems to me a dangerous phrase and a dangerous conception of the task. A political party can do what it likes to make its programme acceptable. A government department must at least try to draw a line between blowing the trumpet of its policy and explaining its objects.

This line used to be drawn, and is still drawn, between bureaucracy itself and the government.

It is a well-known rule of the permanent services that its members may not write to the Press, criticize government policy, or defend their own actions. They were, in short, forbidden to have public relations. This was a sound rule, in so far as it forbade bureaucrats to use their influence in party politics. Imagine the effect on public efficiency if a member, say of the foreign office, were allowed to get up in public, and, with the advantage of his special knowledge, to attack his own secretary for foreign affairs. On what sort of confidence could the secretary and the official meet and work together in future? And how would a party in power regard the intervention of a paid permanent official, not elected but selected by examination, against their political will.

Bureaucrats must stand aside from politics.

But this does not mean, as it is too often meant, that the great departments of state, the colonial governments, should have no relations with the public. They cannot avoid such relations; for the public is always interested in them. State departments, and especially colonial governments, in the past, have too often translated the rule that they must stand aside from politics into the creed that they stand aloof from the people. They have too often regarded the people as an ignorant and stupid mass, always prejudiced, always mischievous.

I have watched the expression of a senior official in Africa, while reading, in an English newspaper, a speech on colonial policy. His face was a study in resigned contempt. Contempt is too strong a word. His very expressive set of features, rather Roman than Greek, seemed to say: "What can one do with such a fellow? He can't really be such an idiot as he talks."

The speech in this case was in fact silly. But its silliness was that of a man who applies a formula to political conditions of which he had no knowledge or idea. He had in short only one relation with colonial government; he misunderstood it, he distrusted it, and he hadn't the faintest idea even of what it had achieved.

But to the colonial official, as I am afraid, to myself, when I heard the empire attacked by critics who did not know the facts, criticism like this was not worth answering. We withdrew into our ivory tower and if we were accused of aloofness, we answered that by the rule of the services we were not allowed to defend that service. That was the business of our minister.

I suggest now that this attitude is not only impolitic; it is not democratic. The people have a right to know what is done by their consent, and now, with much of their own money, in the great spending and administrative departments. A public relations department and its appropriate offices in each colony is a necessity of the modern democratic state.

It is a necessity not only for a government to know what a people are feeling, but for that feeling to be, as far as possible, well informed. For public feeling makes public opinion which presses, for good or evil, on all governments, not only the democratic.

Nazi and Fascist eagerness to control mass opinion, by propaganda, was proof of that urgency.

Propaganda should not be thought of as lies invented to deceive the people, but as things which ought to be known to everybody. A lying propaganda may be effective but not against the truth, put with equal force. The terrible mistake of the democracies, and especially Britain before this war, and for a century before that, was to ignore altogether its duty of giving information, to leave all over the world a clear field to its enemies. The damage has been enormous. The state of Anglo-American relations, in which even friends of Britain are obliged to apologize for that friendship, is one result which may throw an exceedingly long shadow upon history.

This mistake is now, I think, acknowledged, but I am not sure that all members of the older ministries yet understand the need of a branch, or even department, of the service devoted only to public relations. They do not understand that this is also a subject requiring technical experience.

They would not deny to the Foreign Office its right to exist. What is the Foreign Office but a department of public relations, limited to foreign countries, and limited therefore in scope, since it does not attempt to educate opinion.

Finally, not the least merit of a public relations department, fully developed, is in bringing officials themselves into touch with public feeling, at home and abroad. It breaks through that invisible wall, which is so quickly built between any bureaucracy and the real world, by the practice of unquestioned authority, the habit of security, and above all, that independence of the scholar and the expert, which, like all independence, is a supreme virtue, always skirting the precipice of a dangerous vice.

11:
Adult Education: General

THE SEPARATION BETWEEN minds, in Africa, is even more profound than that in Europe between an expert bureaucracy and the people. For it is a difference not only of knowledge but a whole life experience.

A few months ago I sat listening to a white African farmer complaining of his labour, that they would not work overtime, for any wages. He was, I found, a good employer. He treated his labour well. The tenor of his complaint was therefore, "It's no good expecting loyalty or a real job of work from the African. Here we are in the midst of war and very short of labour. And my men won't do an extra hand's turn even for double pay."

It was no good explaining to him that, for the African, both wages and war had a different aspect. A European may strike for wages in the middle of the war. He is loyal enough, but he thinks he is being treated unfairly in comparison with some other worker. The African does not want more wages, nor more work. He has enough wages and he wants his leisure. As for the war, he feels that it has little enough to do with him. A new white ruler cannot give him much less than he is getting already; *or much more.* In short the African, like every peasant, is a sceptic towards life. He expects very little from it and he's not surprised if it gives him less. He is used to disappointment of all kinds, by flood, locusts, famine, fire, disease, the death of children, the incalculable accidents of the law, the whims of tax collectors, village heads, policemen, and witch-finders.

His demands are small, and his pleasures very simple. Neither does he want to go far outside their narrow circle. He suspects and dreads the outer world. He will go immense distances to earn a little money; but he wants the money to make for himself his own village life a little more tolerable; to pay his debts, to ransom his family farm, to buy a wife. Though he is willing to fly from the village to get money, he takes with him the village mind, limited, sceptical, superstitious, and timid of adventure. If he settles in a town, he makes there what is called a slum, but is actually another village, in the town.

The European employer in Africa who complains of his workers that they won't work longer hours even for good wages, should ask himself first. "Do they need more money?" and secondly, "What would they do with more money? What would they spend it on?"

In a place like Arusha, high on the slope of the Kilimanjaro massif, you see a double row of Indian and European shops. Some of them could be taken up bodily and planted in any European town, without seeming out of place. The smart wives of settlers go from window to window, admiring silk frocks and patent leather shoes; while some of the most primitive tribesmen in the world, and their skin-clad wives, dawdle through the streets on their way to the native market. The one thinks in pounds; the other in pence. And the difference is not one of poverty but of mind. The European woman asks a good deal of life—in interest, in variety, in beauty, the satisfaction of a hundred tastes and ambitions. The African asks only that she may escape starvation, mysterious sickness, evil spells; and the same for her children. She does not want change even under the name of progress. Why should she? And her husband, having satisfied his wants at a few shillings a week, does not want more wages.

In short, economic development in Africa is useless or harmful, by itself. It can only be local and superficial. It can create only the mining camp where temporary workers come to earn a few pounds, or the town slum where casual labourers and the misfits of native life, neurotics, petty criminals, prostitutes, and wasters form together an Alsatia like old St. Giles or the Edinburgh Canongate.

Modern civilization requires a modern mind, modern ambitions and needs, and the mind logically comes first. I say, in logic, because in practice economic development is so closely interwoven with changing standards of life that they cannot be separated. Take, for simplicity, the case of a pagan village, just brought into touch with the world. Some wandering trader, Hausa in the West, Indian in the East, brings a load of bright cloth. Some of the enterprising young women want it. Some of the enterprising young men, eager for wives, seek paid work to obtain such cloth for their girls. They return with news of an outside world; of a hospital, a magistrate, and a mission. Some take work at the mission and begin to have new ideas about cleanliness and comfort; hammock chairs and metal cooking-pots appear in the village. One of the men begins to mend chairs, and then to make them. A new industry has appeared to answer a new demand.

This is the natural process. Improvement in idea, in ambition, in hygiene, in industry are tangled together in one complex development. But it is slow.

It is quickened by education, when the village children go to the mission school. But school education is also slow in its effect on a whole population. Few children go to school at all, and not all who go are able to learn anything.

In Africa now, as in Russia twenty years ago, nothing can push forward needed education, in the time available, except adult education on the widest scale. Without it, little will be accomplished; and only by its means, a revolution is still possible.

Schools and more schools, hundreds of more schools are needed; and now that there is money available, we may hope to see them. Some directors of education are already preparing plans for giving at least the beginnings of education to all the children. But what we have to grasp is that children are a minority and a minority with very little influence, especially on economic and medical progress. An African child, like an English child, with new ideas on any subject, is very likely to be laughed at, or to be told that he is talking nonsense. His elders know better.

Thus elementary education of children loses seventy or eighty per cent.

of its effect without adult education of their parents. In fact it is largely wasted. For children, in Africa as in England, are fond of their parents, and respect them. The prejudice of a mother, especially with her own daughters, will outweigh years of careful and expensive instruction. A suggestion from the father that new ways of farming may offend local spirits of which white men know nothing will instantly destroy all the influence of an agricultural instructor. Prejudice, superstition, fear, ignorance must be attacked in their strongholds, the adult mind.

It is not too much to say that if available funds allowed only for children's education or adult education, the latter would be the best choice. For children eagerly learn from their parents, but parents seldom consent to learn from children. The very fact that children are the first to offer a new idea is, often enough, all over the world, to bring it to derision.

It has been a great misfortune to Africa that no government, until very lately, has thought of education other than as school teaching. Perhaps this, too, was the fault of the bureaucratic specialist who tends always to divide the functions of government into separate departments, each with a label and an expert; to say of a witchcraft case: "This is a law business —it belongs to the legal department"; of an outbreak of rinderpest: "This is for the veterinary department"; of education: "We want the opinion of an M.A. with teaching experience," with the result that some English barrister, new from home, tackles a question which is half psychology and half superstition; the veterinary department advises brush burning and quarrels bitterly with the forestry officer who is attempting to save the trees, and nothing is done by either; and the experienced teacher sets about organizing a system of schools, primary and secondary, at which perhaps one native boy in a thousand may learn to be a clerk.

Clerks and children's schools are necessary, but they will not procure, in time, the background necessary to progress. That requires a change of mind and taste in all classes and all ages, and it cannot be obtained except by the vigorous use of all means.

Films, wall newspapers, broadcasting, lectures are all suggested; keyed if possible with some local problem. But I believe very strongly that for the present, in dealing with illiterates, nothing will be achieved without practical example.

An agricultural instructor must not only tell the people of new methods, but show them. A new crop must be cultivated and grown under the native's own eyes, so that he can see the results. Once he has seen them, he is very ready to enjoy the pictures of a wall newspaper or poster and explain them to others who have not had the privilege of understanding them. He can then become an enthusiast for the new ways.

I had great difficulty in persuading Borgu farmers to use seed maize from Jamaica, until one of my policemen grew a patch. After that, I could not get enough seed; I did not need to tell the farmers about it. The ones who had seen the corns on the new maize went running about the country, telling of the prodigy, and even exaggerating it. I believe many who planted, on those reports, were disappointed. They expected even better than they got.

With this proviso, that practical instruction must come early, everything may follow: the newspaper, the film, the comic strip.

An officer who had to carry on the teaching of hygiene and agriculture in a primitive village might well join to the practical instruction, the comic strip, illustrating the lesson. He should invent local characters, male and female, and show them doing everything wrong and suffering every kind of ludicrous misfortune. But the wall newspaper should have some text, for in many villages there would be some child capable of reading it, and his ability to do so would give prestige to that art. Where no one could read, the mysterious signs would still be a challenge to the curious.

Such a newspaper, full of pictures and strips, would of course deal in the first place with local work and local problems. It would be stupid to expect cattle grazers to be interested in the troubles and follies of a coffee grower or a yam farmer. Dress, racial characteristics, hair-dressing, landscape, all these must be local. For a native, like a peasant, may enjoy a picture, even understand it, and yet say, because of some small difference in dress or implement, "That doesn't apply to me." Like other people, he is much more ready to see in his neighbours faults which he himself practises every day.

But all this must follow the practical instruction. I feel that there is a danger that African adult education may begin and end in a great outlay of paper and paste. It must begin like all education with a personal contact between minds, and with a practical experience.

No amount of paper or even talk will make a primitive African understand why it is better to save top soil, to drive his furrow across the hillside than up and down, or teach him the need of preserving cover belts. He must be shown, and he will need repeated lessons.

And these lessons must be given preferably by one of his own race, who knows how to teach. This point needs emphasis. It is much harder to teach grown-ups than children; harder still to teach primitive illiterates.

Native teachers must be taught how to be patient; and picked for flair rather than academic knowledge. It is the commonest of mistakes to choose for instructors those with the highest technical skill, when the real question is—can they teach? I sent out a man to organize well-digging, a first-class well-digger imported specially from Kano, but he created a riot in two villages. I was not surprised when I heard him stating his case against the villagers. He shouted at them, called them fools, bastards, and as a crowning insult, pagans. All this because, like all villagers, they had been slow to take his advice, and critical of his suggestions. They had never dug a well, but they were sure they knew better than the expert, who belonged to a family that had been digging wells for hundreds of years, who had himself constructed some famous wells more than a hundred feet deep.

Villagers always know better. The more remote the village, the greater its conceit. A native pagan who has never seen a white man can only laugh at all his ways and words. A friend of mine, in the last war, when our column was embarked on a river steamer to be carried up the Benue, thought to surprise a pagan boy rescued from some broken village deep in the Cameroons. He said, "Look here, Tommy," and he turned on the electric light. The boy assumed a contemptuous expression and said, "My father can do that." One of my own boys, who had never seen electric light, criticized it thus, "A stick from the fire is better—you can carry it about."

You cannot surprise the ignorant and stupid. The measure of surprise is the measure of genius. It is only the greatest minds which have perceived the extraordinary nature of such simple daily things as growth, persistence of character, change and alternation, freedom itself.

It is harder to teach the ignorant and stupid who know nothing than the scholar who knows a great deal. That is why teaching the primitive African has discouraged so many enthusiasts, why it needs a special skill, a special technique; above all, patience and wit. A good joke goes far to remove prejudice. The ability to tell stories will win over the most hostile. For this reason, too, instruction should, if possible, be mixed with amusement. That is why the comic cartoon, the comic strip would be valuable; and why the broadcast is so important. A wireless programme can give everything: instruction, music, stories, news. It has been used already in India with great success. There, before the war, it required years, and the lucky combination of a far-sighted governor in Madras and a technical enthusiast like Lionel Fielden, to overcome the apathy of the central government, and native jealousies and corruption. In Africa now, under the new idea, I hope that there will not be the same delay. When I was in Lagos, I saw a cinema show given free, by the information office, for children. The films were bad, but the excitement and enthusiasm of the audience was indescribable, and their discussions afterwards as they went in groups down the street could have been heard a hundred yards away. They were walking broadcasters of novelty, of interest.

But even with broadcasting, with films, which should often work in co-operation, as in civil defence training, with the wall picture newspaper, and with the local instructor, I think that adult education may still disappoint, without some direct teaching on general lines.

Man's mind is a strangely divided organ. It seems to be formed of small compartments with sense-tight bulkheads. A native expert on agriculture will be found living in a filthy house and going to a witch doctor for medicine. An old police officer, whose home is spotless, may allow his farms to be conducted on the most ancient and wasteful system; not because, like many old English gentlemen, he is attached to that system, but because he never heard of another.

In short, I don't think adult education will accomplish very much, certainly not what we want of it, unless it makes a fair proportion of the mass, in the next ten years, literate.

The next ten years are going to seem a long time in history, twice as long as the last twenty. Progress will have to be more than twice as fast, and education, at the best, is slow.

If we are going to set up new industries we shall want workers; and illiterate workers, as Russia discovered, are almost useless. They are inefficient not only because they can't read instructions, notices, reminders, directions, because they are so difficult to teach a new job; but for some deeper reason. It seems that the act of reading exercises some part of the mental apparatus which is essential to the modern man: that with which he co-ordinates ideas. It is a power of reflective imagination, quite different from the illiterate's sharper apprehension of immediate events, from which arises his vivid memory. The illiterate's mind, that is, tends to consist of numerous unrelated impressions; and he has the greatest difficulty in conceiving of process, of function. He ill-treats machinery because he has no grasp of relation. In politics he is either immovable, from suspicion of the unknown, or extreme and dangerous, from inability to judge of consequences.

And when we say that the illiterate has a quick eye for detail, we do not mean that he is easily taught by example. He must have an example, or he learns nothing; but again, he is apt to observe the whole process, not as a related and logical development, but as a string of details.

A man who can read, even in the most primitive fashion, will learn ten times more quickly, even by oral instruction, than the illiterate.

But the object of making readers, of bringing in the habit of literacy, is not only to produce capable workers; it is much more to encourage the new mind, to drive forward that social development, without which economic progress will be slow and localized.

What is wanted above all in Africa is internal markets: local demand and local supply. Nothing can give that except a change in the social idea.

Here, again, the first approach should be to those more active and curious minds, found often in the most primitive villages, which desire knowledge for its own sake. They are perhaps more than one supposes.

In Tanganyika, volunteer native readers in the villages, attracted hundreds of listeners, and, what is still more significant, caused a demand for adult reading classes. The cost to the government of this great and real advance was nothing.

Education undertaken by grown-ups, in this way, to please themselves, has another great advantage. It does not produce clerks before there is work for them to do. A man who learns to read in order to enjoy a book of tales or the newspaper, does not expect to change his status or his craft; he is delighted with his education because it gives him pleasure. But the boy who leaves his village to go to school and who learns writing and arithmetic from a teacher, expects to make a career. He expects his education to give him work, and if it fails to do so, he is embittered not only against his teachers but against education itself. He is ready even to support the nationalist reactionary with the old cry, "Back to the primitive—down with everything new." Yet anyone who has told or read stories to natives, in their own tongue, knows the breathless delight with which they follow each development and acknowledge every point.

I have heard my own carriers, after a long and heavy day's work, discussing over their fire for a whole evening a short story read to them that morning by the roadside, during a rest. They went over it a hundred times, discussing its furthest implications from every point of view, repeating its phrases over and over again. The African, like nearly all illiterates, has an astonishing memory. He is accustomed to carry everything in his head. Your servant will carry a long message verbatim; a sergeant will reel off not only the tale of equipment received and issued, but the details of stoppages on a whole section's pay sheet. A boy of mine, after fifteen months of war, was able to tell me exactly the contents of each of ten or eleven boxes of clothes, food, crockery, equipment of all kinds left in store at the bottom of a room-high pile. Only two boxes of leave clothes had to be taken out and they held exactly what he had described. He knew the boxes, plain black uniform cases of exactly the same size and shape, by marks imperceptible to anyone else.

This kind of brain, sharply and minutely observant, and accustomed as a matter of course to memorize exactly great masses of detail, is typical of Africa. It learns, as I have said, quickly by demonstration; but it delights also in the story, the fable, of which it will store away a library full. Travelling story readers in Africa would pay their own way. They would be welcome in every village. The only expense would be the printing of their books; the only difficulty the writing of them. They would need to be like the native's own stories, racy, fast-moving, and full of dialogue. There would be no restriction on type: history, myth, animal stories, epigrams, ribald exchanges and fable, all have their native prototypes. The African does not at all object to a strong moral, provided that he agrees with it. Neither would he mind translations. He still admires the white civilization and is interested in stories about it, or descriptions, provided that they are short and dramatic. Not only Æsop, but Brer Rabbit and extracts from a great variety of European authors, would be suitable.

It would be stupid to aim always at a low level of understanding. Apart from the African's quickness to appreciate a witty turn, he has an unexpected grasp of a situation which, though apparently unfamiliar to him, is natural to mankind. It appears that the sense of wit and plot, like the sense of beauty, has factors common to all the world.

Another advantage in a system which reaches everybody is that it reaches the more intelligent, the natural leaders in ideas; and this is another reason why it should not be aimed at the most stupid. Education needs to seek the good brains. But the most intelligent among the primitive natives are often the most modest, the most reserved. They do not even recognize their own powers. Anyone who has taught African children or adults will agree that it is not those who look the most intelligent, or come most eagerly to class, who always possess the best brains.

I remember gathering a class of Mallams, Mahomedan scribes of any age from twenty to seventy, who were to learn to write the A B C and to do simple sums. We were going to make the first nominal census of Borgu. I myself had been shown by a famous district officer how easy it was to teach such a native class. They sat on my office veranda in a semi-circle, before a lime-washed board on which the letters were marked in charcoal, and I went out between the court cases to look at their copies and answer questions.

The oldest Mallam, who had once been a native judge, was visibly anxious and frightened. He was, by his own calculation, about seventy, but he looked at least ninety; and obviously he did not believe himself capable of learning anything. Yet he badly wanted a job. His struggles with the A B C depressed us both. But when we came to sums, and the whole class was puzzled by a multiplication sum in double figures, it was the old man who first perceived why I put down five and carried two. He said so, in the nervous and wavering tone of one who could not believe his own senses. The discovery that he was right and that he was the best mathematician in the class affected him like a stroke. He sat with his toothless gums apart, his little bloodshot eyes staring in the utmost amazement at himself. A moment later he was laughing and looking around like a child who says, "Look what I've done." After that, he was full of confidence, mastered even the A B C with his shaking hand, and became one of the chief census clerks.

When one is enquiring into some boundary dispute or customary land titles, after much questioning and arguing, and general confusion, it is often some young and shy farmer, who, being asked how he holds his land, or what he knows about the boundaries, gives so clear and logical a statement, and grasps points so quickly, that the whole village listens in a kind of unwilling surprise.

Such minds can be reached, if at all, only in their villages; and when they are reached, they are best left where they are, to become natural centres of illumination.

But even if these natural pioneers are willing to teach, they are not likely to provide enough teachers for the work in hand. There will not be enough teachers, from any source, and I wonder if it would not be possible to revive, with necessary adjustments, the Lancaster method used in this country, at the beginning of the last century, to meet exactly the same emergency; a huge illiterate population, few instructors, and the need for economy.

The Lancaster system, invented by a Quaker, was based on the use of pupil teachers. It would have in Africa an additional advantage of providing African instructors. But such details are for experts. The point I want to make is that vocational training, or mass education keyed upon a single motive like erosion or hygiene or some special crop, is not enough. It will not achieve the purpose expected of it without a very great increase in literacy. And for that, special instruction and special measures will have to be taken.

12:
Importance of
Women's Education

I WROTE OF the children's delight in that free film show on the West Coast. That audience, when it first stormed the hall, were all boys. The few girls whom I had seen in the road, standing by themselves under the wall, had been pushed aside. They didn't dare to come farther until the European in charge made the boys give room and brought in the girls, tearful and holding close together, under his protection.

African girls are still much more shy of novelty than the boys. They are much more under their mother's control; and their mothers are always the conservatives of the village. It is over and through the women that the juju man still exerts his power—still great and far-reaching power —because the women are its tools.

Adult education in Africa will be more than half wasted unless it reaches the women. More than half wasted, because the women, in the home, exert more than double the influence of the men. They have absolute rule over their daughters, not merely by command but affection; and they have powerful influence with their brothers and sons.

African women from no fault of their own are backward, and I believe this backwardness is the greatest single cause of African stagnation; greater even than poverty, and bad communications.

We have been educating the boys, in some places, for generations. What choice have these boys when they look for a wife. There are educated girls, of course. I spoke with many as I could speak to an English girl from a good school. But they are few compared with the educated men, especially those of the artisan class.

Village heads, court clerks, civil servants, engineers, educated men are obliged to marry girls who, in everything but the most superficial details of dress and speech, are as primitive as their grandmothers in the remotest bush. And these wives, in nearly every case, rule the home. They form the minds of their children. They have behind them not only the whole force of tradition and the sympathy of all the other women in the same case, that is to say, the huge majority, but something even more formidable, the profound responsibility which every woman feels towards her home and her children. She means to do her best for them. If she believes, as she must without education, that the best has been given to her in the experience of her mother, in the traditional rules handed down to her from a hundred generations of mothers, she will maintain it with a persistency and courage that defies all argument and even violence.

The conservatism of women is more formidable than that of men because it is anchored to her deepest feelings and to natural responsibilities. I think the happiest surprise of Africa this year was in a dark passage where after some moments of eye straining, I could just make out a group of children, girls, huddled against the wall.

"What are they doing there?" I asked. And the district commissioner, who was taking me round the schools, said, "These are the first girls ever sent by their own parents, in this town, to a Mahomedan private school. Things are moving when poor Mahomedan parents demand education for girls at their own expense. Of course, the school isn't quite used to the idea and so the girls haven't got a proper classroom yet. But there's going to be a classroom."

A stranger to African politics, faced by that dismal hole and the silent group of small girls pressed together in a heap, as if for mutual defence and comfort, might not have understood the D.C.'s pleasure. But I could understand it. I had never before seen a girl pupil except in a government or mission school.

The adult education of women is not only the most urgent part of the whole problem in Africa, it is one of special difficulty.

I hope that no one will make the mistake of treating women simply as a statistical quantity, of saying, "In this village the adult population to be dealt with is a thousand, chiefly farmers." The statement should be: In this village there are five hundred men, chiefly farmers; and five hundred adult women, all housewives, whatever else they do. Two schemes of education will be needed instead of one."

For the approach to a woman's mind, especially that of a primitive woman, is quite different from that of men. I doubt very much if men can even find it. I think that it can only be found by women; and women who have not learnt to think and teach too much like men. Even in agriculture, and though most African women work on the farm, they will need a different approach. If possible they should be taught by women. And all their vocational education—in midwifery, child welfare, hygiene, cookery—should be designed by women who are not afraid to abandon masculine tradition, already so damaging to girls' education in Europe. I have a notion, for what a man's notion is worth, that women, especially primitive women, are better taught in small groups, by someone they know and like. The liking is all-important. A boy may learn from a strange instructor of a different race; though I think the African, boy and man, learns better from someone with whom he is familiar; but girls, and especially grown women, learn nothing at all. Shyness, or something that is deeper and more primitive than shyness, which mounts guard over their feelings, closes up to the strange face and voice, their feelings, and therefore their intelligence. A primitive woman cannot think, much less learn, in the presence of one to whom, in the words of a court scribe, her heart is closed.

In thus excusing a young woman, in a court case, for being unable to utter one word of evidence, after she had presented herself voluntarily for the purpose, he did not mean that she had taken a dislike to the magistrate, but only that she did not know him; and that there was, therefore, no way yet open between her feelings and her actions. She was in a neutral state; and in that state she could not form ideas, or speak.

"Wait a little," the scribe said. "Let her sit over there and listen." And after the end of an hour or so the witness was ready to speak; and spoke very well, with animation and force.

It is a good rule in an African court to let women witnesses sit in the background for some time before they are wanted. They need to get used to the place and the judge.

Men as well as women, of all races, mix a great deal of feeling with their thought. But many African women might almost be said to think with their feelings, which is probably the original method.

I do not imagine that wall newspapers will appeal strongly to the women. Broadcasting for women alone, the small party, taken not as a class but as a party of friends; the demonstration, private and secluded from the men and often from women of a different status, are the methods worth experiment. This last point, again with diffidence, I urge for special consideration. From experience of women's cases, and some attempts, mostly unsuccessful, to interest village women in elementary hygiene, I believe that women, more than men, dislike to be mixed. Grandmothers should not be taught with their daughters; the elder wives should form one group, and younger wives another. On no account should married women be mixed with girls; or girls above the age of puberty with those below.

In all this, I dare say, I shall be contradicted by experienced African teachers. But I am not thinking of classes of town girls, broken in to white tradition from childhood. I have in mind millions of village women who, all over Africa, toil from dawn to dusk, and keep themselves to themselves, in a fashion unknown even to European peasants. African women are not merely, as somebody remarked of women as a whole, a sex by themselves, they are a sex apart; secret and reserved to an astounding degree. An African woman has commonly only one male intimate, her brother, and even from him she hides, out of superstitious fear, out of loyalty to her sex, all that mass of women's customary and traditional lore, taught her by women and transmitted by her only to her daughters.

All that we said about choosing the right teachers for men has double force in choosing women teachers. For the women won't protest, as my Borgu villagers did, against a rude and hectoring instructor of either sex, they will simply close their minds and learn nothing. But the failure of the class will be imputed to their stupidity instead of the teacher's unfitness. As, no doubt, disappointing results of adult education, if women are left out of it, will be put down to African stupidity rather than to his strong love of home, and his ancient respect for his mother, his sister, and often his wife.

It should not be forgotten, either, that in many African tribes, like the Ibos of the West Coast, the women are the chief traders; that in almost all tribes they have their own sources of income, by small trading or industry. Women, in Africa, as in England, do nearly all the marketing. They are above all gregarious, social; and discuss everything among themselves. Their opposition, merely as members of the community, is massive and dangerous; as women, with women's power in the home, it can be decisive.

13:

English and the British Institutes

THE BRITISH COUNCIL was founded in 1934. It is not a department of government. It acts under royal charter, and its purpose is the development of cultural relations between the United Kingdom and other countries. It has set up, in various foreign capitals, a British institute, with a library, clubroom, sometimes a lecture hall. It arranges exhibitions of pictures and films. It is in fact a valuable international service which, we can only hope, will be imitated. Similar institutions in Britain, supported by foreign nations, would be of the greatest value to mutual respect and understanding between the peoples.

It does not deal in propaganda. In fact its policy is to stand aside as far as possible from contemporary politics. Its affair is the humanities: letters, arts, science.

The Council, with small funds, had no mandate for the empire until last year, when the empire division was set up. Its policy in the colonies is to associate the local institute in each place with a local committee, and above all to make the institution a common ground for all colours and classes. It will provide, in short, a much needed club where Africans and Europeans can meet on equal terms, of a common culture, and a common interest in things of the mind and spirit.

The Council has only just started work in Africa, and I hope to see that work very quickly extended. I hope, too, that if it does not undertake the teaching of English, it will encourage that teaching by every possible means, especially by making available for African readers the treasures of literature. Not only of English literature, but of world literature translated into English. That is to say, I hope that it will serve to encourage, if only indirectly, English studies, and the spread of the English language.

This is a controversial point; but it is of such vital importance that it must be dealt with. What is to be the language of higher education in the African colonies: Hausa, Swahili, or English. We are about to set up new schools and universities on both sides of Africa. We know that mass education cannot be more than elementary; and that it will by itself create a need for more secondary schools, to be filled by the cleverer and more ambitious boys released from primitive discouragement by its action. We know also that more men and women of first-class education will soon be required by the new social advance. More doctors, teachers, instructors, inspectors, clerks, and foremen will be wanted for the new schools, new social services, and new industries.

That work is already being planned by directors of education. It has had more attention than mass education, which should have preceded it. But no one has yet decided the fundamental point of language; whether, for instance, the object shall be to produce in Africa, as in India, an educated class, reading, speaking, and thinking in English as readily as in their mother tongues; or Swahili speakers, Baganda speakers, Hausa speakers, to whom English, if they know it at all, will be a grammar-book subject, useless for real intercourse.

This was the old idea, to give a native language, where possible, the first place. It sprang from the same root conception of imperial duty as that which sought to maintain native institutions for their own sake.

But it did not ask two important questions: "What is the object of our education? What do the Africans want?"

If the object of education is to maintain the traditional character of native states, then native languages help to secure it. But it must be said that the natives themselves do not see it in that light. They think of it as an attempt to put them in an inferior position. The war, by bringing Swahili- and Hausa-speaking troops in contact with English speakers, has increased that suspicion.

It is in historical fact a wrong suspicion. But it has for the African a logic not always perceived by the European. For he looks upon Europe and its civilization as things far superior to anything in his own inheritance; and he thinks of the English language as the sign and agent of that superiority; a key to power and prestige.

This should have been obvious, one would think, to Europeans. But it does not seem so. The Englishman takes his civilization as a matter of course. For the last thirty years he has often had the fancy to depreciate it. And among colonial officials there is a high proportion of men who prefer bush life in Africa to town or even country life in Britain.

Abuse of civilization is partly a fashion, begun by Rousseau and continued by reformers, by neurotics, and of course by those who, wishing to be unconventional, succeed only in being commonplace; it is partly a genuine reaction of idealists who, having no practical experience, judge society on ideal and abstract grounds; and it is also escapism. Many of those who have gone to Africa and described some primitive native regime as, compared with England, a golden age, are pure escapists. Their strongest illusion is that in settling among natives they become part of native life. They are of course always travellers, utterly outside that life, which they see with the romantic eyes of that English civilization which they despise so much.

They do not ask how the native women, whose subordination in the native scheme seems to them so proper to their happiness as women; how the chief's poorer subjects, whose filial relation with him strike them as so much better than the legal relations of ruled and ruler at home; feel in that narrow bondage.

The final question, in short, is, do we believe in freedom, or not? Freedom runs great risks, and suffers great misfortunes. It is not the key to a golden age, which will never exist on earth or anywhere else. It is not a formula for perpetual peace of mind or body; it is not the sesame of an escapist. It is only, in the strictest sense of the words, the life of the spirit; eternal life; the power of the individual soul. A free man is one who has mastery, so far as possible, of his own life. And since his life is joined in greater or lesser degree with every other life; with the national life; the world life; with all knowledge and religion; with all the movements of the spirit; he needs for that mastery as much wisdom as he can get. In so far as he refuses, consciously or unconsciously, to seek the truth, or to take responsibility, he is abdicating from freedom; he is making himself a slave of prejudice and fear.

A man can, of course, believe in freedom for himself alone. He can say to himself, "I want as much power as possible to do what I like, to realize my will; but that's no reason why others should have it." He can set out to be a Hitler. Or he can take an intermediate position and say, "It is good for the world that certain men like me should form a caste with special knowledge and authority." He is then a fascist. But we believe, rightly or wrongly, that such men not only propose something which in the end brings them to ruin and proves impossible of realization, but that they are morally wrong. When we say that we believe in freedom we are finally asserting a moral, or, if you like, a religious belief. First that freedom is good for the personal soul; and then, that what is good for one cannot be denied to others.

It is for this reason that we say in England, everyone should have the means of education. For without education he cannot begin to be free.

But language is the very root of education, even at school; and after school, it is almost the whole of that greater education which continues throughout a man's life. It is by conversation, thought, and reading, that he learns. For many great men books have been the only university. Suppose such men had been confined to Swahili or Hausa, how many books would they have read, and how much would they have learnt?

I am not surprised that East Africans incline to think that English had been kept from them in order to make them dependent; because that has been the consequence. Nothing is more striking, when one passes, as it is now possible to pass, in these days by air, from one side of Africa to the other, to see the difference between Africans of the same age and the same education, in the West and the East, the first taught in English, the second in Swahili.

Education is a total experience. A man's reading is a very important part of it. No man can become fully educated without wide reading; for only so can he have that experience of great minds, in other ages and other centuries, without which he must remain parochial in outlook and childish in imagination.

English is already the lingua franca of India. The Indian congress, bitterly hostile to the empire, carries on the major and the only really important part of its business in English, because it is the only common language of the continent. English is spoken in every part of the colonial empire and the dominions, in the U.S.A. It is being taught to all races. Why deny it to some of the most intelligent of the African races, who themselves desire it.

14:
Small Industry
and Co-operation

AS IN POLITICS, so in industry, there are two schools of thought. One is all for mass production, the large unit, the plantation, the collective farm. The other is for local crafts, and small ownership. The two parties are already preparing for battle when reconstruction begins.

Both have right on their side. Large units, centralized planning, are necessary in many industries, such as mining. The factory, in many trades, is the cheapest means of production; and so earns a better wage for the workers.

But small industry, the local craft, all over the world, not only exists in its own right, but grows by the factory. The motor factory brings work for the blacksmith; and begins the new local industry of the garage. The furniture factory supports the village turner, who makes chair legs from the nearest beechwood. And many industries have always been local crafts, and will continue so, such as those of preparing special foods, butter-making, fish-curing, building, basket- and box-making, coarse pottery, and all the repairing trades.

Large and small industry complement each other. All large industry ends in local employment; small industry provides the income which buys the product of the factory.

But I begin with small industry because, at the moment, there seems to be a danger that the experts of reconstruction, in the excitement of paper planning on a large scale, may give too much weight to the factory, the monopoly.

The commonest question asked just now on both sides of Africa is, "What's going to happen after the war to our new local industries? Are they to be sacrificed to the U.A.C.?"

The U.A.C. is the United Africa Company, a powerful firm, engaged in every kind of enterprise. Rightly or wrongly, many people in Africa believe that it is jealous of all that small industry—dairying, soap-making

—which has sprung up during the war, and that it will destroy it afterwards. I know nothing of the facts of this case. I repeat only a suspicion in which West and East, for once, seem to agree.

But if monopoly were allowed to crush local industry, it would injure its own markets. It is in England and the U.S.A., with their countless small workshops of local industry, that the big factory finds its biggest sale. If this is forgotten, the new subsidies may become a hindrance instead of a blessing. We shall have great factories in Africa planted among poverty-stricken tribesmen, and selling, or trying to sell, their whole product in Europe. Africa will become still more dependent and parasitic.

We saw, in administration, that the central plan and devolution, each have their place in social economy. It is in the fostering of the local industry, local transport, local markets that devolution is necessary; that the district officer, or development officer, should have more power and discretion.

It has been the complaint of every district officer up to this moment, that his local schemes of improvement have had to wait, sometimes years, for the approval of some technical department before he can carry them out.

Public works departments, like the government medical service, are mistrustful of the amateur work of native assistants and bush officers. They despise the wooden bridges which fall down after four or five years, the unmetalled roads washed out at every rain, the thatched huts which serve for court houses, schools, and dispensaries; they think in terms of the brick bungalow, the girder bridge, the railway, or the cement motor road.

These must come, but it is going to be, even now, a long time before they come fast enough. Do not let anyone be deceived by the conducted tour which shows a magnificent road, a beautiful new school or hospital building; or photographs of those masterpieces in the Press. Ask only what proportion of villages are on a motor road, what percentage of people can get hospital treatment, of children go to school. No other kind of information is worth having. The most backward regions in the world can show at least one fine hospital, or road, or school.

Main transport lines are of first-class importance, but do not let any central technical department, engaged in planning them, say, "The village roads can wait—we have no time for them just now."

Native roads and bridges in the remote districts are the very roots of the progress so much desired. They may need much repair, but they are cheap, and they pay for themselves.

I had myself the experience of fighting the Treasury for money to build public inns, or *zungos,* as they are called. Private inns are, of course, unknown in primitive Africa. A *zungo* is the Nigerian equivalent of an American auto park, without the motors or the conveniences. It offers nothing but shelter, security from wild beasts and local savages, wood, water, and the simplest food; at a cost of a penny or halfpenny a night. I think our charge in Borgu was a penny for a man, an ox, or a horse, a halfpenny for a woman, a goat, or a donkey.

When we planned the new trade routes, feeders for central native markets, we found that they would have to pass through stretches of un-inhabited bush, too long for a day's journey. Small parties of travellers could not sleep in the bush in danger from leopards and lions, in fear of ghosts and werewolves, and we wanted the small parties. It is the solitary pedlar, or one who travels with only his family, who makes trade flow in the remote bush. He deals in small quantities and studies the local demand. He finds it worth while to make trade friends in the humblest compound and he will go out of his way to visit the loneliest hamlet, some hunter's settlement hidden in the forest, or a fisherman's hut in the islands, lost among the entangled streams and swamps of the Niger valley.

We planted some small villages on the roads by remitting taxes to settlers; and the villagers were glad to produce and sell food. But the African native is not hospitable to the stranger of another tribe. Complaints came in of extortion and assault. We decided to build *zungos.*

The Treasury refused the money, less than a hundred pounds. We guaranteed that the *zungos* would pay at least twenty per cent. after deduction of all charges for caretakers and maintenance. But we heard only from some junior clerk that money was not available for "temporary" works.

It is worth saying that there are "temporary" works in Nigeria, that is, native buildings, eight hundred years old. The provincial resident, who gave me all help and sympathy, finally scraped together a few pounds from the provincial treasury. I added my own allowances for police uniforms, stationery, miscellaneous and secret services, and we built two small *zungos.* The result was far beyond our greatest hopes. The flow of traders doubled in less than a month; in a single year the new markets had become too small. Money and goods began to flow into the villages with immediate effects on their local economy. Demand for products, such as shea butter, dried fish and hides, went up, and poverty visibly went back a little. There were not so many appeals, at the end of that dry season, for remission of tax; not so many children with swollen bellies and skeleton faces; and casual labour was very difficult to hire.

The *zungos* paid not only a native caretaker and guard in each; they paid their whole capital cost in a year. This money, of course, was brought to account under the head of "*Zungo* receipts."

I expected now a query from the Treasury, "Where is all this money coming from? What are the *zungos*? Have they appeared out of the air? But I heard nothing whatever. The Treasury is always willing to accept money; it is only particular about regulations when it has to pay.

These *zungos*, this trade route, which was, in fact, a narrow track cleared through the brush, with half a dozen stick bridges across streams and swamps, did not make a figure at headquarters. But they cost nothing, they produced more than their value, and though they did not lead directly to a railway or motor road, they fed the halfway markets. Trade is like a natural river system. The great tributaries seem to be the chief source of the main stream; but as conservators know, they themselves are only the runout of ditches and field drains, of water-passages unseen by the eye, of a trickle among the stones in far-off hill slopes. If many farmers cut mole drains and clear out their ditches, all at once the river begins to swell. There is no other source for a great increase in yearly volume.

So a river conservancy that wants more water in its estuary begins with drainage in up-country farms. It does two good things at once, educates the crofter and improves its own waterway.

For as education is necessary to economic advance; so economic progress can be part of education, especially in the simple and cheap forms open to native enterprise. A hundred hand presses, each worked by a group of oil-nut gatherers, may not yield so much palm oil, or such even quality, as the factory supervised by a trained manager, but they are more than a hundred times better experience for the natives, not only in economics but in organization. Above all, since each focus of any industry gathers about it dependent crafts, local experts and judges of quality, carpenters, mechanics, engineers, the effect of many small units in widening the native economy is incomparably greater than that of the central factory. Villages providing such a factory may live at its very doors, in their compounds, unchanged in every respect from the tribal way of life, except for the degeneration of the tribal economy. They have ceased to be communal farmers and they live on a pay check; but they are still an undifferentiated mass. They suffer all the disability of the tribe, narrowness of life, monotony of ideas, restriction of liberty, without any of its advantages, mutual confidence, the response of mind which comes from undisturbed faith and tradition.

Small industry has this other advantage, that it is the only kind which lends itself to co-operative production. A factory, even though co-operative in name, is actually run by its paid managers, and the nominal owners are little more than shareholders and dependants.

This is the case even in an Irish creamery. But it is not true of the Irish machinery society owning ploughs, disc-harrows, even threshing machines, for in them the members handle the machinery themselves, on their farms, and are responsible for its upkeep. Ploughs are not yet to be encouraged in most parts of Africa; for they destroy too fast the cover for the remaining top soil; but the small co-operative group owning an oil mill, a crushing press, a cocoa oven, a coffee drier, possibly a lorry or old car, has great value, both economic and political.

The co-operative producing society, growing a cash crop for export, with a common buyer of seed and seller of product, flourishes already in the Gold Coast, and among the coffee-growers of Kilimanjaro. Co-operative societies are encouraged by the Belgian government in the Congo, and there is an interesting experiment in French West Africa, where the government has organized compulsory co-operative societies, one in each administration. Compulsory co-operation is a contradiction in terms, and if the French variety were simply a government machine for collecting dues and developing agriculture, it would have no advantage over direct compulsion by government.

In fact, the members have certain powers to elect local committees and a general council, which can offer advice to the government.

If, as I believe, the members of committees do actually have some voice in policy, then the value of this method in educating the natives in political responsibility, in the use of freedom, is considerable. For though a voluntary society demands far more energy and intelligence from its members, the French type covers more ground, by including the whole farming population. Its economic success is apparently great. It not only distributes seed, but makes small loans to members. Every farmer knows the necessity of credit to schemes of improved cultivation, and for many reasons the co-operative society, especially the small group in which all members are known to each other, is one of the best agencies for giving credits. Several African governments are attempting to found them for that purpose.

Objectors to co-operation are, of course, many. It is said that the members are too sanguine in prosperity and disloyal in any reverse. They take all they can get from the society in good times and desert it in bad.

It is quite true that young co-operative societies stand their first set-back very badly. Especially in Africa, members are so pleased by good results that they think they have discovered a magic formula for wealth. At a big fall in prices they are astonished and then enraged. They shout "treason" and look for the cause, not in the fluctuation of a world-demand, but in some plot or swindle. It is at this moment that the independent buyer, if he wants to break up the society, gets his chance. In Ireland, I remember, it was when butter prices fell that the independent buyers, who hated the co-operative creamery, were able to seduce its members. They offered a better price. The creamery got no supplies, could not fulfil its contracts, and went smash. Then, of course, the speculator could buy at any price he liked. Butter won't keep in a farm cottage.

Anyone who has attended a meeting of small western Irish farmers after the ruin of their creamery, and the loss of their money, can understand the opponent of co-operation, who says: "It is putting too much, both in foresight and risk, on the poor. In Africa it has caused already more bitterness and suspicion than half a dozen famines."

This may be true, but it cannot be helped. It is said that the way to learn to ride is to be thrown off a great many different horses. I can say from experience that the advice has merits. In the same way, the only way for a people to acquire political and economic experience is to take risks and to fight set-backs. The very charges urged against the native co-operative society, its risk and its responsibility, are two of its great merits.

A second objection is that the co-operative society, when successful, undermines tribal authority. This is certainly true. But what then? Are we to say the African must not learn to conduct his own affairs because he will be less subservient to the chief? Which is most desirable in Africa? A population growing richer and more self-reliant, more capable of individual progress and intelligent co-operation, or the continued autocratic rule of the chiefs? The chief, it may be recalled, is not even the traditional representative of communal health. He is no longer the rainmaker, the fertility bringer.

Almost everywhere he has become or is fast becoming, by imperceptible degrees, merely an autocrat or chief magistrate.

Some, as in French West Africa, are becoming agents for the European authority. Others, as in Nigeria, are achieving the position of independent princes, with a guarantee of security from the suzerain power. The change is inevitable. But whatever a chief is called and whatever his relation with government, he cannot be allowed to stand in the way of African reconstruction. It is too urgently needed. Merely to check the rapid and continuous degeneration of the soil will take an enormous effort by every African government, and the greatest possible help from the native. But that help is not to be expected from ignorant, oppressed, poverty-stricken wretches, who cannot conceive that life could be worse than it is.

The fact therefore that a co-operative society among natives, in educating its members and improving their standards of life, tends to undermine the chief's authority, is something to its advantage. The chiefs must learn to accommodate themselves to a rising democracy; the governments must face a rapid change in the structure or balance of native authority. This, in fact, is progress in action.

It follows also that those who support co-operation as a natural alternative to the tribe, will be disappointed. Supporters of this kind are usually the idealists, spoken of above, who have been accustomed to think of the tribesman as a noble savage and the tribal life as a golden age of simplicity and social happiness. They argue that co-operation is the ideal substitute for the tribal life of communal interests and fraternal equality. But just as the equality of tribesmen is not that of brothers, but of slaves, so the community of co-operators is not that of equals, but of ambitious individuals. The members co-operate not to produce a communal wealth but a better return for themselves. A flourishing co-operative society does not produce equality, but inequality. The more energetic and intelligent members, taking full advantage of the society, soon grow richer. The slack and stupid stay where they are.

This is again a solvent of the tribal life, the old idea. It is also the beginning of African advance, and African democracy. The stagnation of Africa is chiefly due to that jealous tribal law which forbade any man to be wiser or cleverer or richer than his neighbours. For thousands of years, Africa, like a modern dictator, has oppressed the natural freedom of the mind, and thrown away all its increase. The hard and fundamental truth, which has been long recognized in the new Russia, is that men are born unequal in ability, in character; and that there is no substitute for either. Moreover, in the last resort they can't be compelled to give what they alone have to give. They can only be persuaded, bribed. So in Russia, or a western democracy, the old abstract notion of equality, broken upon the real fact, gives place to the new conception, "Equal opportunity, and protection of the minimum standards."

Let us abolish, they say, ignorance, poverty, insecurity, but let us, at the same time, cherish the best in quality, wherever we find it. Let us build freedom.

This is the only policy that can break the long trance of African history and give it life.

15:
Large Industry and Finance

SMALL INDUSTRY HAS always existed in Africa. It is the large units that she has lacked and she cannot afford to build them for herself. She has neither the capital nor experience.

Fortunately all the African powers are now prepared to spend capital on her development.

I write spend, rather than invest, because much of the capital will give no immediate or visible return, except in a gradually increasing public wealth, and taxable capacity.

Reclamation and reconditioning of land on the necessary scale is beyond the powers of any native government. In great areas, nothing or very little has been done to check it.

Lord Hailey, in his report on Kenya, says of the Kamasai reserve that about £6000 had been spent in six years on attempts to check erosion and over £9000 on famine relief in ten years; that is an average of £1000 a year on reconstructive work, and nearly £1000 a year on relief. The reason, of course, is that famines must be relieved but that reconstruction can always be put off. But Kenya has at least an officer detailed for the duty; in many districts it is still left to the magistrate.

The process of degeneration is going on faster every year; and every year more vigorous efforts, more money, are needed even to check the fall. But if the effort is not made, then the money will be needed, very soon, for famine relief on a continental scale.

The choice is between subsidies now, education, every possible expedient to make a real and quick change in African economy, even among the pastoral tribes; or later, famine relief and the same effort at reconstruction in a country far more seriously damaged. Millions of acres, even now, seem beyond help. The soil has gone and left bare rock.

Reconditioning of the soil cannot wait, but as we saw, even regarded solely as an economic question, it can improve only the yield of farms; and farming, by itself, cannot pay the cost of modern social services, even on a very simple scale.

Co-operative farming, in a few favoured districts, does produce the highest incomes in Africa, amounting on the Gold Coast to over twenty pounds; but even an average family income of twenty pounds a year, throughout Africa, would not pay for the hospitals, schools, and maintenance of services needed to give her the most modest standard of life.

Neither can small crafts make up the necessary social income; or even develop, without large industry. Their absence of development, over hundreds of years, is due chiefly to social stagnation; but also to the want of factories to provide those cheap products of cloth or metal which become the raw material of small industry, as well as the stock-in-trade of the small shop.

This point must be maintained in its turn because many people who agree with enthusiasm that local crafts and local enterprise should be encouraged, grow silent or find difficulties when factories are proposed. And those especially who have romanticized the tribal native, are apt to say now, "Yes, by all means give them *hand* presses, *village* industries," because these adjectives continue the primitive idea. It is the old secret nostalgia for a golden age, a kind of eternal peace, breaking out in a new form. So Gandhi wishes the Indian peasant to weave his own cloth because it seems to him that by so doing he simplifies his life and approaches more nearly to the golden age, where no one is afflicted with unrest and unsatisfied desire. So Tolstoy, one of the most complex and divided of men, wore peasant's dress and slept on a peasant's bed.

But poverty does not bring simplicity, only ignorance, disease, super-stition; and much village handicraft does not mean cheaply satisfied wants but expensive production. The Greeks disliked slavery but they could not do away with it. For there was no substitute but the machine and, by fatality, they had little mechanical genius. *Hand* presses, *village* industries are not to be admired because they smack of the Anglo-Saxon, but because they make a good beginning for economic development. No one must think that African economy should stop there.

Factory production is already needed where village industry cannot do the work; for instance, meat factories in Kenya, the large sugar re-fineries in the Belgian Congo, and ginneries in all the cotton-growing areas. To these factories, dealing with local products, can be added a few others in southern towns, catering for native demand.

Mining remains the greatest African industry, and in the Union whole tribes depend upon it; the best hope of many African governments, at least in the near future, of enlarging their incomes, is in the improvement of the mines. But mining itself, at least in the Union, has created a lop-sided and dangerous economy, and it leaves Africa still primitive in industry. She still depends chiefly on agriculture, often of the lowest grade, for her livelihood.

Those who advocate a deliberate extension of African industry be-yond the present point are usually met with the objection that it would begin at once to compete with European industry. European governments, it is said, are not likely to encourage or subsidize cotton mills, soap works, or metal-working trades.

This is true. If any European government did begin to develop com-peting industries in its African dependency, it would certainly be fiercely attacked by representatives of those industries at home.

But such a development is absolutely necessary to African economy. Africa is a poor country, and a poor country especially must have the best possible industrial organization to support itself at a reasonable standard. The fact that Africa is so far from such an organization now must not prevent understanding of its need; as a final aim, it should be in the mind of all responsible governments. Fear of competition has prompted obstruction to every development of industry, in the East, in India, Russia, Southern Europe; but the actual results of that advance have been an enormous increase in the world's wealth and in immense expansion of markets. It is true, for instance, that the immediate effects of competition by cotton factories in India have been felt in the old-fashioned European market; but so also, in the national market, a new factory with new methods, competes with the older business. Competition has been the result everywhere of progress, and it cannot be avoided unless progress is stopped. Its evil results in causing unemployment may and should be avoided; but any attempt to prevent the use of new processes, better machinery, in order to avoid competition between factories or unions, and the dislocation of trade routine, is reactionary and stupid. It would prove a certain method for bringing any country that practised it to decay and ruin. That tendency is seen already in modern big business, and is likely to increase with bureaucratic control over industry. It is one of the chief dangers in the modern state, whatever it calls itself: whether the bureaucracy is that of industry itself, organized in cartels and combines, or of a socialist state.

The tendency to limit international competition is an equal danger to the world's progress; it is short-sighted as well as wrong to condemn any part of the world to poverty and backwardness, for the prosperity of each is in the end the prosperity of all. It does not seem possible even to avoid competitive industry in Africa, when improving agriculture leaves a surplus of labour which can find work only in some kind of industry.

European governments must be prepared therefore to encourage the development of competing industry in Africa, and when the setting up of such an industry would be of advantage to local economy they should not be frightened from it by clamour at home.

Government encouragement will be necessary in almost every part of native Africa because of the difficulty of obtaining private capital. Except in the mines, there is nothing to attract investors.

A government share in industry is no longer a novel suggestion. The whole trend of economic development and control everywhere is towards a new modification of the capitalist system. The British government has long been a direct partner in the Suez Canal, in Persian oil, and indirectly, through the various agencies for reconstruction after the slump, in a great variety of enterprises. It is now, during the war, rapidly taking control, direct or indirect, of the whole of British industry. It is on the one hand limiting dividends, on the other, providing new material at fixed prices; capital and machinery.

The various African governments have always taken part in colonial development; they built the railways and most of the ports. The French have made loans to the co-operative societies of their own West Africa, Togoland and Dahomey; the Belgians advanced a great part of the capital invested in the oil, mining, and sugar syndicates of the Congo; the British government is a partner with the Sudan plantation syndicate in a cotton-growing enterprise, and takes forty per cent. of the profits. In the Union of South Africa, the government is a member of the Diamond corporation.

I think it may be assumed that a trend which began fifty years ago, and has increased ever since, will continue, probably with greater speed. Government co-operation in industry, not only in Africa, will be a normal part of the economic system. It appears likely, too, that it will follow the plan of the Belgian and Sudan enterprises, in entering industry rather as a partner than a master.

The benefits of this arrangement, even on paper, are great. It allows variety in the relationships of the state to each undertaking, and it enables the government, when it chooses, to attract private capital, while keeping the power to supervise the conditions of labour.

In real economic fact it has the immense advantage of allowing freedom to private initiative, and scope to local management. It may prove a means of combining the drive and flexibility of the old purely competitive age with the social security of the new; and the protection of labour.

Such syndicates of state and private investors, taking preference capital, might be the best means of developing new central industries in Africa. At first these will be in the thickly peopled districts; afterwards, wherever power is available, in centres to which labour could be attracted from greater distances, and settled.

Some African writers seem to fear the development of the manufacturing town in Africa. They are thinking in terms of the nineteenth-century anarchy. Planned townships in Africa, able to afford irrigation for gardens and parks, can be incomparably better living places than any native village. Moreover, it is only in towns that any development of the indigenous native civilization can be expected.

Labour coming to such industrial centres, placed near sources of power, the great rivers with their falls, or the coal-fields, would not be drawn from one tribe or political division. It would be the surplus labour drained from wide areas.

For industry will grow up, or will be set up, where conditions are suitable, and labour will go to it. This will be the rule in Africa, much more than in Europe, for the African native already shows readiness to settle at great distances from his home. The last century emigration from Europe to the U.S.A. has its parallel in the native emigration from the poor to the richer parts of Africa. Many Nigerians, for instance, have covered the whole width of the continent to grow cotton in the Sudan under the Plantation Syndicate, and in the South the drift to the towns has had to be checked by legislation. But the checks merely increase the pressure of unemployment in native areas where there is not enough land for cultivation.

African unemployment had not yet been surveyed. Much of it could be described as under-employment. This is the characteristic form among agricultural peoples. All have work to do if they choose, but much of it is unproductive, and half the number of hands could do it without any extension of hours of loss of production. In France, during a depression, many workers go back to the family farm and work there. But they share out the work and they do not make any adequate profit or wage. That is typical under-employment, and its existence in Africa is one reason why the opening of any fresh industry, like the Rhokana copper mines in Rhodesia, brings, even in the most primitive areas, a rush of labour.

16:
African Nationalism

A LAST OBJECTION, dangerous because it is not often stated in print, but only by word of mouth among officials, is that industrial development in Africa will cause political trouble.

I have heard this answered: "Not at all—I was greatly struck at K——— craft school by the good manners of the pupils and their sense of gratitude for what we are doing for them there."

But the atmosphere of a craft school is as different from the open air of social politics as that of drawing-room games from St. Giles' fair. The pupils know their teachers; the labourer knows only his work, his hours, and his pay. Gratitude is not an active principle between abstract bodies, such as nations and races; it affects only individual members and even there it is neither deep nor lasting. It never occurs to the mass of people of any country to modify their private ambitions out of consideration for the services of any other country, however valuable and generous.

The first effect of education, of improving standards of life, is to encourage and release private ambition, as well as imagination, so that they are very likely to produce, in Africa, social turbulence and probably nationalist movements.

Nationalism is not the creed of the poor. They find the struggle for life too hard to trouble about such romantic and abstract ideas. During the Napoleonic wars the French were often better received in poor German homes than the Germans; especially when the Germans were in retreat. The enthusiasm which raised armies to drive Napoleon out was middle-class. In the same way, the Fascist and Nazi parties were originally middle-class movements. The socialist revolution in Russia, from its early stages, was middle-class, and had many middle-class or noble leaders, and the reason is the same. This revolution too, especially in its beginnings, was romantic and abstract. Even when in its later stages it adopted an economic theory and a mechanist interpretation of history, it was largely romantic. It did not stop to examine facts but repeated slogans. This might be expected. As we have seen, man is not a professor of economics and he does not live by statistics; he is a poet and a dreamer, a sentimentalist, and he lives by his feelings. His brain is the tool by which his feelings look for satisfaction. When he is poor, and hard driven for life, he feels only the crudest appetites, hunger and thirst, fear, greed, and lust. The agitator who appeals to the very poor plays always on one of these nerves. He does not talk of patriotism or citizenship, or duty to the great ideals of the race, but he excites fear and hatred by warnings, or promises loot. To the countryman he says, "We will give you the land"; to the factory worker, "We will make you rich."

But even then the poor do not lead social revolution; they can be persuaded only to take advantage of them.

The French revolution did not begin among the poor, but in the salons, with Voltaire, Diderot, and it ended with Robespierre, the lawyer, poet, and scholar, most ruthless and cruel, because he was the most abstracted in thought. The typical revolution leader, everywhere in the world, is the mystical fanatic, to whom no reason can appeal because he lives in a world of fantasy; he is indifferent to human values, self-centred, merciless, because for him real men do not exist but only the abstract "Revolution," spelt always with a capital letter because it is thought of as something real and independent. The nationalist leader is inhuman, dangerous, an enemy of God, because he has abandoned reason and lives with abstraction. For him such phantoms as the Race are much more real than living and suffering men.

Fascism, communism, socialism, the nationalist revolutions, all these are some of the dreams of poets and idealists who have the leisure to read, to dream, and to use their imagination. Some issue in evil and some in good. They are the driving forces of modern politics; just as science, scientific research, and economic progress, blind and irresistible, are the driving force of change. The latter produce the wealth, the material body of a new world; the former attempt to carve it into the ideal forms of their desire; the new society, the new architecture, the new art and literature. It is the battle of ideals which fills the world with violence.

Wars are no longer for the glory of a king or the power of a dynasty; they are nationalist wars to glorify the ideas of a Race; and those who defend themselves against the nationalists invoke the ideas of international order and liberty.

As the world becomes richer, better educated, it becomes both more turbulent and more resolute to manage its own affairs, national and international. What is true of the world, is true also of the smallest divisions within it. Whenever the people escape from the pressure of famine and begin to enjoy a little leisure, a little security, some education, they develop new ideas and demands, new revolutionary movements.

Those who perceive this and understand the dangers of African nationalism among a people highly emotional and open to suggestion, are strong opponents of African progress. They no longer dare to say, "Keep the African poor and ignorant, as near to slavery as possible, for as soon as he escapes from his prison, he will make trouble," but they think it.

They are right in assuming that he will make trouble. Already, when the African has achieved any small degree of economic independence, he begins at once to show political energy. The Chagas of Kilimanjaro, having made a success of their co-operative society, are far more suspicious and difficult to manage than the primitive tribes in the plains below; the Gold Coast native, who enjoys the highest average income in Africa, has organized strikes against the European cocoa buyers, and criticizes the government, in his own Press, with the utmost vigour. As other regions of Africa are developed to the same level, there will be growing agitation and more angry criticism. For the one will encourage the other. Industrial expansion will certainly produce strong nationalist movements and the demand for self-government, or at least a great development of local government.

But self-government is itself the only cure for irresponsible violence. As we saw above, the Chagas' strike in Tanganyika instead of ending, like so many in South Africa, in bloodshed, served only to teach the strikers the folly of losing their heads. For the damage they did was to their own property and business.

Nothing is more striking, in political history, than the change affected by responsibility in the demagogue or the nationalist fanatic.

A man who finds himself answerable to the people for their welfare very quickly discovers which are the real values in administration and which are the false. He begins to think more of economics and less of spell-binding.

But this does not mean that nationalist violence can always be cured by a sudden grant of political freedom. All the evidence seems to show that after the agitation has passed a certain point nothing can cure it. Violence and bloodshed have become inevitable, with the usual consequence of egotism, hatred, bitterness, and a calculated attempt to deceive history itself and to educate whole generations in lies and spite.

The greatest danger of an autocratic government is that it may lose its chance of delegating power until too late. This was the fate of the Russian and Spanish monarchies. It might have been the fate of the imperial government in India.

The only safe and wise course in African native districts is to hand over power gradually and continuously so that native responsibility increases at about equal speed with economic and political development.

There is no other alternative to revolution. For even if it were possible, against the conscience of the democratic peoples who now share between them the responsibility for nearly the whole African continent, to keep Africa poor and wretched, the people would remain open to propaganda. If the African nationalist parties, working for the most part from outside, fail to make headway among the poverty-stricken masses, then the communist agitator or the anarchist, who tells the people they have nothing to lose by revolution except misery, will find there a field exactly suited to their energies. The opposition of race is fortified by the difference of colour, the contrast between rich and poor is great; the conflict between exploiter and exploited, capital and labour, is clearly seen and even acknowledged. Even in the bad days of capitalist absolutism, no European employer would say openly: "The people are born to be my slaves and I shall keep them down." He did not even think it. He imagined himself and the workers as subject to the same economic laws which alone could produce wealth. But in Africa, it has been written and said a thousand times, that the African is fit only to be a wage slave and that he must be kept in his place.

If then, Africa, poor and ignorant as it is now, does not encourage a nationalist movement, it does threaten with ever-increasing urgency a social war of black against white, poor against rich.

The world, after this war, is not going to be a more peaceful and reasonable place, but much more violent and excitable. There is a new tempo of life. The last war quickened every activity; it left whole nations restless, so that they no longer had any patience with rulers who said: "We can't go any faster." They demanded impossibilities, listened to no excuse, grew violent and dangerous at the least check; and nearly all their impossible demands were satisfied. What seemed a Utopian dream to the politicians of 1910 or even 1920, was a commonplace by 1940.

This war will leave an even greater impatience; a fiercer resolution in all countries to see the world remodelled more nearly to the ideals of liberty and justice; and again, struggling and perplexed governments will be forced to answer that demand.

Does anyone suppose that Africa will escape that agitation from within or without? More than forty years ago, public opinion in Europe and in the U.S.A. finally obliged Leopold of the Belgians to hand over the Congo to the Belgian government, in the interests of the natives. A similar agitation today would have plenty of material; in five years, ten years, it would have a great deal more. It would not need to urge particular atrocities; an account of African standards of health, of the condition of living, of the misery of children suffering from every kind of preventable disease, and dying every day by hundreds to Europe's tens, would be quite enough. If it could add that nothing had been done and conditions grew worse every hour, or if it could point to famine over great districts, then it would bring down more governments, and their successors would be pledged to a development far more expensive and far less productive than it could be now.

The choice is not between leaving Africa poor and primitive or developing her resources at the cost of African nationalism; but between an early and vigorous development before resources are further injured and wasted, or a late enforced effort to avoid a general disaster.

All objections in detail, to expense, to competition, to the destruction of tribal custom, to possible nationalism and political turmoil, are met by this wall of economic fact. Africa, already a vast slum among the nations, is growing poorer every day and cannot save herself. She is sinking deeper into wretchedness, disease, famine, while the world's demands upon responsible governments, the world's conscience, become every day more impatient of excuse.

17:

Political Reality

THE GREATEST POLITICAL MISTAKES, both in practice and in theory, have arisen from abstraction. Men talk of England, France, the U.S.A., what England thinks, what Germany is feeling, and forget that these names are only labels applied to millions of people all more different from each other than black and white. They are even surprised when "England," "France," "Germany," or the "U.S.A." suddenly produces a government which contradicts all these imaginary thoughts and feelings. It is only when the majority of a nation are agreed, that the statement "Ruritania feels so and so" has any value whatever; and such majority agreement happens rarely except upon the simplest issues of war, peace, or hunger.

In real history, if not in written history, the real overcomes the abstract; that is, the feelings and needs of human nature gradually shape politics and destroy or transform artificial divisions and abstract political constructions. They destroy even the work of nationalists, so that many countries, having fought for independence and established the idea, "This country is self-sufficient and asks nothing of anybody," have found themselves, in fact, dependent on world economics, exchange, and have been compelled, little by little, to take up once more a subordinate and dependent place in the real society of the world. The reason is that the nationalist leaders invent a world of fantasy and maintain it by an effort of will; while the people have real appetites, real hunger, for which they demand satisfaction. That is why all nationalist leaders nowadays are demagogues, and why even Hitler calls himself a socialist, and pretends to represent the people. The strongest modern governments feel increasing pressure from below. For the unique unit of every state, the most civilized as well as the most primitive, is the individual. He is real and everything else in the social order is derived and conditional. Without him there is no state, no people, no nation, no family, no organization, no politics. He requires the state for his security, education, health, transport, a thousand services which he can obtain only from an organized society; but his need is not absolute. Robinson Crusoe on his desert island had no state to work for him. He was therefore deprived of almost all liberty except the indestructible source of freedom which belongs to the human will and brain. And he survived. He did not need a government to put food in his mouth, to breathe for him. But no state exists without men, for it is made of men, and the quality, the power of a state, arises from the quality of its members. And as modern experiments show, the powers of men are different in kind as well as degree. Among the hard cases of unemployment, the unemployables, the men who never keep a job, is always a proportion of those who never had a chance to use special ability, possibly great ability. They are completely wasted, not only in themselves but to the state. Apart from them, there are hundreds of misfits in every kind of work who do the job well enough, but could do another far better. These are partly wasted. If to them is added the enormous waste of intelligence everywhere, due to bad or indifferent education, we can say fairly enough that even the most highly organized states in the world waste nine-tenths of their potential. A great deal of this waste is unavoidable. For various reasons there must always be misfits, and there will never be for every man the perfect education and the right kind of job. But the ideal state, that which gives to all its members the best chance of happiness and realization, and makes the best use of their different powers, is obviously that with the greatest variety of social and economic organization. It is not the tribe with its simple pattern of existence into which all must fit, but the highly complex modern state, like the U.S.A. or the northern European democracies, which gives to its subjects the greatest liberty of will and action.

The reason why the broad attack on African stagnation, even if superficial, has quicker results than specialist concentration on one point, is just because it gives to the natives a choice of new ideas, and so attracts a greater variety of interest.

I write social, as well as economic, because they cannot, in real life, be separated. It has often been noticed that the civilized man works harder than the primitive pagan. The reason is not that he has a larger appetite, but that he has higher standards of achievement. He feels more strongly the social demands upon him; he wants a finer house, a better education for his children, travel, books.

The word "economy" must not hide the reality of a social order which is not fundamentally economic. Men and women are not units in an economic structure, they are living souls who are ready often to ignore even the primary needs of their bodies for some ideal satisfaction; glory or learning, religion or beauty.

They seek pay not for its own sake but because it gives them freedom to enter this richer world.

It is quite wrong to suppose that the savage lives more fully and intensely than the civilized man. From my own experience, the reverse is true. Among the natives themselves it is the better educated, those with more leisure, more experience, who show the most quick and deep appreciation.

I remember a pagan chief whom, in Gombe, we invited to watch a polo game. He was a man of forty or more, in that country already middle-aged. But his interest and delight was such that he insisted on mounting a pony and trying to hit the ball. While the greater part of the crowd, including his own courtiers, looked on with mild amusement, of which the dignity was merely the form of their apathy, he joined our game, charged wildly about the field and felt the misfortunes of his side so deeply that we had to let it win.

The same man was never tired of studying an illustrated paper and asking countless questions about the pictures; not in mere curiosity, but in sympathy. You felt at once with him a quick deep movement of sensitive feeling.

This man was, of course, by native standards, rich and leisured. He had, from earliest years, been at the centre of events, especially novel events in his remote hills. He had had more power than his subjects, more freedom; and this form of liberty, in a chief, has a subtle effect upon the mind. For it obliges him, in reflecting on a policy, to use invention and imagination, which are unnecessary to the tribal clansman. This is the reason why there is so striking a difference among primitive people between the ruling caste and the unthinking horde.

The reason why a complex civilization shows higher standards of imagination and deeper power of feeling, is that a higher proportion of its members are in the position of this chief—with freedom and responsibility, leisure, and variety of experience.

We cannot even say, "Primitive people may be limited in their powers of mind and enjoyment, but at least they don't know it. They don't suffer the frustration that springs, in a civilized state, from disappointed ambition."

Tribal natives do often show strong, if vague, resentment against the harder constraints of their lives. These are the sulky boys and bitter women who appear at every sitting of a primitive court, accused of such mysterious crimes as "a bad heart" or "arguing." I don't know how Tasuki lived before he was sent to me as an unemployed waster, but I know he was a ragged skeleton full of disease and covered with bruises. He had been flogged by at least one court. Yet he had more brains, guts, and powers of leadership than many of those emirate officials who had taken their pay for fifteen years to neglect the Borgu roads and leave the streams unbridged.

Tasuki got his chance of freedom, and seized upon it, not for the pay, but the delight of doing that work for which he had been fitted by nature. Yet what an improbable chance it was that gave him his opening. He was only one out of tens of thousands in primitive Africa who spend their lives either in the dulled apathy of over-driven beasts or a sterile disgust.

For the individual autarchy, whether primitive or modern, is the enemy of freedom and life. For the state, it is a waste of power, and none, however powerful, can afford to throw away its Tasukis. It is because Africa wasted her Tasukis, or flogged and mutilated them for "badness of heart" and "arguing" that she remained primitive. Every nation that attempts to kill the freedom of the soul, by censorship, by regimentation, even by that benevolence which seeks to make an artificial equality between men at the expense of their freedom, will die in its tracks, and stand there a desiccating monument of the past, until some irreverent child among the neighbouring peoples gives it a push and sees it crumbling into ruins. This was the fate of the Spanish empire, the old Chinese empire, the Austrian empire. In Nigeria, the great edifice of the Fulah empire tottered at the noise of a single screw gun, firing one nine-pound shell against the door of a walled city; and fell in a skirmish.

Freedom, power in the people, is a nuisance to rulers; it is insolent, enterprising, vulgar, inconstant, ungrateful. It produces in any state an everlasting confusion and turmoil. It has the manners of a yahoo and the vitality of a mad dog. But you cannot do without it because it is life itself and a dead state does not stink. It gives no warning of putrefaction to the autocrats, who depend upon its size for strength and find at last that size is a drawback in a corpse.

18:

The Future

THE PRESENT WAR, like the last, has powerfully affected Africa in many ways. It has brought the African suzerains into closer relations, as war allies, and as war providers; it has excited the people with new ideas, especially of the division and fallibility of the whites; it has gathered together in mixed armies natives of every kind and of every part—South, East, West, and North, in the sympathy of a campaign.

But this war, far more than the last, must change Africa. The natives who now again come together belong to a new age and generation. Many more have the beginnings of education; nearly all have heard of co-operate and political action. Although as soldiers they may stand aside from revolutionary movements, they are making comparisons between wages, conditions, hopes. The Cape half-caste driver meets the Gold Coast farmer with his free co-operation, and his independent status in a country without a colour bar; the Nigerian Moslem sees, through the eyes of an Indian hillman, the fraternity of Islam; the Congo mechanic describes to some East Coast pagan the garden village built for him by the paternal despots of the "Union Minière Belgique."

But the new drawing together of the subject races in Africa will not be so immediately decisive, after the war, as the co-operation of the victors. Central international planning, for production and currency, for exchange, for the organization of labour and health services, will be absolutely necessary.

It has been suggested that in Africa, Great Britain, having been left predominant among the allies, will have both the power and responsibility to carry out an African reconstruction on continental lines. But Britain is only one member in the Commonwealth of Dominions. She may be left dominant in tropical Africa, but south of Capricorn the British-Boer Union of South Africa and its rulers will have the chief power.

In the great Belgian and French dependencies, representative of the mother countries, a new and vigorous spirit of independence is to be seen.

The chief hope for Africa is in an authority superior to the nations. That authority would seem to be promised in the new league or international council, already proposed on both sides of the Atlantic, to take charge of reconstruction after the war.

But we must not forget that such a council will in the first place be charged with feeding and clothing ruined peoples and rebuilding their industry. It will think largely in terms of economic development and world transport. If the U.S.A. is to be an active member in such a council, it will be the more effective in its power to suggest and co-ordinate policy. But that power will be indirect. Its sanctions will be financial. And they are likely to be exerted chiefly in the protection of markets and trade.

It is likely therefore that the final authority to which the African people, as distinct from African governments, must look for help is still the public opinion which presses upon all those governments. The duty lies still upon the imperial peoples, of Britain, of the U.S.A., of the Dominions, to see that their governments, in pursuing economic advantage for themselves and Africa, do not try by that busyness, to hide from themselves the truth, that freedom is not, in the last resort, economic; it belongs to the man. To leave any man in ignorance, sickness, poverty, or racial contempt, without help, is to hold freedom cheap.

Many theorists, especially those of commerce and science now so influential, many governments of the past, have held cheap the freedom of the poor. They reckoned the people only by a number in their calculations. The history of revolution is their epitaph. For even if the poor are too weak and divided to use their power, it offers to every ambitious man, good or bad, the challenge of its opportunity. He can become great and glorious at one stroke by uniting that power in the name of the people. To have freedom on your side is the only security of all government. And since freedom is never satisfied while it is held back by any bounds not strictly accountable to reason and justice, only one policy is open to government, the quickening of all powers, in mind and body, to the man, that as a responsible citizen he may become his own judge of what is necessary and just; and the devolution of all authority that to the sudden and terrible challenge of freedom cannot answer, "I am your servant."

Britain and West Africa

CONTENTS

1:

The Merchant Adventurers

NO ONE KNOWS what wandering sailor first touched at the West African beaches. He probably did not know himself. He landed, traded, and sailed on. It is said that the Phœnicians had a regular trade south of Cape Bojador. Hanno the Carthaginian reached Cape Palmas about 500 B.C. and saw the bush fires, still lit every year by the African villagers to clean the ground and drive game. But, till the age of print and reference libraries, discoveries were soon lost. Everything had to be refound, re-explored, restated a thousand times. Between Hanno and Henry the Navigator, in 1415, Europe knew nothing of Africa behind the deserts. It is said that some Dieppe sailors made an earlier landfall on the Guinea Coast and set up a trade. It is very likely. Ships of every country, carried on the south-west winds, are likely to have skirted that coast and landed for provisions or goods. But they left no records, no maps. The Portuguese left both, without dispute. Prince Henry, when he landed at Ceuta in 1415, heard talk of gold across the Sahara and in 1430, against the bitter opposition of those who said that everyone who sailed south would turn black, sent his first expedition to Guinea. The Portuguese bought there a few slaves, the first of the trade, and, what pleased them more, gold-dust. From this they named the country Gold Coast. They opened mines, and when they built their first fort, in 1421, it was called Elmina, or The Mine.

They claimed the land by that odd right called "of discovery," and by legal right. Pope Martin V granted to them all they cared to take of Africa not already seized by other Christians. Thus all sailors of other nations who dared to visit the coast risked the fate of pirates. The first English expedition, planned by a Captain Baker in 1481, was actually stopped by Edward IV on complaint of the Portuguese King.

To landsmen the world consists of nations surrounded by a general water; to sailors it is different seas bounded by a common earth. Seamen distinguish Atlantic and Pacific by their several natures, but do not find a notable difference between the rocks and sands of any continent. They understand national rights to the seaboard as hardly as landsmen under-

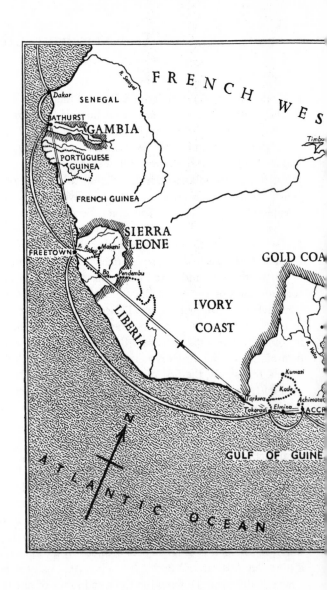

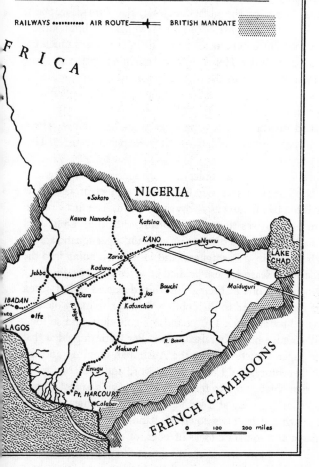

BRITISH WEST AFRICA

RAILWAYS ●●●●●●●●●● AIR ROUTE ══╪══ BRITISH MANDATE ▦▦▦

F R I C A

NIGERIA

● Sokoto

Kaura Namoda ●   ● Katsina

KANO ●●●●●●●●● ● Nguru

Zaria ●   LAKE CHAD

Jebba ●●●●●● Kaduna

● Bara   Bauchi   Maiduguri

IBADAN   ● Jos

R. Niger   Kafunchan

● Ife

LAGOS

Makurdi   R. Benue

Enugu   FRENCH CAMEROONS

Pt. HARCOURT
● Calabar

0   100   200 miles

stand maritime law in mid-ocean. Seamen were the first internationalists and sea empires the first federations. The Pope's edict was often broken and the Portuguese custom was to fire on all strangers within reach of their guns. So they remained masters of as much as they could overlook and defend, and wandering tramp ships of those days picked up their cargoes out of sight.

The first Englishman who joined this African contraband trade was William Hawkins, father of the great Sir John, the Armada captain. To quote from Hakluyt: "Old Mr. William Hawkins of Plimmouth, a man for his wisdome valure experience and skill in sea causes much esteemed and beloved of King Henry 8, not contented with the short voyages then commonly made to the known coasts of Europe, armed a tall and goodly shippe of his own of 250 tunnes, called the Paule of Plimmouth, and made 3 voyages to Brasil."

Hawkins touched on the way at "the river Sestos in Guinea where he traffiqued with the negroes and took of them elephant teeth."* This was in 1530.

But Hawkins called at Guinea, under the Portuguese guns, only as a man going to his office pauses at a stall to buy a punnet of fruit. His voyage is rightly listed by Hakluyt as a voyage to Brazil. The first English voyage express to Guinea was that of Wyndham, with the "Lion" and the "Primrose," in 1554. It was a disaster. Wyndham, a passionate, stupid man, fought with his guide, a Portuguese, and insisted on going into the Benin River at the worst season. Here he died of fever with two-thirds of his crews. "Having sanke one of their ships, they departed and of seven score men, scarce forty returned to Plymouth of whom also many died."

But this remnant brought back 150 pounds of gold-dust, and so their story did not chill courage but only raised hopes. For African gold at that time had even stronger attractions than the Australian diggings and the Klondike in the last century. Gold was a magic word and idea. Not many years ago a Nigerian chief asked to touch my ring, a gold signet ring. I put it into his palm, and, gazing at it with a look of wonderment, he said at once: "What heaviness! It draws down the hand."

It was such magic and romantic ideas of gold, of strange races, beasts and seas, which drew the pioneers, and still draws them, to Africa.

The pioneers who risked their lives must be distinguished from those

---

* Hakluyt, *The Principal Navigations . . . of the English Nation*, Vol. IV, 1599.

who risked their money. But not too invidiously, for the one needed the other. African enterprise has always been expensive as well as dangerous. Hawkins had his backers who, as it was said, "set him forth." The word "adventurer" has changed its meaning. In the sixteenth century it meant "speculator." But the gambler has the merit of courage, and without merchant adventurers there would have been no Greek or Dutch or British empires: empires not of conquest but of intercourse and diffusion.

The early captains were also the earliest explorers. John Lok, sailing in 1554, tells us of the Gold Coast: "The Princes and Noblemen pounce and rase their skins in divers figures, like branched damask." That is to say, they had cut their skins in patterns as they do to-day, "and many of them, as it were, laden with collars, bracelets, hoopes and Chaines, of gold, copper and ivory." Lok was also charmed by the idea and sight of gold.

But Lok, besides the romantic curiosity and the romantic gold-love of all these early men, had advice for the trader which, obvious to him, has not been obvious to stay-at-homes, either critics or capitalists. "Whoever would deal with them," he writes of the negroes, "must behave civilly, for they will not traffique if they be ill used."

African historians, I think, have not always seen the meaning and application of this remark. It throws upon much colonial history one of those sidelights which give the detail without which history is as flat and deceitful as a political poster. Traders, as distinct from conquerors, must be on good terms with their customers. Thus the smallest trading post becomes, merely by force of necessity, a nexus of personal ties which, of themselves, breed obligations on both sides.

This is shown as early as 1620 by Captain Richard Jobson, who sailed more than 200 miles up the Gambia River in search of a famous African trader, Buckor Sano. He writes: "There is, as it were, a certaine combination made betwixt the people above and us, never to faile them of a yearely trade, which if in our parte it should be neglected, may justly cause them to take a great distruste of our fidelities, in regarde we are nowe the first white people they have seen," and he recommends to Englishmen "The Auncient and free commerce, that uniteth nations, wherein our especiall animation is, the certaine knowledge we have gained in discovering the Golden Trade of the Moores in Barbary, which was the first incourager of this businesse."*

* *The Golden Trade*, by Richard Jobson, gentleman, 1623.

In history books, which must be full of dates and institutions, it is easy to lose sight of history itself, which is made by men, all singular, all full of their private creeds and passions. We read of companies and governments, but the chief interest of West Africa lies in the men who made it; adventurers and poets of action; at their worst very close to pirates, at their best not far from monomaniacs, but always free and independent. For this reason they were extremely hard to manage by any kind of government. It is comic or tragic, as you like, to see, century after century, the efforts of home governments—that is, prudent men of affairs—to restrain or control these other kinds of men, far from offices and far from prudence.

First Chartered Company, 1618

We have said that the adventurous seaman was lucky to find in England the adventurous merchant accustomed by long tradition to risk capital in foreign voyages. But the African trade needed backers even more than the Baltic or the Levantine. These seas had harbours open to trade. On the Guinea Coast there were few safe anchorages and no free harbours. The freebooter captain who anchored opposite some native settlement and did his barter on the strand, had the advantage, like the modern tramp, in being able to seek cargo where it was to be found. He needed only local agents among the natives to recommend him as a safe man. But he had also great disadvantages on the African coast, beaten night and day by those huge Atlantic rollers which, even from 5,000 feet up in the air, can be seen to-day like an everlasting fringe of waving lace to the bright ochre beaches. He had to send his boats through the surf, and chance the weather and the Portuguese guardships till they came back. And this might mean a long wait if his African agents were away from home, or had no gold, peppers, ivory, or slaves ready for him.

Slaves especially needed a shore establishment, a barracoon, in which they could be gathered and fed until a ship came. But stations required a staff and, because of the Portuguese and the pirates, a fort. They were expensive beyond the reach of private firms, without some warrant of special profit. In those days this warrant was given by a monopoly secured by a charter from the Crown. There were already chartered companies holding monopolies for the Baltic or Eastland trade, the Russian or Muscovy trade, and the Levant.

In 1618 a group of London traders applied for and was given a charter for the Guinea trade. It undertook to build stations and forts in exchange for a monopoly. The name of this first company was The Governor and Company of Adventurers of London trading to Gynney and Bynney, and it built the first British forts in Africa at Fort James, on an island in the Gambia River, on Bunce or Bence's Island, in the Sierra Leone River, and at Cormantine, on the Gold Coast. It was this company which sent out, in 1620, that famous Richard Jobson, whose book is an English classic.

This company and its successor, the African Company, were quickly ruined, by bootleggers stealing their trade, and by the Dutch who were now all-conquering on those seas. When the Dutch took Elmina from the Portuguese in 1637, they remained masters of the Coast, and defied all comers.

The Slave Trade

The coastal trade had now a value beyond gold, pepper, or ivory. It was turning more and more to slaves.

The slave trade, like slaving itself, was of course an established commerce. It has existed from pre-history, and, what seems strange to us, records a first step in civilization. For at one time men exterminated their enemies. It was an innovation, due perhaps to the change from hunting and herding to agriculture, to spare lives to workers. Prisoners of war were kept or sold, throughout the ancient world. Every African chief caught slaves and kept slaves; and even while the Portuguese and French and British captains were taking Africans in slavery, thousands of Portuguese, French, and British citizens were slaves to the Moors and the Turks. Every sailor ran the risk of being caught by some Algerian pirate and sent into slavery. As late as 1816 there were over 3,000 white slaves in North Africa, found there and freed by Lord Exmouth, who, with five line-of-battle ships, attacked the great fortress of Algiers from the sea and blew it to pieces.

It should be noticed that in the worst times the European nations, though they made galley slaves of their criminals, did not sell them. This was no alleviation of their fate. Many a white slave in Turkey or Barbary had a better life than the naked convicts or war prisoners in Spanish and Venetian galleys. But it acknowledged a difference between man-goods and other goods; and every such distinction of truth, however slight, has in it a seed of liberation. It is a beachhead for the invasion of justice and freedom. As a commodity, the Portuguese bought slaves, but not many, because the demand was small. Negroes did not stand well the climate even of Portugal. Sir John Hawkins, indeed, "being assured that negroes were very good merchandize in Hispaniola, communicated with his worshipfull friendes of London," got a concession from the Crown for an exclusive trade, and took slaves from Sierra Leone.* This was in 1562. But the British slave trade was small in the sixteenth century.

Even in 1620, when Richard Jobson's African friend Buckor Sano, up the Gambia River, brought to him "certain younge black women who had white stringes across their bodies, which he told me were slaves, brought for me to buy," he answered that "we were a people who did not deale in such commodities, neither did we buy or sell any that had our own shapes."

Jobson must have heard of Hawkins' trade. He spoke, that is, like many who claim a special glory for their people, rather what he wished than what he knew. Yet it was true that he did not want slaves; he went to Gambia for gold. His mind was all on the golden trade.

But in the same year, 1620, a Dutch ship called at Virginia and sold slaves, the first negro slaves in America, to the tobacco planters; and the settlement of Barbados in 1628 greatly raised the demand. It was supplied at first chiefly by the Dutch, French, and Portuguese, for the first English company was ruined by their competition and the second by the civil wars. It was not till the Restoration and the Dutch peace that the British slave trade began to grow.

First Committee for Colonial Affairs, 1660

Charles II had seen at work in France the most modern and efficient government of that day. He knew the value of organization, of the specialized government department; and in 1660 he appointed a committee for colonial business. It had no State Secretary. It was merely a committee of the Privy Council that had to act through the Secretary of State for the Southern Department. But it was the first organ of government with an exclusive and, what is more important, a continuous mind for colonial affairs.

Charles warmly supported the new African company, that of the Royal Adventurers trading to Africa founded in 1662, and sent a royal ship down the West Coast, which harried the Dutch so thoroughly that

* Hakluyt, *The Principal Navigations . . . of the English Nation,* Vol. IV, 1599.

is was called the beginner of the Dutch wars. And Van Ruyter, the Dutch admiral who destroyed every British fort in Africa except Cape Coast Castle, soon broke the new company.

But by the Treaty of Breda the British right to Cape Coast Castle was allowed. It has been British ever since. And in 1672 Charles and his brother James chartered a new company, the Royal Company, which built six new forts. It shipped as much as £70,000 worth of woollens in a year, and imported redwood, ivory, pepper, and gold-dust. Both these companies of Charles II bought gold; and it was from this gold that guineas were first coined, stamped with the elephant mark of the trade and named after the Coast. Both also flourished upon the slave trade to the plantations, and in 1715, after the French-Spanish war, the Royal Company took a share in the Spanish slave trade under the contract known as the Assiento. It undertook to export yearly 4,800 slaves to Spanish America. For this reason it is often called the Assiento Company.

Yet it failed. The Whig and Liberal revolutionaries of 1688, detesting all monopolies, would not renew its exclusive rights, and it could not compete with the free traders, as it called them—small men with no overhead expenses, who came in rotten ships, sometimes with pirate crews, and often kidnapped their slaves.

The company, as it pointed out in 1749 when, already bankrupt, it asked Parliament for relief, could not fight such methods. It had to be on good terms with the natives who supplied its trade and its provisions. It had to keep up its forts.

The forts were not defensive against Guinea natives, who freely complained if they were deserted or left short of goods. They were aimed at the Dutch and the French. France, under the old autocratic monarchy as well as the Empire, was always a formidable enemy. It was not till the nineteenth century, in the reign of Louis Philippe and Napoleon III, that she began her great conquests in Africa, but already, in the seventeenth and eighteenth centuries, she was preparing the way for that advance by her consistent and aggressive policy. British merchants already complained that they could not get the same support as did the French from their own government.

2:
The Old Imperialism in Africa

IT WAS TRUE that the British Government never gave traders in West Africa the same encouragement as did the French. The old France had a centralized, autocratic government, accustomed to the idea of conquest wherever it suited her. British Governments, from the time even of Elizabeth, rarely looked outwards, but inwards; they did not seek conquest and prestige abroad, but their own security and popularity at home.

This was not from any special virtue in rulers or peoples, but because the people, protestant and insular, were used to criticizing and opposing authority, and because the rulers were not strong or rich enough to be tyrants.

The map of North-West Africa is a concise record of two different imperial histories, French and British. French West Africa is a great single territory under one central government. The British Colonies, scattered here and there along the coast, are islands, trading settlements, cut off from each other and from the interior.

English government of the seventeenth and eighteenth centuries may not seem to us very democratic, but it had some of the virtues and faults which mark all real democracy. It was representative of different groups and parties in the country and it responded, though crudely, to their pressure. So that the head of the State, at any time, was not an autocrat but a party leader who had to please his party, and who had to give place to any other party leader strong enough to turn him out.

That democracy, in short, like all democracy, had the merit of choosing leaders whose power was based on some measure of popular consent. Its history was that of little revolutions, with less bloodshed.

Such a government combines the merits of revolution, energy, hope, and change, with the stability of a business firm which contrives always to have a popular line. It has also the faults of its quality. It cannot pledge the future, for that may belong to other rulers with other ideas. This again is not wholly a misfortune. It leaves the future free, and if that freedom carries with it uncertainty and conflict, so does all freedom, all growth, all adjustment.

The complaint therefore against British government, repeated every century, that it has never formed a consistent policy for the Colonies, has some truth, but not so much as many suppose. The facts are more interesting. Policy in a democratic government is reviewed by each new party in power; but it may be, and often is, accepted and continued by the new party. Its consistency hangs therefore upon some degree of common belief and purpose in all the parties. Tory and Whig, for instance, might quarrel about religious toleration, but they both supported the Established Church. Their differences, therefore, never produced such violent changes of policy as we see in eighteenth-century France, when the revolutionary party tried to abolish Christianity.

Colonial policy, as we shall see, has suffered at different times from both deadlock of opinion and sudden changes of policy. But it did not do so in the eighteenth century. Successive home governments had almost the same views on Africa. They wanted a share of African trade, but even for that they did not choose to risk valuable lives or much money. And they had no wish for colonies on the unhealthy West African coasts.

End of the Assiento Company, 1749

The appeal of the Royal African, or Assiento, Company in 1749 opens a good picture of the workings of democratic government at that time, in face of a colonial question.

First, on the bad side, Governments had utterly neglected the company and the merchants, until they were ruined. The votes to be had by giving them help were not so many as those to be lost by a new charge on taxes. But now that the company was bankrupt numerous groups of citizens, many with votes and influence on votes, started up and exclaimed: "What is going to happen to our African trade without forts and stores and barracoons?" The free traders who had helped to ruin the company now shouted for defence against the French, for safe harbours. The planters in America, and their friends in England, asked where and how they were to get good and cheap slaves without a company. And the Government saw that it must take action.

But since the different parties, though strongly divided in political and economic views, were not opposed on any fundamental moral or religious ground like, for instance, the Imperialists and the Little Englanders of the nineteen-hundreds, they were persuaded to accept a common policy. And the policy became that of successive Governments for the next forty years.

There was as yet no Colonial Secretary. But the old committee of the Privy Council had given birth in 1695 to the Board of Trade and Plantations, which was now asked by Parliament to look into the mass of complaints and proposals brought before it.

I relate these proposals and their solutions because once more, at a time when the chief parties enjoy a measure of agreement on general principles, we have proposals for corporations which are neither State-owned nor privately owned, but seek to marry State responsibility with private energy and ambition. The experiment of 1749 may be worth modern study.

Experiment in State Partnership: Merchants Company, 1750

The Board of Trade and Plantations rendered down the schemes put before it to three, which it then, with its expert advice, sent back to Parliament. They were:

1. By the Royal African Company, the planters and some London merchants, for a new Joint Stock Company, with monopoly.

2. By some Bristol merchants, for an open, regulated company, that is, a company with settled establishments on the coast, but no monopoly. The Bristol merchants were not so rich as the Londoners.

3. By Liverpool merchants, for Government to take over the forts and put them under a committee of nine merchants.

All schemes required, of course, a subsidy.

Parliament, after debate, combined elements from the last two schemes. It set up a regulated company open to all British traders, and vested in it the whole property of the Royal African Company. The company was to be ruled by a committee of nine elected from the freemen of the company, that is to say, from all traders who, having paid a sum of 40s., were entitled to trade from the company's harbours and forts. The company was not allowed to put any restraint upon trade, and it was not allowed to engage in trade on its own account, except with its fees which, of course, were not enough for its expenses. It received a subsidy of £10,000 a year, for which it was obliged to make annual account to the Treasury and annual appeal to Parliament, when its conduct came under review. Its forts and harbours were subject to inspection by any captain of the Royal Navy, who could then report direct to the Admiralty. Finally, no committeeman could be elected for more than three years running, and the Board could discharge any one of them for misconduct.

This new corporation was named The Company of Merchants Trading to Africa, and its charter was from Port Sallee in South Barbary to the Cape of Good Hope—about 7,000 miles of coast.* In practice it took over from its predecessor one fort on the Gambia and eight more, in a ruinous condition, on the Gold Coast and Slave Coast. Bunce Island at Sierra Leone had been abandoned in 1728. Cape Coast Castle remained the head station.

This odd plan worked apparently as much to general satisfaction as could have been obtained by any plan. The company was attacked, but never with success. Burke himself defended it, in 1772, on a charge of increasing the price of slaves and packing its committee. His defence, it is true, was, in short form: "any change would be for the worse, especially if it gave more power to Government. For that would mean more jobbery."

In fact, the appointment of the first Colonial Secretary in 1768 to sit as President of the old Board of Trade and Plantations, and abolition of the Board itself in 1782, seem to have been changes for the worse. And the explanation given, which should be noticed by those who plan modern development companies on similar lines, is that the West Coast offered little patronage. There were not good enough jobs in the company to make it worth encouragement by a Minister of State. So that West Africa, under a Colonial Secretary, was more neglected even than before under the Board.

Such light as we have upon these lonely stations, perched on the beach between the everlasting pounding of the Atlantic and the salt swamps or jungles of a continent wider even than the Atlantic and much less known, show well why West African jobs were not good value for votes. We read of garrisons three parts made up of convicts, condemned to serve on the coast and treated often worse than slaves, because of less value; of sickness which carried off half the station in a week.

Thomas Thompson, a missionary who left his comfortable living at Christ's College, Cambridge, to serve Christ, went first to the slaves of America and then, in 1751, to the West Coast. His diary records the

* An excellent book on this period is *The British West African Settlements,* 1750–1821, by E. C. Martin. Longmans, Green, 1927.

completeness of his success and failure: a warm and anxious welcome
from some, dying or repentant, who needed to hear an English prayer;
the utter indifference of most; the polite boredom of the Africans. In
a five years' mission he converted fewer than a dozen, of whom, before
his health broke, he sent three to be educated at home. One of these,
Philip Quaque, son of a chief at Cape Coast Castle, was afterwards or-
dained in the Church of England and went back to the West Coast in
1769. He ministered there till he died in 1816, and baptized both black
and white. But again, not many. And he complained to the company
that the Europeans kept coloured mistresses and did not come to church,
that some were violently against the church.

Tropical Africa, in short, then as now, tended to gather to itself men
of independent character, good or bad. But there were prizes, then as
now, for the strong, the bold, and the lucky. William Mutter, who joined
as surgeon's mate in 1752, was Governor of Cape Coast Castle by 1763.
The fearful death rate cleared the way for those who had the talent to
keep alive and the nerve to keep sane. The company highly valued this
attraction among the few it could offer. It made a strict rule that promotion should be by seniority. Also it allowed and encouraged private trade,
as many companies do still in this century. So that a man could invest his
pay in goods, and do barter for gold and pepper.

The fourth African Company lasted longer than all its predecessors,
because the profitable slave trade continued to grow. By the end of the
century it was presiding over an annual export of about 40,000 African
men and women in their prime, out of a total Atlantic trade of about
80,000.

I say the company presided over this traffic, because it must be remembered that it was not in the first place a trading company. Its income
was in dues from traders. Its responsibility for the trade was shared with
the merchants, and each side felt it the less.

The cruelties of that trade have often been described. But of all stories
the one that brings it most home to me is that of the captain who
threatened the slave women on his orlop deck with the whip if they did
not stop singing, for, as he complained, "the dolefulness of their songs
will drive me mad."*

---

* *History of the Rise, Progress and Accomplishment of the Abolition of the African
Slave Trade by the British Parliament,* by Thomas Clarkson. London, 1839.

Abolition of the Slave Trade, 1807

Slavery should be distinguished from the slave trade, because many have defended one in the name of the other. Slavery has often been so mild that slaves refuse freedom, and domestic slavery has sometimes been benevolent. As lately as 1919, when I offered freedom to some African slaves, they refused it. They preferred to stay in their master's family.

But the slave trade has always been an abomination, especially in Africa where the Arab raiders, as late as this present century, would seize a whole town, murder the old and the babies, castrate the young boys, of whom eighty per cent. died, and drive the remnant across country with such indifferent cruelty that half would die on the road. To the Mohammedans African pagans were lower than the beasts.

The original supply of slaves in Africa, as elsewhere, was from war captives. Francis Moore, factor at Fort James in 1730, describes their arrival "tied at the neck by leather thongs." But though war was the immediate source of slaves, as old as settled civilization itself, when the demand for workers for the plantations grew, local chiefs began to raid for slaves and to make slavery the punishment for very small offences. And even in those hard centuries, when, to the most civilized, pain and injustice were familiar acquaintances, when half the number of all children born died young, when the smallest operation was complicated torture ending usually in a miserable death, when prisons, even for debt, were black holes of filth and misery, the slave trade moved consciences and brought protests.

Nothing is more strange and interesting than the movements of the conscience and its impact upon the ideas and conventions in which men live and strive. Slavery and the slave trade were attacked from very early times. Plato rejected it for Greek, by Greek. The Christians and Christian fathers, for the most part, made it a sin. But slavery still continued, without a check, for century after century.

Slave dealers and owners were justified in thinking that it would go on for ever. Yet its abolition, within the British Empire, was completed in little more than a single generation.

In 1767, Granville Sharp, a man of strong Evangelical principle, brought an action against a slave owner who had imported a slave into England. He fought the case persistently until, in 1772, on appeal to

Lord Mansfield, he got a judgment that no man in Great Britain could be a slave. As soon, therefore, as a slave set foot in Britain he became free. This freed slaves in Britain itself.

In 1785, at Cambridge, the Vice-Chancellor gave as subject for a prize essay in Latin prose, "Is it right to make slaves against their will?" Thomas Clarkson, aged 25, of St. John's College, won the prize, and the Master of St. John's advised him to publish the essay. He therefore published a translation, which brought him into acquaintance with Sharp, and soon afterwards Sharp, Clarkson, William Wilberforce, and some others founded the Committee for the Abolition of the Slave Trade. Clarkson gave his whole life to the cause.

These were energetic men, and they were soon joined by others as remarkable—Josiah Wedgwood, Zachary Macaulay, father of Lord Macaulay, and Henry Brougham. They brought not only vigour to their case, but experience in propaganda. They introduced Bill after Bill, and harried successive Governments until, in 1807, the trade was abolished in all British territories.

One point should be noticed, especially in these days of scientific positivism. It is sometimes said that the objection to slavery was logical, based on a mathematical idea of equality. This is not so. The statement that one man X equals another man Y is not a truism, nor even demonstrably true. It means only that, in the opinion of some people, X ought to be equal with Y before the law; and equal in opportunity to use his powers and to satisfy his ambitions. And this is not a truism. It is not obvious in logic, or fact. It is a moral statement, a creed, a belief, a conviction often held more strongly by free and well-off people than by the oppressed themselves. In short, the slaves do not owe their freedom to rationalism, but to a group of evangelicals and Quakers with strong leanings to theoretic anarchism.

This pressure group, as we should call it now, deserved all its fame. It owed much to a change in public feeling, long prepared by Locke, by Rousseau, and by almost all the writers of the century, but without its action the slave trade might have lasted another fifty years.

The Abolitionists, having stopped the British trade, set about stopping the world trade—with the same success, arising from the same cause, a prepared public opinion. The trading countries, not indeed at once or all together, found themselves obliged to yield to public feeling.

The U.S.A. prohibited importation of slaves in 1807; the Congress of

Vienna, in 1814, on the strong representations of Castlereagh, agreed that a general abolition was desirable; and in 1820 Great Britain paid £400,000 to Spain, in 1830 £300,000 to Portugal, as compensation for their giving up the trade.

Emancipation of slaves followed naturally upon the abolition of the trade. It had the same motive. It faced the same opposition from planters. It was achieved by the same means, continued agitation and appeals to Parliament, which passed the Act in 1833. £20,000,000 was paid in compensation to the owners.

The emancipation could not free the slaves in an Africa still under its own chiefs. But it made a general emancipation certain in the course of time. It also had one very important effect on the emancipators. It gave to national action a moral dignity, very rare in history, but enormously valuable to any people and any Government. Governments may perhaps think little of it, and trouble very little about it. If so, they are stupid. A great cause, in which a whole people can feel themselves honoured, is the prime secret of national unity and vigour.

Foundation of Sierra Leone, 1787

Lord Mansfield's ruling in 1772, that no man in Great Britain could be a slave, set free many negroes, who fell into misery. To these destitute poor were added, at the end of the American Revolution, those negroes who had fought for Britain and dared not remain in the U.S.A. at the mercy of the victorious planters. The British Government sent some of these loyalists to Nova Scotia, some to the Bahamas. But there also they were poverty-stricken and dissatisfied.

At this time, some philanthropists, including Granville Sharp, the Abolitionist, proposed a settlement in Africa for "free blacks and people of colour." This was in 1786, nearly fifty years before the abolition of slavery, and twenty before the abolition of the slave trade. A free settlement in slave-trading Africa was therefore a new and bold suggestion.

The Government, embarrassed by its duty to the discharged soldiers, fell in with the plan, offered transport and a ship, and Sierra Leone was chosen as the place of settlement. The first settlers sent out were four hundred negroes, and sixty whites, chiefly London prostitutes. They arrived at the Coast in May 1787, and the naval captain in charge then bought from a native chief, Nainbanna, twenty square miles between the Rivers Sherbro and Sierra Leone.

It is often thought that this land was the first West African territory owned by the British Crown and the parent of the first colony. This is not the fact. For a few years, from 1763 to 1783, the Island of Gorée, and Fort St. Louis in the Senegal River, captured from the French in the Seven Years' War, were joined with old Fort James on the Gambia and made into a Crown colony Senegambia, with a government on the American colonial model. But it did not last long. Senegal was given back to the French by the Treaty of Versailles in 1783; Senegambia was abolished, and the Gambia was returned to the Merchants Company, as the cheapest means of administration.

Senegambia has no importance except in date. Sierra Leone has much importance, both in its idea and its consequences.

The Government, wanting as little responsibility as possible for this strange thing that circumstances had forced upon it, a free settlement on the African mainland, left administration to Sharp, who designed a plan based on what he called the ancient English Frank-pledge. By this, roughly speaking, all males from 16 to 60 possessing their own arms acted as police and elected their own justices. There was no Governor.

But the first settlement was already in dissolution. Many settlers, Africans unaccustomed to Africa, died; others, to Sharp's surprise and anger, went off to get good jobs in the slave business. Sharp, unable to compete with the attractions of slavery, formed a company, to engage "in honourable trade."

A thousand new settlers arrived from Nova Scotia at the same time, a new administration was set up under the company directors, and, in 1792, Freetown was laid out.

The company governors, who included Zachary Macaulay, had still a very difficult charge. In 1793 the French destroyed their capital. In 1808 white agitators, raising the cry of negro nationalism, came out in rebellion. Troops arrived only just in time to save Governor Macaulay and his staff.

In the same year the company went bankrupt, and the Crown found itself once more responsible for a colony on the West Coast, and, what is historically more important, one that was difficult to get rid of. For its obligations to the settlers were recorded in the very name of Freetown.

But a few months before, in 1807, the slave trade had been abolished, and this now caused, along the West Coast, one of those sudden and complete changes of policy which, as you prefer flexibility or consistency, are either the chief virtue or chief fault of democratic government. The Abolitionists represented a powerful party with great command of votes. And the Government, which had once, at the demand of planters and merchants, set up a company to encourage the slave trade, was now even more eager to destroy that trade. This was already proving to be difficult. British merchants were forbidden to carry slaves. But Portuguese, Spaniards, Dutch, and Germans could still legally engage in it, and smugglers, including British and American, were extremely active.

All ships carrying slaves to the U.S.A. or to British plantations were subject to capture, but it was not easy to catch them.

Other Powers had condemned the trade; Denmark had abolished it. But Britain and the U.S.A. were beginning to see that putting down the traffic would have to be undertaken by their own Fleets; in practice, since the British Fleet was much the larger, chiefly by British warships.

The Home Government therefore passed almost at a single step from regretting the burden of the West African settlement, now without economic value as a slave market, to congratulating itself on possessing some stations on the coast from which its frigates and sloops could hunt down the slavers.

As Freetown had then the only sheltered anchorage, it was made the naval headquarters. The Merchants Company lingered on for a few years. But it could not live without the slave trade. And in 1821 it was at last wound up. Its property and buildings on the coast came, by charter, to the Crown, which, not knowing what else to do with them, placed them under the Governor of Sierra Leone.

Foundation of the Gold Coast, 1843

The Gold Coast stations were not yet abandoned. They were useful still to traders, African and British. But in 1826 war broke out between the Fanti tribes on the coast and the rising empire of Ashanti in the hinterland. The Fantis, old friends of the company men, called for help, and Sir Charles McCarthy, Governor of Sierra Leone, and therefore now responsible for the stations and their local allies, came down with his small local forces. He was defeated and killed. The Ashanti chiefs cut off his head and carried it away with them. His skull became the royal drinking-cup.

The Home Government then sent out troops, and in 1826 won a

local victory. But it was disgusted by this unexpected and expensive war. It resolved to abandon the forts, which so long as they remained, would invite the Fanti to seek British protection.

Again the merchants protested. They offered to take responsibility for forts and Fantis. And again the Government, under various pressures, handed over the Gold Coast stations to a committee of merchants, with a small subsidy of £4,000 a year.

These merchants, like so many of their forerunners and successors, now succeeded in finding a good man to serve them, George Maclean. He was not a trader, but a soldier, a member of the Royal Colonials, one of those colonial corps which, down to the time of Lugard, have always attracted young men of enterprise and ambition. Maclean was the true founder of the Gold Coast as it is to-day. With 120 African soldiers, and his own extraordinary prestige, he pacified the hinterland and made a treaty in 1831 with the Ashanti, which secured some independence and peace for the oppressed Fantis. Maclean's triumph ended in tragedy. He was attacked in Britain by those same groups of anarchist evangelicals, who, by a sardonic but perhaps a necessary consequence of their creed, have brought about not only the great glories of freedom, such as the abolition of the slave trade, but many of its disasters and oppressions, in refusing defence of liberties already established, or, as now, in attacking its pioneers.

For the same abstract idea of liberty which told them that all free action was good, tended also to assure them that all government was bad; and all governors tyrants.

Anyone who wants to know what Africa was like before men like Maclean gave it law should read Mungo Park's *Travels.* Then they will know how, without justice, the mass of the people suffered their lives. Anarchy is the prime wretchedness of the poor and weak.

Maclean, with nothing but his own prestige and half a company of native levies, had brought peace and order, the beginnings of justice, to millions.

But he had made enemies of every local exploiter. He was accused at once of encroaching on native rights and protecting the slavers; even of murdering his wife, a poetess then well known under the initials L. E. L. And all slanders were believed. Maclean was poor and far away, and he could not defend himself. Above all, he was a Governor.

Maclean was cleared at last by a Government Inquiry. But the Government dared not reinstate him. Neither could it desert the Fantis, now still more dependent on protection, without a scandal. So it again took over the coast in 1843, and made new treaties, in 1844, to confirm Maclean's understanding with the chiefs. To Maclean, since for fear of his enemies' influence at home they could not make him Governor, they gave a minor post as Judicial Assessor. He accepted it, with what feelings we do not know, and served in it for a few years until, in 1847, he died.

Then at last the Gold Coast chiefs and people had an opportunity to show, by mass demonstration, how great they held him, how deep was their gratitude. They gave him the funeral of an African king. Unluckily, like other heroes who have suffered the same injustice, Maclean could not see his vindication—his friends, since they did not know their own number, could bring fitting honour only to his coffin.

The Government now found itself with a new colony on the West Coast. But it did not want colonies. It did not know what to do with them. For since the Reform Bill, bringing new groups, especially the evangelicals, into power, British democracy was profoundly divided on fundamental principles. Possibly it could not have been worked at all if both sides had not been able to agree in one idea, that government's chief duty was to keep order as cheaply as possible, and let what were called economic laws have free swing. In fact all parties were agreed only upon the principle of *laissez faire,* which all parties now, with equal conviction, would reject and despise. And this principle could not deal with a dependent empire.

There had lately been a rebellion in Canada, and Lord Durham's report on Canada advised self-government for the whole territory. It was expected that Canada, like the U.S.A., would soon cut loose, and this idea exactly fitted the theory of *laissez faire.*

But Canada, it was believed, could look after itself. Colonies on the African coast, which obviously could not do so, were therefore a puzzle. The ruling theory, on which alone British democracy was then able to work, found no place for them. The Government was forced to stay on the Gold Coast, but only as the best of several political evils. And it acted there with the greatest caution and economy. It wanted neither new annexations to offend the native-rights party, nor new expenses to annoy the taxpayer.

It escaped from the first difficulty by a Fanti Agreement, which made the protectorate requested by the Fanti, without calling it so. From the second it was partly rescued by the Gold Coast chiefs, who in 1858, being assembled by the Governor, voluntarily agreed to pay a poll tax towards the cost of the British administration. These two agreements with the Gold Coast tribes, by which they entered into voluntary contract with the British Government for the benefit of both parties, are important in the history of the Coast. But they did not, in the Government's mind, commit it to a permanent occupation. As we shall see, it was soon making a still more resolute attempt to avoid Imperial duty and trouble.

Lagos and the Oil Rivers, 1861

Lagos Island, in the Bight of Benin, had not been much used by British traders. It was too far away. It was not brought into the Empire by a trading company, nor, like Sierra Leone, as a settlement for freed slaves and discharged soldiers, but by the third cause which founded West Africa: by the Navy, upon its duty of suppressing the slave trade.

That is to say, as the merchant was zealous for his store and his native friends about the store; as the War Department was concerned for its discharged men; so the naval officer, seeking not only promotion but also occupation, eagerly hunted the slave trader. Lagos Island, occupied by runaways from the Kingdom of Benin, and governed by its own chiefs, was a nest of slavers. A King's Officer was sent to put down the trade; the chief refused a treaty. The sailor landed, fought him and deposed him.

The Government then set up a new chief, and appointed a British Consul to make sure that the treaty was carried out.

At once traders and missionaries followed the Consul, who, since he had no powers, found himself in the same position as many a British official before him on the same coast: obliged to keep order and organize peace, without any authority but his own character, and an occasional call from the Navy. Also as before, in the Gambia and in Sierra Leone, his position became impossible and the Government was obliged to ask itself which it could do, with the least trouble and expense—go or stay. It decided to stay. The vigorous and reckless Palmerston, Prime Minister in 1861, took over Lagos and made it also a Crown Colony.

And while the abolitionist policy was bringing new responsibilities in Lagos, merchant adventurers, exactly like their Elizabethan and Georgian ancestors, were risking their lives and their capital in the Niger Delta behind and about Lagos, and therefore automatically creating new ties or troubles for the Government.

The attraction was no longer slaves, but palm oil, which was now becoming valuable in the European market. For this reason, the mouths of the Niger, not yet known to be those of the Niger, surrounded by the high rain forest in which the oil palm flourished, were called the Oil Rivers.

These pioneer traders of the Oil Rivers explored much of the Delta for themselves and made their own maps. But the interior of Africa was no longer a complete mystery. African exploration had begun some time before. In 1770, James Bruce went to Abyssinia and the Blue Nile. His stories were disbelieved, but excited all Europe. And in 1788 a group of British scholars and dilettanti formed an Association for the Exploration of Africa.

Thus a third element of the free spirit, curiosity, was added to those two others, ambition and restlessness, which had already been at work in Africa. The Association, like the Merchant Adventurers, found plenty of brave and ambitious men in Britain ready to risk everything for the adventure.

In 1795 and again in 1805 it fitted out, by subscription from its members, the famous Mungo Park.

Park, on his latter journey, had Government permission to recruit an escort from the coast garrison. His plan was to march from the Gambia to the Niger, build a boat, and sail down to the Niger mouth. But of 39 in his party, all but eight died before he reached the Niger, and four more in the next few weeks. Park built a ship large enough for this party by joining two large dugouts together. Five Europeans, the guide, and three slaves bought by Park made up the crew. They were attacked many times, but each man had fifteen muskets ready loaded, and easily drove off all enemies until they reached the rapids at Bussa. Here they were attacked by the chief of Yauri, whose complaint was that Park had not sent him a present. Park had sent a present—one of his silver rings given as a present is still in Bussa—but it was not sent on to Yauri. Some subordinate chief, hearing that Park would not come back that way, kept it for himself. Yauri's men attacked the party at a narrow and dangerous rapid. They killed two slaves, and the boat, out of control, ran among the rocks. Park and the two other Europeans were drowned in trying to escape.

It was the African Association also which sent out Clapperton to Chad in 1827, and the Lander brothers, who explored the Lower Niger in 1830. Clapperton and Richard Lander both died in Africa, and of Africa.

Their work was taken up by McGregor Laird and a company of Liverpool merchants, which fitted out, in 1832, an expedition to continue Lander's exploration of the Lower Niger and, if possible, to establish the new oil trade in place of the slave trade.

Laird himself went with the expedition, which had no commercial success. Of forty-nine Europeans in this party, forty died. But Laird, like so many before him, was much more of an explorer, an adventurer, an evangelist, than a trader. He continued to dream of opening Africa to civilized intercourse. In 1854, he approached the Government for a subsidy.

It was a good moment. The Government had sent out, in 1850, Heinrich Barth, one of the great African explorers, who spent four years in Hausaland, and wrote one of the classics of African travel. Livingstone, supported by the Royal Geographical Society, successor to the African Association, was now at work, and added to the new popular interest in African wonders and African cruelties a missionary zeal.

African exploration had become a popular cause, as well as a scientific and mercantile speculation. Government was under pressure from many quarters to support it. It gave Laird a subsidy for his expedition, to be commanded by a naval doctor, Baikie.

Baikie made a record in African history that must not be forgotten. He gave his crew a daily dose of quinine; he took his ship 350 miles up the main Niger to Lokoja, and brought it back again without the loss of a man. That is, he proved in 1854, that a white man going to the Coast, and even into the terrible Bight, need not take odds of 5–1 against coming back alive.

The Government, impressed by this feat, agreed with Laird for a subsidy to keep a ship on the river for five years. Baikie set up a post at Lokoja, where he was Consul, and travelled through the northern lands as far as the great Mohammedan city of Kano, already described by Barth. But the whole enterprise depended on the characters of these two men, Laird and Baikie. When Laird died in 1861, and Baikie in 1864, the Consulship at Lokoja, and the post, were given up.

Yet private trade on the Oil Rivers was growing fast. This was the beginning of the Earlies, described by Aloysius Horn, where men of his kind, wanderers infected by a passion for the wilds and the solitudes, made their homes in stranded schooners, or moored hulks, along the lower river, and traded with the jungle tribes.

And these men too, like McCarthy, Maclean, Baikie, Laird, committed their country. For though one or other of them might be murdered without causing attention, their very presence was a factor in a political situation which was growing rapidly in complication.

This fact was not, however, noticed by a Home Government busy with the exciting and difficult politics of the day, the ambitions of Germany, the revolution in Italy, the complex instability of Napoleon III. It had little time for the obscure and troublesome problems of the West Coast. It called together, in 1865, a select committee, which advised, of West Africa, that the Government "should transfer to the natives the administration of all government with a view to our ultimate withdrawal from all except Sierra Leone." This committee was appointed by the same Liberal Government of Palmerston and Russell which had occupied Lagos four years before. Again it is easy to accuse democracy of inconsistency, of having no colonial policy. In fact it had two or three, belonging to different persons or groups. The impulse for occupying Lagos came from the anti-slavery group, and from Palmerston himself, always ready to take positive action in the cause of freedom which he identified with British supremacy. The motion to withdraw came from the economy group, represented by Gladstone, combined with the antimilitarists. These differences may be food for satire, but they are the very stuff of integrity and freedom itself. Deadlock is the chief danger of free States. It may destroy them. Conflict on first principles held back social development in England throughout the century. Autocratic Germany surpassed it in organization. But authoritarian States have their own diseases still more fatal. Sooner or later, but inevitably, they rot and infect the world.

The Government, glad to escape from a dilemma, accepted the committee's findings and made a first step by placing the Gold Coast once more under the Governor of Sierra Leone. But the rest of its suggestions were found quite impracticable. And the Colonial Office had hardly become aware of its commitments in the Gambia, Sierra Leone, Lagos, the Gold Coast, and the Oil Rivers, when it was once more drawn into an Ashanti war.

It had inherited from Governor Maclean his agreements with the

Fantis, for protection, chiefly from the King of Ashanti. This King was the most powerful on the Coast. He had a large, well-organized army and a centralized Government. The tyrannies of that Government are too well known for description here.

The Ashanti had several times invaded the Gold Coast territories since the war of 1826. Now once again they were on the march.

The Dutch had decided to give up Elmina, their last fort on the coast, useless to them since the abolition of the slave trade. They sold it to Britain, who, in spite of the committee's advice, found it expedient to buy. But the King of Ashanti had an old claim to Elmina, and the Ashanti had always wanted access to a Coast station. They resented having to trade through the Fanti middlemen. They came down, therefore, with a large army, and beseiged Elmina.

Unluckily for the Ashanti this was in 1874. Germany had lately defeated the Austrian Empire and the French Empire in campaigns of a few weeks each, and had declared its own unity at Versailles. Europe was startled. Every nation looked to its defences. In Britain, a new War Minister, Cardwell, set to work and carried through, between 1868 and 1874, a complete reform of the Army.

The British Government remembered old defeats on the Gold Coast. It dared not risk another, in the face of the new Europe. It sent out, under Garnet Wolseley, a force which was, for the first time in colonial history, properly equipped and trained. In six weeks it defeated the Ashanti and took their capital of Kumasi. After this the Gold Coast was again returned to colonial status with a Governor of its own. Thus, in spite of the committee of 1865, in 1874 Britain was more firmly established, that is, more deeply entangled, in Africa than ever before. She was the sole European Power on the Gold Coast, with enormous prestige among the tribes which, for centuries, had trembled before the terrible empire of the Ashanti. She was settled at the Gambia, Sierra Leone, and Lagos; and her independent traders were far up the River Niger. Her explorers, Clapperton, Barth, and Baikie, had taken her name even to Kano, the capital of the Fulah emirs, and the trading capital of the Western Sudan.

Again it was shown that a first-class Power with any footing, even a single trading station, upon the coasts of one divided and confused, cannot avoid the growth of its connections, until it finds itself drawn into the politics of the continent. That is proved by the histories of India, China, South Africa, as well as the West Coast of Africa.

An expansionist policy had not been needed to entangle Britain in West Africa. But that policy, a true imperialism, now suddenly, from many different elements, precipitated itself, and finished in twenty-five years what had been hardly begun in three hundred before, the division of the whole African continent.

3:

The New Nationalist Imperialism, 1870

LOUIS XIV, Frederick the Great, and Napoleon had all set out to make empires. But Napoleon III was beaten by a new imperialism, not so much dynastic and military, as popular. The nations of the past, made up of a despot, a small ruling class, a vast peasantry too poor and stupid to count in politics, had been replaced during fifty years of industry and education by a new kind of nation, in which a huge middle class of traders, distributors, clerks, and artisans exceeded the upper class in wealth and power.

This new nation set Governments of all kinds new problems of management. It was literate and had some historical imagination; it was therefore at once more romantic than the old, more easily led by slogans, and more excitable, more difficult to drive by decree. The old cosmopolitan aristocracy, ruled by reason or interest, to which wars were a game, had gone for ever. The new dominant class had no common sense, but it had great technical ability; its organized power was formidable.

Its first appearance on the battlefield in 1864 and 1870 shocked the world. For everyone felt, even if he did not clearly perceive, that world politics had turned a corner so sharp that history was no longer in one perspective with events. The future must be new and blind.

The brilliant little Ashanti campaign of Wolseley in 1874 was the first small effect on British colonial policy of this revolution. The second was more unexpected, and much more decisive.

Conflict of the Powers in Africa, 1876–1885

African exploration from east to west had now been almost completed by Livingstone, Speke, Baker, and Stanley. The deep and cunning politician Leopold of Belgium, assessing the popular interest in Africa created by these discoveries, and the new force of mixed evangelical and scientific feeling, formed, in 1876, an International African Association, with himself as President. Belgium was weak, too weak to seize great colonies by power of arms. But Leopold, recognizing the new imperialist age, had devised a means of acquiring for himself, as King of the Belgians, at least a share of the African booty.

The Association was private. No Governments were officially represented among its members. But its expeditions, as Leopold foresaw, gave it, and therefore himself as president, a first claim upon the territories explored. In 1878 he met Stanley, a British subject, and engaged him to open up the Congo Basin. Stanley made treaties with the Congo chiefs and when, in 1884, he was succeeded by another Englishman, de Winton, he was in fact Governor of an enormous territory.

He was Governor, by the letter, for the International Association; but in practice, for Leopold, the richest and by far the most powerful member of that Association, a reigning king.

Other nations of Europe—France, Portugal, Germany, and finally Britain, which had been, so to speak, holding their breath since 1870, and waiting for the immense dust of that campaign to blow away and discover to their eyes the new political landscape—now perceived that Africa was at least one part of it. And each considered, "If I do not secure my position, I shall be thrown out of it." That is to say, each separate Government feared a loss of prestige, now become so important in this new age of nationalist and romantic competition. As now the loss of a football match may ruin the manager of the club, so then a loss of face might bring down a Government or a Dynasty. The French quickly reached out towards Timbuktu and the Upper Niger. Their agent de Brazza competed with Stanley in the Congo. He took over the northern bank of the river. Portugal made great claims also to rights on the Congo. Italy took a port on the Red Sea. Germany occupied South-West, and in 1883 a German warship suddenly appeared on the West Coast. It seized Togoland and the Cameroons, which had long asked for British protection, and where British traders had been established for fifty years.

The British Government had sent a Consul to take over these territories, already in a British sphere of influence. He was in time to save the Oil Rivers, that is, the Niger Delta; but five days late for the Cameroons. So close was this famous race when, after several hundred years, it started.

European Ministers, under pressure from their peoples, were in violent competition. But none of them, certainly not Bismarck, wanted war over Africa. Bismarck, indeed, from the older generation, was contemptuous of the romantics who sought colonial expansion. He sought power over the peoples and wealth of Europe; not over deserts and jungles, however large on the map. Nothing shows more plainly the force of the new popular nationalism than that the cynical aristocrat Bismarck had to give way to it. He sent his Consuls and his warships. But at the same time, to avoid bad consequences, he called an International Conference at Berlin and showed plainly how much he desired a peaceful settlement of African conflict.

The Berlin Conference, 1885, and the Partition of Africa

Bismarck's Conference recognized the Congo Free State and secured its neutrality. It declared that any Power wishing to occupy new lands in Africa should first notify the others. And it laid down that an occupation, to be valid, must be effective; that is to say, roughly, that the Power in question must have actually entered on a territory, and acquired some standing there by treaty with the chiefs.

This ruling was to the immediate advantage of Germany herself and France, which had long encouraged the policy of penetration by treaty. Her agents, soldiers of fortune, had already made treaties to cover the greater part of North Africa. She was now able to cut off all the different British settlements from one another, and sometimes, as on the Gambia, from a natural hinterland. The Gambia is still a wasted river, because it is divided from the territory which should feed it with trade.

But in some other ambitions the French were disappointed at the Conference. They had, like the Germans, long coveted the Niger Delta. They had in the 'sixties and 'seventies given support to French firms which opened stations on the Lower Niger and they would certainly have been able to claim the river, had it not been for the founder of the Royal Niger Company, Sir George Goldie. Goldie, who had seen the ambitions of France, and who, like Laird before him, and Rhodes afterwards, was moved more by patriotic ideas of empire than trade, in 1879 brought together all the small firms on the Niger into the United African Company, which was too strong for the French, and at last bought them out. Thus at the Berlin Conference, Britain, thanks to Goldie, was able to claim as a sphere in her effective occupation the Lower Niger, which has since grown into the great Colony and Protectorate of Nigeria.

The Conference had avoided or postponed war, but it had not allayed competition. On the contrary, it had, in effect, thrown open Africa to the new popular imperialism. It said, "Take what you can, but don't fight about it." The Congo, after this invitation, did not long remain international. It became in the same year, 1885, the Congo Free State under the sovereignty of Leopold. That clever man had now his private empire. France, too, proceeded by annexation. She brought new African colonies under the government of the Republic. But Britain was still deeply divided. A strong party under Gladstone, which disliked all colonial adventure, was opposed by the new imperialist groups now rising to power. Traders and missionaries who saw the moves of France and Germany, who had seen the Cameroons snatched away from them and enclosed within a tariff ring, demanded vigorous action, and they could count now upon the support of millions, where, in the eighteenth century, they would have found indifference. They had a Press and a popular cry. The death of Gordon at Khartoum, in 1885, was still fresh to every mind, and no Government could forget the reaction of public anger against the ministry whose carelessness or neglect was supposed to have brought it about. Yet Gordon, too, had been a soldier of fortune. Leopold had offered him the Congo. And in the Sudan, as Governor for the Khedive of Egypt, he had acted upon his own independent will, refusing to withdraw when ordered to do so.

Gladstone wondered at the enormous effect of Gordon's death upon public opinion. Gladstone saw him as a kind of buccaneer in the Elizabethan manner and resented the power of an independent egotist to divert the policy of H.M. Government. But Gordon had power because he appealed to the romantic and the religious feelings of the new age, so much stronger than economic or even logical argument.

The Government dared not risk humiliation in Africa. At the same time, it did not care for the risks and expense of direct annexations; it preferred the tried method of the chartered company, and three new African companies were founded. The first of them, in 1886, was the Royal

Niger Company, with Goldie as President. The other two were the British East Africa Company in 1888, and the British South Africa Company in 1889.

The Royal Niger Company, 1886

These companies differed fundamentally from the old merchants companies. They did not possess only trading posts and forts meant to protect the sea trade with Britain. They entered upon great lands. Their charters were not in the first place for a trade monopoly, but for administration of those lands. They undertook, therefore, the responsibilities of a government to establish peace and open trade routes.

Moreover, as before, obeying that rule by which an ordered State becomes entangled with its neighbours, either by attraction or repulsion, they soon found themselves drawn into wider engagements. No sooner had the Royal Niger Company established itself at Lokoja, on the Niger, than it came into conflict with the emirs of the north, who raided for slaves down to the very river.

France, which had now pushed forward into Dahomey, claimed Borgu, on the river bank, which was also claimed by the company. The Royal Niger Company, like the old Gold Coast merchants, now looked round for an enterprising young soldier to lead its forces. It pitched upon Captain Lugard, who had already done brilliant service for the British East Africa Company in securing and pacifying Uganda. Lugard in 1894 led his small force of Niger Company police two hundred miles through unmapped bush to Nikki, suzerain town of Borgu, and made a treaty which justified the company's claim to Borgu and the right bank of the Niger. Captain Decoeur, the officer sent by the French Government to get the same concession for France, arrived a week later.

French public opinion resented this success, and two years afterwards, while the company's main forces were engaged in war with one of the slave raiders, the Emir of Bida, French troops marched across Borgu and seized Bussa, on the Niger. And now at once what every British Government had feared, to be drawn into European war by a quarrel over a few square miles of African bush, seemed close. For though the Royal Niger Company was the governing body in conflict with France, public opinion at home regarded British prestige, and therefore Government prestige, as offended.

Joseph Chamberlain, the Colonial Secretary, was in sympathy with that feeling. He represented the new imperialism of Britain, indeed, of all Europe, and he was not to be outfaced by the same imperialism of France. He guaranteed the expenses of two battalions of troops and three batteries, as the nucleus of a new West African Frontier Force, under Lugard's command.

At the same time British and French armed forces had met, gun to gun, on the Nile and in the Gold Coast hinterland, north of Ashanti, where British officers had also made treaties with the chiefs. The French and British peoples were in an angry mood. Excited crowds seemed to be eager for war. But their rulers hesitated. For the new democracies, though touchy and bellicose, were not designed or prepared for war. The French Government was no longer controlled, the British Government never had been controlled, by its Army. Thus, while the popular Press was full of warlike threats, the ambassadors were anxiously seeking peace and, using a method already proved useful in dealing with the new democratic nationalism, part of the new technique of government, they prolonged these conversations, privately and almost secretly, until the people had found another diversion and the Press another sensation. It was then possible for each side to declare concessions, which, if they had been even suggested a few months earlier, would have caused riots, adverse votes, possibly the fall of governments, and the war which they were meant to avoid. By a convention of 1898 signed in Paris the new boundaries were fixed. France was given Nikki and a large piece of country bordering the upper north-western course of the Niger; Britain kept Borgu and about 35,000 square miles north of Ashanti. Each people was able to regard itself both as a victor and as a civilized member of world polity, unwilling to quarrel about trifles.

The new country north of Ashanti was called the Northern Territories of the Gold Coast, and put under a British Commissioner who reported to the Gold Coast Government.

Foundation of Nigeria, 1900

The Royal Niger Company was now left in a strange position. The Government paid local troops, over which the company had no authority. At the same time it was criticized, as a company, for using its unique position, as an administration, to set up a trade monopoly on the Niger, a thing expressly forbidden by its charter.

Sir George Goldie, the pioneer who had formed the company, and who had been its only President, himself declared that this charter had been meant only as a step towards Imperial control, to which he himself had always looked forward.

The Government therefore resolved, in 1899, to take over the whole administration of the company's lands, which by Goldie's policy of treaties with chiefs had been extended from the Oil Rivers Protectorate to Sokoto on the edge of the Sahara Desert, and Bornu on Lake Chad.

This large region, the south of jungle, the north of open bush, was divided into two Protectorates, of Southern and Northern Nigeria. Neither was yet fully under control. Many of the Mohammedan emirs of the north, some of the powerful southern tribes, still raided for slaves and carried on a regular traffic. But the territory, as a whole, included within the boundary settled by conventions with France and Germany, was acknowledged as British.

Thus at the end of the century, after thirty years of quick expansion, the British Government found itself in charge of the Gambia Colony, Sierra Leone Colony, Gold Coast Colony with the Northern Territories, Lagos Colony, and the two Protectorates of Nigeria. Of modern West Africa, only Ashanti was still independent.

All African chiefs had felt the pressure of the new forces and new ideas in Africa. Some gave way and made their peace. Some resisted. Ashanti, a military empire, which lived by slave raiding, whose religion demanded human sacrifice, would not or could not change its political system, even though it brought it into conflict with Protecting Powers, especially Britain. There were two more Ashanti wars, and at last, in 1901, Ashanti was annexed and placed under a Chief Commissioner.

Europe in Africa: Problems of Government

Europe had now occupied all Africa. And the popular idea of Africa was that of tropical forests full of rich and valuable products to be had for the gathering. In fact, Africa was poor, full of deserts and swamps. Its new owners found that it could barely pay the expenses of administration; sometimes not even so much. Development, the opening up of the interior, was plainly going to be very expensive. In this difficulty, some Powers had already followed the policy of giving large concessions to private or semi-private corporations. And this policy led to oppression and cruelty, which had a strong effect on African policy during many years.

The European occupation itself came to be looked upon as a crime. This was stupid, but it was a logical result of certain political changes in the democracies, especially British democracy, where new classes had risen into power—classes traditionally and religiously taught to be suspicious of all governing authority, and especially of imperial development, which they regarded as the exploitation of the African by foreign capital. Neither did they distinguish between one kind of development and another.

A planter's or forester's concession is quite different in effect from a trader's charter such as that of the old companies. Traders, selling or bartering goods with anyone who may choose to deal with them, can do little harm, and may do much good. A trader's store in the early days was often the only neutral ground for large territories. There, like animals coming to a water-hole, hereditary enemies could meet without flying at each other; and lonely storekeepers became often, by mere force of their independence, centres of freedom and peace. But the concessionaire who takes over native lands or forests is in quite another place. He is not the servant of the people, obliged to be of use to all comers, but the master, compelled by need to persuade or force an alien peasantry to work for him. This does not mean that all planters must exploit, or that no foreigner has the right to employ those of an alien race. Exploitation is a matter always of local standards, of conditions and wages. Good pay, fair conditions, for willing labour, is a boon whoever gives the pay, and whoever works for it. The greater part of the world, not only in Africa, cries out for such employment. But primitive labour, as Russia discovered, is usually bad. The peasant cannot or will not learn a new job. Thus the early African concessionaires found that their labour costs, their overhead expenses, were high. And fearful cruelties were committed by desperate men seeking to grind profits out of labourers far more helpless and discouraged than slaves. All Powers, nowadays, if they still give grants to concessionaires, even to great modern companies, know that they will need close watch and strict regulation.

In 1900 the scandals of certain foreign concessions were fresh in mind, and the British Government would not risk grants of land.

The imperialism of the 'nineties which has now, by this same democratic process of representation that brought it forth, been thrust aside, was not entirely greedy or selfish. The force with which it drove European Governments, after three hundred years on the West Coast, so deep into

Africa sprang as much from the missions as from private ambition and adventure.

Many of the traders were actually missionaries for whom trade was the best means of approaching the people and winning their sympathy. All emphasize the importance of friendship and fair dealing with the Africans. This motive, in various forms, recurs again and again throughout these three centuries of West Coast history. We saw it in Jobson, we find it again, strongly expressed, in McGregor Laird, whose expedition has been mentioned above.

Laird writes, as preface to his book of 1835, that the object of the Liverpool company was not only to "establish a commercial intercourse with Central Africa via the River Niger," but to open new fields of enterprise to the mercantile world and of usefulness to those who labour for the amelioration of uncivilized man.

A later witness to the value of the trader, apart from the slave dealer, was the celebrated Mary Kingsley who went out to the Coast in 1893. Her object was, in the first place, scientific—to examine and classify tropical fish. But she took a lively interest in all West Coast affairs, commercial and political. Her *Travels* and her *West African Studies* are well worth reading.

Mary Kingsley, expecting to find in the trader her chief enemy and the native's chief enemy, found him her best friend. She even supported the trader against the missionary, on the ground that he interfered less with native customs and did good where it was most needed, in bringing prosperity. She was a strong imperialist, feeling that trade expansion in Africa was good for both parties. "I think," she told the Liverpool Chamber of Commerce, "that trade is the most important thing in Africa and the most interesting."

And it is interesting to see that when, in 1898, she came out in support of the eastern tribes of Sierra Leone which had risen against a new hut tax, she had strong support from the Liverpool traders. Both parties were against interference with native ways of life.

Mary Kingsley's views have appeared short-sighted; her imperialism, her romantic admiration of the bush native, belonged to her period. But nowadays her opposition to a purely bureaucratic and political government, her insistence that trade prosperity was more important to Africa than restrictive laws or Sunday-school teaching, her suggestion of a mixed government for the African colonies, in which the traders should give their expert advice on improving African conditions, have a very modern look. Mary Kingsley was an enthusiast and a Kingsley. An adventurer herself, she loved adventurous men. And one cannot read her life, or her letters, without feeling a very warm affection for a nature so brave, honest, generous, and simple. She had no vanity, no conceit, and she loved justice. She was not only just, but understanding with the many enemies who attacked her, as they had attacked one of her heroes, Maclean of the Gold Coast, with the malignity of the sentimentalist. She was incapable of carrying on a feud, of bearing a grudge. And though her opinions were not so modern as they seem, though she was not, and could not be, a very good judge of political values, she was right at least in seeing that her friends, the traders, as pure traders, could be in Africa, as they had been in Ancient Greece, Asia, India, in every continent and age, a centre for the diffusion and mingling of ideas.

As she saw him, the trader was a civilizing force beyond either government or missionary, because he sought for the natives only the peace and prosperity which were also his own.

The partition of Africa, whatever the complex of motives behind it, was a blessing to the African masses. Its worse evils, even of the Congo under Leopold's concession, were not so bad as the perverse and ruinous cruelty of slave raiders and despots like the Ashanti kings. I rode once through a city gate in a mud wall. Half an hour later, I reached another gate and passed out from the wall. There was nothing between but grass. That whole great city had been wiped out, not many years before, by the Emir of Kontagora, whom I knew—a tall, grave man, handsome, and of most distinguished bearing. To him, a Moslem aristocrat, as to the early Dutch of South Africa, Christian patriarchs, the pagans were animals designed by God only to be hunted and enslaved.

Talk of the white man's burden is now a joke. Probably it is good that it should be a joke, for it was too easily used to cover a mean complacence and to breed that hypocrisy which of all vices most quickly corrupts a nation. But the responsibility of Britain towards her dependants was not a joke to the Whigs who impeached Hastings; to the men who fought the slave trade; to the church people who have always supported the missions; nor to a thousand humble officials in the British service, whose duty, as they were taught, was to the African people.

And behind this official policy there was a vast public opinion at home which from imperial pride, or vanity, if you like, demanded from those

Empire servants the highest standards of justice and sympathy. We can call that public romantic. It made heroes of the pioneers in Africa. But it made them romantic heroes, and asked much of them; it made a policy of exploitation impossible for any British Government.

British West Africa, 1900: Resources and Population

The new British West Africa had neither economic, racial, nor political unity. The Gambia was simply two hundred and fifty miles of river, with a small area of forest and bush on each bank. Its whole area was about 4,000 square miles, and its population not much more than 100,000 all told. Bathurst, the capital, built on St. Mary's Island, with some fine old colonial buildings, had about 5,000 inhabitants. The chief export was groundnuts, and most of these went to France. The annual total of exports was valued at £240,705.

Sierra Leone had an area of about 27,000 square miles and a population of about 1,000,000, chiefly negro tribes, such as the Timni and the Mendi. But in the capital, Freetown, and thereabouts, the descendants of the original settlers, numbering over 30,000, represented over a hundred different tribes, and were regarded by the rest as a separate race, the Sierra Leonis. These were English-speaking Christians, many of good education. One of them, Sir Samuel Lewis, a pure African, had been Chief Justice of the Colony from 1882 to 1894. The exports of Sierra Leone were chiefly palm oil, palm nuts and ginger, valued at £360,000 annually.

The Gold Coast, with Ashanti and the Northern Territories, had an area of about 78,000 square miles and a population of about 2,000,000. There was no deep-water harbour. The old coast towns, mostly with ancient forts, such as Accra, Axim, Sekondi, Elmina, Anamabu, Cape Coast, Cormantine, were all small. The chief exports were rubber from vines, palm oil and nuts, kola nuts, gold and cocoa, valued at £885,000 annually. Gold in 1900 amounted only to £38,000.

Lagos Colony and Protectorate, and the Protectorates of Northern and Southern Nigeria, amounted together to over 330,000 square miles, with every kind of climate from the delta rain forest, full of mangrove and oil palm, to the semi-desert edge of the Sahara. The population was estimated at from fifteen to twenty millions, of many great tribes speaking different languages and ruled by different ideas of life. Exports from the north were as yet very small. From Southern Nigeria they had a yearly value of £1,130,000, chiefly of palm products and rubber.

The whole area of the new West African Empire was therefore about 440,000 square miles, with a population of about twenty million people. The area of Great Britain, that is, England, Wales, and Scotland together, is 88,750 square miles.

4:

First Colonial Development Policy: Trusteeship, 1900-1929

EXPENSE IS, as we know, the first problem of all government. Any kind of government costs much money; and good government costs a great deal of money. It was the problem of financing a government which, in the major degree, brought Charles I and Louis XVI to their deaths. For people demand services that they do not want to pay for; and each generation demands greater services.

In Africa the problem was ten times worse than in Europe. The physical obstacles to government, bad communications, bad climate, absence of educated help, were much greater; and it was impossible for tribal natives with a total income probably of five pounds a year to pay the taxes required by a modern budget. That is to say, the new Empire could afford, by itself, only the crude government which belonged to its barbarous condition, an administration, let us say, like that of William the Conqueror, securing peace and rough justice. It could not afford great schemes of development or education, and those who criticize the small reach of government plans for Africa in those early days must remember that no one at that time dreamed of the Colonial Development Funds, of 1929 and 1940, set up to give subsidies to the Colonies. In 1900 both parties were agreed, when they agreed on nothing else, that a Colony should, as far as possible, pay its own way. And their grounds were not only economic, but ideal.

The conception was that of trusteeship. The Colonies, like children under a trust, were to have every kind of help and encouragement; but out of their own funds. The principle was not so selfish as it appears. It was argued that great development loans to the Colonies would put upon them debt charges too heavy for their resources.

In this difficulty the Colonial Office resolved to use all funds available in the different West African Colonies on opening main trade routes, especially railways and ports. In Sierra Leone, the Gold Coast, and Nigeria, railways were quickly built to join chief towns on the coast, Freetown, Sekondi, Accra, Lagos, and Calabar, with the interior as yet undeveloped.

At the same time, ports were improved. Lagos was dredged to give water for large steamers. On the long and dangerous Guinea Coast, where the steamers of this century, like the caravels of the first Portuguese traders, were still forced to anchor at sea and ship their cargoes in surf-boats, 'Takoradi was begun. Its huge breakwaters, which protect an artificial harbour, were finished early in 1928. All was paid for out of Gold Coast revenue or credit.

This economic policy was attacked. It used almost all the surplus revenue of the Colonies. Officials had to live in mud huts, and all the services were starved in order that the railways might be built, the harbours dug. But I think it was a right policy. The first need in Africa has always been communications. Trade, order, peace, the intercourse which comes from trade and which is the very beginning of civilization and the education of peoples, all start from the free and safe harbour, the open river and the cleared road. Africa had never had them and could make no progress without them.

I am not saying that the other services—education, medical, veterinary, forest departments—were entirely neglected during this first period. Schools and hospitals were built; new crops introduced and old ones improved. Some of these crops, like cotton and cocoa, seem on the face of it to have had more effect on the returns than the railway policy. Cocoa on the Gold Coast and in Southern Nigeria quickly became a main cash crop and made the growers rich beyond other Africans. Mines were opened. Between 1903, when modern machinery was set up in the Gold Coast, and 1927, production of gold was valued at twenty-six millions sterling. Cocoa exports, valued in 1899 at £16,000, were worth in 1926 nine millions sterling. In Nigeria, an export of 3,000 tons of groundnuts in 1900 became 127,000 tons in 1925, an increase of more than forty times. Tonnage of tin concentrates grew five times in the same period. And these figures mean an immense change in national wealth. In

1900 the currency of most of Nigeria was cowrie shells, at a rate of 2,000 to the shilling. Pay and standards of living were among the lowest in the world. By the 1920's money circulated everywhere, sustaining an internal trade of which these exports are only a fraction.

In Nigeria, the Naraguta Plateau, rich in tin, was made accessible by a light railway; and the Government opened, at Udi, a Government colliery which supplied not only the State Railways and the Marine, but also the steamer lines. In the Gambia, groundnut farming was so much improved that the crop was doubled. In Sierra Leone, the railway was pushed forward; new roads were built; and, more lately, platinum, gold and hæmatite were discovered.

Progress therefore, even on the old policy, was great. Critics tell us that it might have been greater. That is true. But the practical question is, could it have been greater having regard to the political and economic situation at that time?

We have to remember again that democracy, for good or evil, is a representative government. It cannot act against the will of the people, or of any large groups of the people. And the governing people, from the year 1906 down to the 1920's, were divided in mind; powerful groups of voters were in direct conflict on every colonial question. No Minister could have carried an expensive plan to subsidize the Colonies at the expense of the British taxpayers.

This was not the fault of successive Governments. It was due to the nature of democracy itself, and an irreconcilable division in British democracy at that time, between two great bodies of opinion, which could agree only on the idea of trusteeship, because it did not involve legislation or dangerous quarrels in the House.

British Political Policy, 1900: Indirect Rule and the Land

When Lugard was made first High Commissioner of Northern Nigeria in 1900 he had not only to bring this vast region to order, but to devise for it an administration. Some of the great slave-raiding emirs proposed to fight. But they were not popular with their own subjects. Lugard's campaigns were short and almost bloodless, and by 1903 the whole of Northern Nigeria, except for the remoter pagan areas, was at peace.

A new administration had been built up at the same time upon a system already tried in Southern Nigeria under the company, that of Indirect

Rule. The European magistrates, that is to say, did not govern the people directly, but through and by means of their own chiefs.

Sir George Goldie, in 1879, had laid down the principle for his officials: "If the welfare of the native races is to be considered, if dangerous revolts are to be obviated, the general policy of ruling on African principles, through native rulers, must be followed for the present."

Goldie was obliged, of course, to economize on staff. And Lugard wrote at a later date: "The staff of a tropical dependency must necessarily be small in comparison with its area and population."*

But it is false to say that Goldie and Lugard, in setting up Indirect Rule, merely followed a line prescribed by necessity. They had a choice. A small staff of one race, ruling over another, of course, employs subordinates from the people native in that country. But such a staff, however small, can still give direct orders through its subordinates. It can set aside native tradition and rule absolutely. This, in fact, was the common practice in Africa. It had been followed by almost all the Colonial Powers so soon as they attempted any real government.

Goldie and Lugard, therefore, could have ruled directly. They chose the indirect system, not from poverty, but for ideal reasons.

The idea behind indirect government, briefly, is that any given civilization, however primitive, in Africa as in Europe, has a life of its own. It consists of people who have grown up with certain ideas, certain ties, obligations, expectations, and a certain relation with their own government. Any sudden and violent change in such a civilization, or its method of government, is like the dislocation of a human body. It breaks what was a living and homogeneous social unit, possibly crude and simple in form, but self-respecting and energetic, into a mere scattering of human units, despondent and usually corrupt.

And the principle of indirect rule as designed by its pioneers was to avoid these disasters by maintaining the power and prestige of native chiefs, and the continuity of native rule, as a system familiar to the people, and to the natural sphere of native local government.

Native Africans, it was said, would learn better how to govern themselves in the traditional setting than in one imposed from above and strange to local experience.

I cannot give here an extensive description of Indirect Rule. It varies

* *The Dual Mandate* (1922), p. 141.

greatly in practice. But I can describe, shortly, its working, as I knew it, in a Nigerian emirate.

The Emir, an old man, who had fought against us in 1903, lived in his palace with a large staff. He had his own Council, his Treasurer, Chief Justice, Chief of Police, and Vizier, or confidential chief minister. He had his own police organization, treasury, prison, etc.

The British Resident lived about half a mile from the Emir's capital town, in the European station. He had here his own Residency, in my time a large mud hut, his office and court house, his European staff, that is, one Assistant Resident, a doctor, two African clerks, and a detachment of African infantry under European officers in charge of a mud fort. In the office was a safe with the petty cash; in the fort, a cash-tank full of bags of silver.

The Resident, in this case, was one of three in a Province, under a Provincial Resident, who, in turn, was under the Governor of the Protectorate. The Emir, on the other hand, was a feudal monarch ruling over numerous district chiefs and village headmen, but he had no African superior. He came under the Governor, who had Africans on his Council, but as part of the British Government. Indirect rule, therefore, began, and begins, with the local chief, and the British Government is the paramount chief over all the emirs and chiefs.

Laws, financial estimates, were made at the centre, in consultation with the Secretary of State and Parliament, and referred downwards.

The Resident in each division promulgated the laws, and assessed the taxes in bulk. But the final assessment on each household, and the collection, was carried out by the Native Administration.

Taxes, when collected, were divided between the two treasuries, the Native Treasury or Beit el Mal, and the Government Treasury. This is an important point in indirect rule, for though the Government keeps check upon native expenditure, the Native Administration handles the money and pays its own officers. The Emir takes his salary out of the Native Treasury. Any surplus falls into the native reserve. Many Native Treasuries are now very rich and have large accumulated reserves.

The Government Treasury pays for the European administration. It is usually poor. But, of course, European salaries to civil servants, clerks, police, and troops are much higher than those paid by Native Administrations.

The Emir's police kept order and controlled the prison. But if they needed help, they could call for the Government police, or troops. The Emir's prison is open to inspection by the Resident at any time.

Resident and Emir met at intervals to discuss public affairs; but the real liaison was through the Vizier, who came every day to the Resident's office to bring reports, and to receive news or orders. The Resident also examined the Native Treasurer's books at least once a week, and, from time to time, checked his cash balances.

The Emir had his own courts administering native law—in this case, Mohammedan law. The Resident also had his court, administering English law. The Emir's court tried all cases concerning natives of the emirate; but anyone could appeal to the Resident, who then reviewed the case, with the help of Mohammedan assessors. Cases concerning Europeans, or Africans not native in the emirate, came before the Resident's court.

Thus a typical morning's work in the Resident's office which I am describing might be:

From six to seven-thirty: office work; the mail.

At eight, after breakfast: a call from the Vizier with reports that cattle disease had broken out in a certain district; that certain highway robbers had been caught; that the Emir wished to depose a district chief for incompetence, etc., etc.

The Resident would ask if stand-still orders had been given to the cattle men, and if the old grass had been burnt. He would suggest a meeting with the Emir to discuss the headman's case. (This particular Emir was autocratic and quarrelsome.) The Resident would then open his own business; new roads were proposed—could the Emir's roadman come up to discuss labour and material? And complaints had come in from some village, of extortion by the chief—would the Emir look into this? Etc., etc.

After the Vizier's departure there would be complaints and petitions, usually lasting a long time. This Resident kept open house night and day to complaints. He made it a rule and he taught me the rule to receive anyone who approached him anywhere, and not to allow any junior official, clerk, orderly, or court messenger to stand between him and the people. The rest of the morning might be spent on court cases or office work.

The evening after four, if office work was finished, might be kept for a stroll through the town to see a new market, or a new sanitation ditch.

At least half of this Resident's time was spent on tour through the villages. He would spend a day and night at each village. Timid complainants, as I found myself, will often speak to an official in the small hours, especially if his bed stands out in the open, well away from servants or police, when they would not approach by day. A whisper out of the dark will often throw light on mysterious trouble and discontents. And a very important duty of a Resident is to know the people, to know what's really going on in his division or district.

This sketch of a Resident's work is taken from an Emirate. Among primitive tribes there would be differences in detail. A primitive chief has more limited judicial powers and a less experienced staff. He depends more on the Resident for advice. But the general principle is the same—to delegate responsibility to Native Authorities, to keep the traditional native system in working order, both as an actual government and a training ground for native officials.

As a policy, Indirect Rule was an immediate success. It won general consent, and the Nigerian experiment became a model.

As a practice, or an ideal to be aimed at, it has been brought in throughout the Colonial Empire. Native Governments have been everywhere strengthened and encouraged. After the last war German East Africa, now called Tanganyika Territory, was alloted to Britain under mandate, and Sir Donald Cameron, because of his experience of the indirect system in Nigeria, was in 1925 chosen for its Governor.

Tanganyika, in one important respect, differed from Nigeria. It was a country of small chiefs. But Sir Donald, following Nigerian practice, looked for native organization, native social tradition, and set about building on these foundations. He was very successful. In Tanganyika, perhaps even more than in Nigeria, one finds among the natives and their chiefs not only trust in the District Officer, but a friendly regard for British administration as a whole. That is to say, there, as everywhere, it has produced a harmony between Government and people not common in a dependency.

Indirect Rule, like all popular successes, has now become suspect. It is said that it is merely a means of dodging responsibility for real government, that chiefs take advantage of their immunity, and officials of their vicarious position.

It is true that chiefs soon grasped the theory of the scheme. They knew that their prestige was to be maintained. Thus I, as a young and humble officer, at a public assembly of dozens of sub-chiefs and hundreds of their courtiers, summoned by the Emir and myself jointly to publish our agreement, reached privately over the tea-cups, that a certain feudal tyrant should be deposed, had the mortification of hearing the Emir announce, through his chief minister, that he, for his part, would prefer to give the rascal another chance. Bribery had been at work between the tea-party and the durbar. In this dilemma, I was glad of my orders to do nothing to break the chief's prestige. I said therefore that the Emir, of course, should have his way, adding only that he would also have the responsibility for any crimes or follies that the sub-chief might afterwards commit. The Vizier was up at my bungalow the same evening to explain that his master could not really take responsibility for such a fool as the sub-chief. He was much agitated, and the reason was simple. The chief was in debt and had asked for a rise of pay, which he could not get if I gave him a bad confidential report.

I describe this incident because, small as it is, it shows better than long analysis the real position under Indirect Rule, that is to say, the real power of the chief, the responsibility that arises from it, and also the power of the District Officer or Resident to make his will felt, if he chooses.

He has ultimate control not only of the force which lies behind every Government, but also of the purse. He can refuse to authorize payments out of the Native Treasury, just as the Secretary of State or Parliament can refuse to pass Government votes.

This does not mean that Indirect Rule is a sham. As anyone with political experience or imagination knows, government is finally a conflict or co-operation of forces, and these forces are largely personal.

One cannot set up a Native Authority and support its prestige without giving it the real power which arises from prestige and without which, in fact, no one would trouble about prestige.

A native chief, like any party chief, can appeal to the people, or to the District Officer's superiors, against him. In my own knowledge, an Emir who quarrelled with his opposite number, a Divisional Officer, threatened to go into voluntary exile with his whole administration. He conveyed this threat to the Provincial Resident and caused at once a political crisis. The Provincial Resident himself hastened to the spot and it was necessary to reach a compromise. A political crisis, however caused, does not please Provincial Residents and Governors. It does not assist District Officers in their careers.

Thus the relation between a Chief and a District Officer actually approximates to that between sovereign Powers, or their representative diplomats, in the essential point that each, openly or tacitly, and having regard to his real strength, brings to negotiation some power of making his will respected. And this depends largely on the characters of the two men.

In short, Indirect Rule, like every system of government, may be likened to a garden, of which the boundaries, climate, and quality of soil are all to be considered by a buyer; and yet, when he has bought his garden, and kept it for some years, he will begin to think that the only difference between one garden and another is the gardener. Indirect Rule, in practice, has quite different results even in different Provinces.

I have described one Resident's work and his determination to know the people. I might have described another whom I knew who did not care a pin for the people, and who was almost inaccessible to complaints. His aim was progress on all fronts. He was a driver in the modern style, who thought that some injustice was a negligible, or at least a necessary, price for rapid advance. A third was an enthusiast for education, for roads and markets, for the people; but he was reputed to be too innocent for the natives of his Province. They took him in. All these men did excellent work in their own ways under Indirect Rule—as they would have done under any other system. What we have to consider is the nature of indirect government as a principle: that is, the soil and climate of the garden. And this inquiry had better wait until we deal with another fundamental question—the land.

The Nigerian Land Ordinance

Africa is still an agricultural country. The enormous majority of its people are farmers dependent on the land. Land ownership and regulations, the Land Laws, mean more in Africa to the people than in Europe. Yet nothing in Africa has been more mishandled. The first settlers in Africa, the trading companies, even the Sierra Leone Company of Philanthropists, had assumed that African land, like English land, was owned by persons, either individuals or governments. These companies all bought or rented land from chiefs, as they would have bought or rented land in England from a large proprietor. They had no notion of tribal or common ownership, with all its complex and often mystical roots in the African past. The companies were followed by the colonists and their assumption of British land rights was succeeded, of course, by British land law. The new Colonial Supreme Courts brought in British tenures, freeholds, leaseholds, with right of sale. Anyone who chose could buy from native owners lands which really belonged, not to them, but to the community or the chief, and great evils followed: the land speculator; the absentee landlord; the waste of good land in neglectful hands.

Lugard's Land Ordinance was founded on the same root principle as his theory of Indirect Rule—to defend as far as possible native life and native customary law from violent and harmful disruption. He laid it down that the land should belong to its native people, under their own customary law, but that it should not be saleable to foreigners. The Government might give leases to foreigners—for instance, to missions, to storekeepers; or develop, for public good, lands not in use; but the amounts leased should be small and be strictly controlled. And the increment value of leased land should return to Government. In short, this law, for the first time, secured to Africans their own land. It absolutely prevented alien speculators from buying them out. Above all, it set a precedent and showed an example, which together, I think, have had quite as important an effect on colonial history, not only of West Africa, as Indirect Rule. Much of the Nigerian land law is still in advance of that in Britain. This is an achievement of which the Nigerian Government has a right to be proud.

Criticism of Indirect System

The Land Ordinance, like Indirect Rule, has been sharply attacked on the same grounds of standing in the way of progress. Many say that the policy of leasing large tracts to companies, so that they can lay out plantations in the most modern style, would pay Africa far better in the end than peasant ownership. The smallholder, they say, is always inefficient. He wastes most of his labour. Where large landowners with much capital and machinery do not exist or have disappeared, they must be replaced, as in Russia, by the collective farm, with State or company management.

We have again a conflict between two fundamental points of view about the duty of government. For there is no doubt that the indirect system, as a whole, has been a success in producing that result which was intended. It has brought peace and harmony. And the tranquillity of the State, the good feeling between ruler and ruled, is not, as sometimes represented, superficial, due only to the repressive powers of the chiefs. It is felt by the people themselves, the masses. It arises from the sense of continuity, which makes everyone feel he knows where he is. No un-expected or mysterious acts by an alien Government will throw his life out of gear. He sees that Government as a friend.

Shortly before I was sent to take over in one remote district, the people rose, murdered sixty members of their own local Government, and then rushed out of the district—not to escape from a white Resident, but to find one, and tell him their case. Their complaint was that, in the absence of a District Officer, the Emir had been making them pay double taxes.

Again I tell this story to compress a volume of argument into a para-graph. The critics of Indirect Rule will welcome it. "Here," they say, "you have a people kept back by a primitive tyrant. They do not value that tyranny even for its tradition. They are much more concerned with the taxes. They want, like all proletarians, to get on in the world. And they know that the white man can help them. Your Indirect Rule is not only a weight upon progress, but a fraud. It keeps in poverty and sub-jection, for the sake of a theoretical local culture and tradition, people who do not care a farthing for culture or tradition, and only want modern civilization, comfort, and security as fast as they can get it."

This, of course, is also the standpoint of the critics of the land policy, who say: "Peasant ownership and the small-holding are out of date. They get in the way of real progress in African agriculture. Already, plantation-grown palm oils are beating the wild forest products."

This criticism is important and must be answered, for two reasons. The first reason is that if this system stands in the way of modern progress it is in direct conflict with the new colonial policy. The second is that since it is now the approved system for all the Colonies, the Colonial Government would find itself opposed in its new policy, at every point, by the open or silent enmity of local Governments; and that opposition, as every official knows, can be ruinous. We have seen that colonial economic policy did secure, even in early years, great progress in all the West African Colonies, especially in Nigeria, so that Indirect Rule did not prevent progress. The questions are: Was it a hindrance—did it hold Africa back and keep it primitive? Will it do so in the future?

Lugard saw such a danger. He instructed all his officers that their duty was not to keep Africa primitive, but to press the chiefs forward. He laid it down that chiefs were not to be regarded as absolute rulers of their people, but colleagues in the new Government.

Yet Sir Donald Cameron, on his return to Nigeria in 1931 as Governor, remarked upon a tendency "to what I can only describe as reaction in dealing with the affairs of the Emirates."* He writes also that: "the absence of public opinion in Nigeria, and the extraordinary seclusion in which it was attempted to maintain the Native Administrations . . . undoubtedly encouraged stagnation."

Sir Donald fought that tendency. But I think it may be a fault innate in the system. Every kind of government has its special faults. All totalitarian systems tend to cruelty and injustice. They are, so to speak, an element in the climate and soil of a centralized and abstract government, run by experts from an office. So in Indirect Rule, with its devolution of power, its respect for traditional attachments, there is an easy-going quality of the air which affects the gardener as well as his work.

The danger of *laissez faire* under indirect rule is therefore real, and some critics of it are fair and valuable. Others are not fair, who forget the deep split between the political notions of this generation and the last. The pioneers who founded West Africa lived under Chief Secretaries and democracies who conceived their duty thus: to ensure peace, justice, tolerance, to make the way open for trade, and to do all this without putting upon each Colony a weight of debt beyond its power to pay.

They had to be economical, and they were not to make any drastic change in the life of the people.

But already, before the last war, in Europe and especially in Britain, new ideas began to eat into this ancient and simple conception of a ruler's duty. The people asked of government service as well as local justice; not only roads for trade, but the fostering of industry. This was an idea of government quite new in the world, and whether it affected autocratic or democratic systems, it divided them from all before. The Russian Revolution, the organization of two continental wars, deepened that split into a chasm. It is impossible for anyone who has not lived in that old world to pass to it now, except by an effort of the historical imagination. Those critics who complain of Indirect Rule that it did not develop Nigeria, Uganda, Ashanti with enough speed, are often making the mistake of judging the past by the light of the present. And that past is dead. For good or evil, the new ideas rule the world. All Governments acknowledge their power; and when the British Government in

* *My Tanganyika Service and Some Nigeria,* 1939, p. 15 and p. 182.

1929 opened the Colonial Development Fund, it began a policy so different in conception from those which had, up till then, disposed its relations with the African peoples, that I am not very sure it has yet realized or faced the consequences. Partly because the new departure, like the source of a great river at the top of a watershed, was a small stream. It was seen only long afterwards to belong to a different line of country.

5:

The New Colonial Development Policy: State Partnership and the Colonial Development Acts, 1929 and 1945

IN 1929 the Colonial Development Fund made it possible for any Colony to receive from the British Government a grant, free of interest, for schemes of capital development. Thus a Colony could build a port or motor road free, but it would have to maintain it. The last clause perhaps tended to hide the real meaning of the new step. For the free grant is not one of a trustee's duties. It begins a new relation and a new responsibility. It says in effect, "I am going to set you up in life," and as every student of politics knows, such an offer creates an expectation on the other side which changes the whole balance.

It was inevitable that the Colonies should ask for more and greater help; that in Britain strong groups should press the Government to give more help and would accuse it of neglect of duty if it did not do so.

This pressure was the stronger because almost all parties were agreed, as they had not been agreed for a century, on general political aims. The confusion of the 'sixties, when *laissez faire* wished to abandon the Colonies, the deadlock of the 'seventies and early 'eighties between the old Gladstonian economists, still chary of all Government action, and the Disraeli new Conservatives, eager to intervene at home and abroad; the conflict of the first ten years of this century, when powerful new parties detested the Empire, simply as an Empire, had been resolved in a completely new idea of the functions of a Government. It was regarded no longer by one party merely as a policeman; by another, as a taxgatherer; by a third, as an enemy—it was to all the universal provider. Both sides of the House of Commons were at one on the need for a constructive policy, for social services; they differed only on the amount and cost of the services. And the most convinced lover of liberty had perceived that freedom was not merely a matter of equal laws, but that a man with money in his pocket and skill in a job had more freedom of action than an illiterate pauper.

It was the Colonial Office itself which recognized the new political idea, and accepted it. It demanded new powers, not only to subsidize capital works, but to assist any development or research likely to promote the welfare of the colonial peoples. And Parliament and people being once more united in their conception of a Government's duty, they willingly passed, in 1940, the new Colonial Development and Welfare Act, which gave £10,000,000 for liquidation of debt, and £5,000,000 a year for ten years to start new welfare schemes and to encourage local industries. A further half a million pounds a year was to be spent on research.

In 1945, a second Act allotted £120,000,000 for welfare and research during the ten years up to March 31st, 1956.

The war has, of course, prevented much of the development proposed. Material, and especially men, are not available for the new schemes. But plans are made and more are being made. And the all-important point is that the whole idea behind the Fund is new and positive. It says, in effect, that Colonial Governments are no longer merely protectors, trustees, guardians, for the colonial peoples. They must plan for the future on the widest scale; they must, therefore, form some kind of idea of what they are aiming at in Africa: what kind of civilization is desirable for Africans.

New schemes of education, of industry, of town planning will profoundly affect that civilization. Is such an idea of positive development compatible with Indirect Rule? Many say that on the face of things they are directly opposed in idea and in practice. And certainly some of the pioneers of Indirect Rule did think of it as a means of allowing African civilization to grow, rather than as a method of imposing new ideas on Africa. But I have shown how flexible it is as a system. And I think that there is a danger that just as it was once too uncritically admired, it may now be too hastily damned. Its principle, local self-government, should be a powerful help in development. For in any new government policy there is nothing more valuable to the innovator than the sympathy and understanding of the people. And there is more chance of getting that support under Indirect Rule than under direct. What we have to remember is that though great changes are to take place, they need not appear as violence done to a way of life. A people can be driven to school, but they will hate it and close their minds to teaching. Or the instruction can be brought to them, through teachers of their own race, and through their own administration, so that they will welcome it as something that gives them valuable help in their own African interests, their farming, their households, and their trade.

People can be forced to work in a collective farm or factory, but their work will be unwilling and inefficient. Or they can be brought into co-operatives, and have all the benefits, the machinery, the expert advice, of the large farm, without more loss of freedom than that involved in a contract. What we have to remember is that statistics of any social group, especially in the modern world, are very delusive. They show certain facts, but only facts. They do not show the real conditions of life among actual families, covering in their ages anything up to seventy years of history; they do not show the complication of old and new; the overlap of ideas; the assimilation and transformation of one culture by another, which goes on all the time.

The word "plan," applied to great schemes, calls up the notion of a blueprint. But blueprints apply only to machines, and people are not machines. They never behave like machines. Thus we must be careful, in criticizing a system founded on respect for living people, not to argue as if we were dealing with robots. Africans at any time, like ourselves, are grown men and women attached to a society. The society may be in decay, like tribal society everywhere in Africa, or it may be in rapid change, but it is still quite unlike a factory full of machines. It is a nexus of personal attachments, of tradition, experience, feelings.

A primitive society, brought into the presence of modern civilization, faces two great dangers: of complete breakdown; of artificial preservation, when it quickly becomes mummified. We see in Africa plenty of both, town slums full of wasters and parasites; tribes preserved, by natural isolation or by local policy, in primitive stagnation.

Indirect Rule has the merit that it can put a brake upon disintegration, the fault that it can lead to mummification. And the fault must be guard-

ed against, especially where powerful native kings govern large territories.

But if this fault can be avoided, its merits are great. It can help very
much to give native life some innate coherence during a period of rapid
change.

Statistics of Development, 1900–1937

How rapid that change has been can be read from the table below,
which shows that the wealth of the Coast as a whole since 1900 has
multiplied more than ten times. And though we have to remember that
this progress, as in Russia, starting from a very primitive agricultural

		Imports* (less bullion and cash) £	Exports* £	Total Trade* £
GOLD	1900	1,099,000	864,000	1,963,000
COAST	1937	12,306,555	15,949,533	28,256,088
NIGERIA	1900	1,735,000	1,887,000	3,622,000
	1937	14,623,674	19,242,197	33,865,871
SIERRA	1900	553,000	318,000	871,000
LEONE	1937	1,691,930	2,820,178	4,512,108
GAMBIA	1900	194,000	241,000	435,000
	1937	705,165	665,000	1,370,165

* Figures for 1900 from *Capital Investment in Africa*, S. H. Frankel, Oxford University Press, 1938. Figures for 1937 from *An Economic Survey of the Colonial Empire*,
His Majesty's Stationery Office, 1937.

economy, cannot be compared on equal terms with that of the pioneer industrial and organized nations which are obliged to invent, as they go,
the new techniques of which beginners can borrow and use the results,
it is a remarkable success for the old colonial policy. The Gold Coast,
for instance, now produces much the greater part of the world's total
cocoa crop.

Such an economic revolution in forty years means great social changes,
and a stress far greater than any felt in Europe, except Russia, during the
same time: a stress which continually increases. Figures of imports and exports do not mean by themselves a general prosperity. Africa is still a

very poor country, and Africans generally have a standard of living far below European poverty lines. But I think that the improvement in average conditions of life has been widespread, at least in West Africa. On the other hand, this economy has become more insecure in the last fifteen or twenty years, and the insecurity tends to grow. A fall in commodity prices affects the West Coast as powerfully as London or Paris.

And the African has found not only his income unstable. His social order, hung in the vast gap between a Bronze Age culture and that of modern Europe, is still more dangerously placed.

He cannot go back; so he must go forward. The only way to deal with the modern world is to have modern knowledge, a modern apparatus of living.

The Future

In a modern world, where ideas are carried in a few minutes from one end to the other, and where already the remotest places are more easily reached, by air, than great capitals before, the forces of ambition and invention which drive forward society have very great and strong effects. They could not be kept away from Africa if Governments wished it. That is to say, West Africa could not even be defended from European culture. But she does not want to be defended. She is anxious everywhere for a modern civilization. She wants to learn English, as a lingua franca, as the key to a world literature; she wants modern education as well as modern services.

She wants it though it might destroy her. And she will now be able to get it quickly. The British Government, therefore, in its new policy of education, of modernization, is acting like a man on a runaway coach, who picks up the reins and takes upon himself the duty of steering the horses over a very rough road, and down many dangerous hills. And like such a driver, it will find that often the only safety is in speed, in urging the horses forward, before the wheels overrun them.

I think, that is, that the new policy of a general all-round development is the only means in West Africa of keeping the social balance: of giving stability to a new set-up.

As for those who fear that Africa, in gaining a modern equipment, will lose by that its own quality, colour, humour, its exuberance and native dignity, and, above all, that positive affirmation of life, which in extremest misery and oppression has been the strength of the Negro and the Bantu, one can only ask if any great and rich culture ever weakened a race. Did Greek scholarship ruin Italian art in the fifteenth century? Did the Renaissance destroy the French architecture and English poetry of the sixteenth? Did English philosophy and science bring decadence upon the French of the eighteenth century, or the painting of Turner and Constable discourage the native genius of contemporary Paris schools?

The secret of a rich local and national culture throughout the world is not the shutting out of foreign ideas and arts, but their assimilation. The process can be seen already in Africa. The great co-operative societies of the Gold Coast have had profound effects on the real structure of society and the position of chiefs. But the new forms of Society are still local and indigenous. They are full of that energy which, like the sap of the growing tree, springs from roots deep in their own native soil. The new Africa is no longer that of the primitive tribe but neither is it an imitation culture taken from Europe. It is as racy and native as it has ever been.

You could not make an imitation Europe in Africa if you tried. Freetown, I suppose, was such an attempt. It was formed of refugees, without African tradition, and speaking only English. It was Christian from the beginning. It is still a small town, grouped about the old tree which shaded the slave dealers and which is still called the Slave Tree. Its parishes are St. George, St. James's, St. John's, St. Paul's. Its suburban villages, Wilberforce, Regent, Gloucester, Leopold, Bathurst, Charlotte. But these villages, with their European names, and Freetown itself, have a character, a quality, so intensely their own that it stays in the mind long after that of up-country villages, more primitive but more bare, has faded quite away. And that quality seems not only richer but more African. There is no fear that tropical Africa will lose its local qualities when it is permitted to take its place in the world; rather it will bring to the world a new African civilization, new arts, new religion.

Appendix:
The War Years and After

By E. MAY ALLEN
(late Education Officer, The Gold Coast Government).

NO ONE REALIZES the need for a modern pattern of living in West Africa more fully than the Governments of those countries, and since 1938, in spite of war and the aftermath of war, definite steps have been taken towards social, economic and political progress. Some constitutional changes were due to come, having been thought out during the pre-war years, and also much economic and social development was moving slowly forward during those years. When, however, offers of financial help under the Colonial Development and Welfare Act were made available to Colonial Governments, more extensive and more highly organized social and economic planning was made possible.

Constitutional Development

In all four West African territories it is intended that Africans, in increasing numbers, shall assist in the local and central government of their countries, with a view to eventual responsible self-government by Africans for Africans.

Orders-in-Council establishing a new constitution for the Gold Coast came into operation on March 29th, 1946. Under the new constitution the Gold Coast becomes the first British Colony in Africa to be granted an unofficial majority for African members in its Legislature. In place of the fourteen unofficial members, there will in future be eighteen elected members with twelve official and nominated members. The Governor no longer provides for the administration of Ashanti by direct ordinance; instead, Ashanti, through its five representatives, takes its part with the Colony in legislative procedure. Representation of the municipalities in the Colony is increased from three to four members. The remainder are Provincial members, of which the Western Province provides four and the Eastern Province five. The United Kingdom Parliament's control is maintained by the provision, in the new Orders, of re-served powers for the Governor. The transference of responsibility for the acts of the Legislature from a Legislative Council with an official majority to one with an unofficial and elected majority is a decisive step in progress towards self-government.

The new constitution for Nigeria proposed in 1945 (Cmd. Paper 6599) came into operation on January 1st, 1947. As stated in the introductory note of the Command Paper it is designed

(*a*) "To bridge the gulf between the people and the Government by a measure of decentralization,"

(*b*) "to widen the basis of representation which will bring the established Native authorities within the legislative machine,"

(*c*) "to provide, by the grant of unofficial majorities on the Legislative and Regional Councils, for an immediate advance along the road to responsible government."

The existence of Nigeria as a single political unit dated back to 1914, but under the new constitution the country has been divided, for administrative purposes, into the Northern Province, the Eastern Province, the Western Province and Lagos Colony. Regional Councils have been formed. In the Northern Province the Council consists of a House of Chiefs and a House of Assembly, in the Western and Eastern Provinces the Councils have only Houses of Assembly, while Lagos has a Municipal Council. The members of the new Legislative Council will be as follows: the Governor as President, thirteen ex-officio members, three nominated official members, twenty-four nominated unofficial members, and four elected members. Of the nominated unofficial members, eighteen will be appointed by the various Regional Councils, six by the Governor, and two will be chiefs appointed by the Governor from those chiefs who are members of the Western House of Assembly.

The Legislative Council will have an unofficial and an African majority. While direct election will be retained where it exists at present, that is for the townships of Lagos and Calabar, the majority of the unofficial members will be appointed from their own bodies by the Northern House of Chiefs and by the unofficial members of the Houses of Assembly. The Houses will act as electoral colleges for the Legislative Council apart from their other functions.

In Sierra Leone, the Legislative Council already has a number of African members. With the Governor as president, there are eleven official and ten unofficial members. Of the unofficial members three nominated Protectorate members are Africans and three elected African members are for the Colony and urban and rural communities, in addition to two nominated African members and two nominated Europeans.

In July 1946 a Protectorate Assembly was opened at Bo, Sierra Leone. It consists of ten official and thirty-two unofficial members, twenty-six of whom are elected African representatives of the District Councils. Though a purely advisory body, without at present any legislative powers, the Assembly has within it the germ of a parliament, because it voices the general opinion and wishes of nearly 2,000,000 people. Not only will this new organization provide for the Protectorate a most valuable education in the higher arts of government, but it should be an effective link between local self-governing authorities and the Central Government.

In the Gambia, in March 1944, the first Joint Conference of Chiefs representing the Protectorate as a whole was held. The Chiefs present were invited to submit a list of suitable candidates to the Governor for nomination to the Legislative Council. On this occasion the Governor announced the appointment of a special Commission to act as a link between the Central Government, the four British Provincial Commissioners who administer the four provinces into which the Protectorate is divided, and the Native Authorities.

The goal of responsible self-government in a colony cannot, of course, be attained overnight. Preparation is required which involves social research, the setting up of improved political and judicial machinery, and the specialized training of native personnel for posts of responsibility, as well as the improvement of social and economic conditions. It is realized that much of this preparation can, in West Africa, be achieved by the development of responsible local self-government which would run parallel to, and in close alliance with, the Central Government schemes of social and economic development. It should be a process which is acceptable and satisfying to the people concerned and which would include the nurturing of existing rule under chiefs and the extension, where required, of municipal administration. Local self-government is no new venture in these countries. It has been known since the most primitive times, and its early varieties (patriarchal, tribal and kingship) can still be seen there; for instance the rule of the House Father is still to be found in the isolated compounds of the Gold Coast Northern Territories, the Sierra Leone hinterland, and the Gambia Protectorate; the chiefs' rule of villages can be seen in all the more populous areas of the Gold Coast and Nigeria; and kingship rule is clearly demonstrated in Ashanti and the Emirates of Northern Nigeria.

A description of the fostering of local Native Authority administration of the people through Indirect Rule has been described in Chapter Four of this book, and Lord Hailey in "An African Survey" (Chapter IX, Section XX) shows how, in areas of non-tribal populations, township and municipality rule was encouraged. Such places as Bathurst in the Gambia, Freetown in Sierra Leone, Accra and Kumasi in the Gold Coast, and Lagos, Calabar, Ibadan, and Kano in Nigeria are examples of non-tribal areas. In the earlier days of colonization under British rule the ideal of law and order was gradually accepted by the chiefs. To-day both Native Authorities and Municipal Authorities are being urged to accept an enlargement of that concept to include responsibility for the social and economic development of their localities. They are being asked to finance their own schemes from treasury funds and recruit their own labour from local sources, but at the same time they are being offered some initial help in the form of money granted under the Colonial Development and Welfare Act and also technical advice from specially appointed Development Officers. Details of this are given in local bulletins and Governmental Development Programmes, and special mention was made of Development Officers by the Colonial Office in "Post-War Opportunities in the Colonial Service" (June 1945).

The new vision of local self-government encompasses increased care and modern guidance for the people. It may be said that the ideal before each Native and Municipal Authority is, primarily, to safeguard the individual as well as the family and tribe, and to encourage the private enterprise of both employer and employed, while at the same time dovetailing local effort into the large-scale development schemes of the Central Government. This will entail a local endeavour to promote public education (juvenile, adolescent and adult), public health (personal and civic), public welfare (social and economic), and improved production, marketing, and transport, within the political and judicial framework already existing, so that the people may learn modern citizenship and in addition be afforded the facilities for its practice.

The growth of responsible local self-government ensures a practical and comprehensive training for potential candidates for higher political administration posts on a much bigger scale than has been hitherto possible, but it is a means to the political education of the native people on a sound practical basis, democratic in trend and with self-government in each colony as its goal. To some extent research, improved political and judicial machinery, and the training of Africans have always been a part of Political Administration in West Africa, but with the proposed general development of the territories, aided financially under the Colonial Development and Welfare Act, an organized movement towards responsible local and eventual central self-government can be launched. In fact, it appears to be materializing as part of the general Mass or Fundamental Education Scheme, the planning and implementation of which is now being evolved in the four West African territories.

Economic and Social Development

It is fully realized to-day that the need for economic and social development of backward countries is urgent. The gradual growth of the pre-war years must be speeded up. With this in mind the four Governors of West Africa, with the help of Development Advisers and Development Councils, have formulated full-scale plans of development for each of their four territories.

In Nigeria (Sessional Paper No. 24 of 1945) it is planned to spend, over a ten-year period, £55,000,000, of which £23,000,000 will be allocated from the Colonial Development and Welfare Vote and the remainder found from

Nigerian loans and revenue. A full programme covers every field of activity—Water Supplies, Health, Education, Communications, Electrical Undertakings, Town and Country Planning, Agricultural, Veterinary, Forestry and Fishery Services, Mineral Development, Social Welfare. A Department of Commerce and Industry has been set up and a Local Development Board established.

In Sierra Leone the amount estimated for development is £5,256,575 over a period of ten years. Part of this amount will be raised in loans for local investment and the rest granted under the Colonial Development and Welfare Act. The development programme is designed to be of mutual benefit both to the Colony and the Protectorate. It falls into three main parts: the improvement of communications, the full exploitation of the natural resources of the country, and the expansion of welfare services. The first three years, 1946-48 inclusive, are to be regarded as years of preparation, that is, a period in which detailed plans and designs will be made, and in which the main task will be to press on vigorously with certain key schemes.

In the Gold Coast a general plan of development is in preparation. To the £3,500,000 allocated from the Colonial Development and Welfare Vote, it is proposed to add £4,000,000 raised by loans, as well as surplus balances from revenue, estimated at perhaps £5,000,000. The expenditure of a total of some £12,000,000 from these sources on welfare and development objectives is being worked out, in particular on educational and health services.

In the Gambia similar schemes of development have been planned and work regarding them is going on.

In all four territories action has been held up by lack of manpower. Under Colonial Office directions extra European staff in the form of Development Officers is now being made available. (See Post War Opportunities in the Colonial Service [1945].) These appointments are usually for technical officers and, owing to the nature of the work required, which is largely demonstrating skills to the people generally and teaching skills to picked Africans, the appointments are temporary.

In the Gold Coast and Sierra Leone special Social Welfare Departments have been set up, but in Nigeria social welfare is considered the responsibility of the Provincial Administration, assisted by such advisers and co-ordinating officers as may prove necessary. In this territory it is felt that practically all the development schemes have a social welfare bearing and it is impossible to regard welfare as a separate, self-contained subject.

It will be seen, therefore, that each territory in British West Africa is working to its own pattern within the larger plans devised for the whole.

Africa Yesterday: One Ruler's Burden

Africa Yesterday:
One Ruler's Burden

IT IS A GREAT PITY that some of our political theorists can't enjoy a short spell as dictators. Nothing is more instructive in the problems of actual government. I have always thought myself lucky to have had such a spell when I was sent, in 1917, to take over Borgu, a remote district of the British colony of Nigeria which at that time had not even a telegraph office. Letters took anything from a week to ten days, according to the state of the Niger and the morale of its ferrymen, for an answer.

I was told, therefore, by my Provincial Resident, Hamilton Brown, that I should have to act on my own in any crisis, and rely on him to back me up.

This was not an idle or conventional promise. Some months earlier there had been a rebellion in Borgu. The people had risen, murdered sixty members of their own native administration, and then rushed off to find some British magistrate and state their case.

A friend of mine, Diggle, was sent down to look into it. He found plenty of reason for grievance: extortion, stealing of women, blackmail, corrupt judgments. He turned out the worst offenders and handed over a peaceful country to me. But he warned me to keep my eyes open. "You can't get rid of corruption in these parts; you can only hope to stop it from going on the bust."

Then he went off on leave and left me with my first independent civil command, in a country of about twelve thousand square miles. My staff consisted of one clerk who could not spell (we had no typewriter); twelve police with single-shot carbines and ten rounds apiece; a Political Agent —a Hausa Negro who spoke the local languages and was supposed to be an expert on local affairs; and a couple of office messengers to sun themselves on the court veranda.

Government has been called a relationship. This is a misleading half-truth. The essence of government, the nub, is rule. That is the hard part. But it is true that to rule efficiently, a relationship has to be formed: one of confidence, or fear, or hope, often all three. And in forming such a relationship the first need is knowledge. My relationship with Hamilton

Brown was one of mutual confidence based on knowledge of each other. Any other would have made my job in Borgu impossible. But in the other direction I had neither knowledge nor confidence.

William the Conqueror understood very well what he needed, when he ordered the Domesday Book compiled. It gave him the foundations for his system. But I am pretty sure that it gave him no more. He had to rely for the really important question (not what things people have in their possession, but what those people are doing with them) on what he was told from day to day, on opinion, on reports from spies, on his own guesswork and knowledge of human nature. I am sure, too, that the success of his rule was not due so much to his system as to some method by which he did get reliable information about the working of the system, and the men who worked it. Systems, ultimately, are men.

My first immediate discovery, quite unexpected in its force, was that I could not trust anybody or anything—that is, any appearance. All information was vague, contradictory, palpably false (like the news of a ship-load of Negro nationalists just arrived fom the United States to drive us British into the sea), or trivial. The Wazir (Vizier) to the Emir came up every day on his official duty to give me the news and consult upon it, but the Political Agent had different news; each implied, deviously but resolutely, that the other was a liar. Each gave broad hints of the other's plots to benefit himself at the expense of a "new judge"—that is, myself.

My secret-service men, a few ragamuffins recruited by the Political Agent, either gave wild reports like that of the Negro invasion from America or told me solemnly that some chief had cursed me, which I could guess for myself and which did not matter. (As a dictator I could not pick my own men. Every action of a dictator is watched and known immediately, and if I had chosen an informer he would have been corrupted or beaten up within the same day.)

No one not placed in such a position can fully realize the sense of blindness and distrust which took possession of me in those first months of solitude in Borgu. I say "took possession" because it was at once like a foreign invader seizing on my mind, and a sort of demon. I would wake up at night and feel as if the dark itself were an immense black brain, meditating, behind its thick featureless countenance, some deep plan for a new and still more surprising outbreak.

I could not forget that the last rising had been caused by nothing but the failure of the district officer, in exactly my own position, to know what was going on under his very nose—and that officer had had much more experience than I, and besides had done nothing but his duty. It was the rule then in the Nigerian service, and has always been one of the guiding principles of British colonial policy, to preserve local law and custom as far as possible, and to do nothing that might break the continuity of the local government. Tribal chiefs and tribal councils were to be maintained, and progress made by educating chiefs, by improving their administrative machine, and by a general development of trade, roads, and public services, which (as experience shows) by itself modifies the whole situation and can (if that end is kept in view) quite quickly build up a class capable of some share in the government, on the first elementary representative committees.

But the first principle was absolute: Do not break the continuity. Do not attempt to force a constitution on the people. However good it may seem, however suitable to the place and time (and this is granting a lot), it will be hated and sabotaged. So it will serve only as a bar to all constitutional development.

My predecessor (let's call him Smythe) had done no wrong in supporting the Emir who provoked the rising. He was, I learned, not only astonished but aggrieved when, having been sent on leave in a hurry with acute fever, he heard in England that his people, of whom he was so fond, had burst into revolution as soon as they were left to themselves. He felt that he had been badly treated by fate. I dare say every dictator feels the same in the same case. And in fact Smythe's only fault had been trustfulness and ignorance. He had simply failed to know in time how badly the native administration had been behaving and had failed to use his powers to keep the Emir in order. A political officer, though he must keep in the background, has great power over a chief. He can always warn him, either through his Wazir or at a private interview, that if he does not behave himself he will be reported to the governor or fined, or even deposed in favor of some other member of the dynasty. On the other hand, a good chief can be rewarded with a raise in pay or some special honor.

Smythe thought that he had a good Emir, a really progressive man. And so, I believe, he had. The Emir was a clever fellow who supported all Smythe's favorite schemes. He perceived that they were actually to his advantage. They cost money, and the more money there was floating about, the more he could steal. In fact, it is just the clever, the active,

the really valuable chief who can be most dangerous. How was I to discover that the new Emir, a very distinguished and reserved old gentleman, who had been a slave raider in his time (he had been passed over
for the succession partly because of his conservative background and was
now brought in as a popular choice to restore public confidence), was
not another more sedate and conservative crook?

I remembered the casual remark of an old official that in Africa, even
an honest and loyal subordinate never told all the truth to a district officer, because he never knew what use would be made of it.

I realized that the man in absolute power is not only dangerous to all
his subjects; he is also a mystery to them. And this, I think now, is true
of all men in power. Even the foreman of a labor gang or a senior office
clerk is, I suspect, so far as he has power, an uncertain quality to those
below. That is to say, the uncertain element in all human relations becomes, in power relations, a source of mistrust. All subordinates say to
themselves, "I'll tell the boss no more than I need to—for no one knows
what he'll do with it." Everyone in authority has seen in the face of the
most trusted subordinate that peculiar look of discretion which means
"How much must I give away—how little will satisfy him?" And the
greater the power, the more the discretion that surrounds it, even in the
stooge, who seems to be within the iron curtain but in fact chooses his
words so cunningly.

The way I escaped, simply by good luck, from this invisible jail that
shuts off every dictator from the sense and sound of the actual world was
still more illuminating. And old friend, my first commanding officer,
meeting me by chance on trek and hearing of my difficulty, said that for
his part he had found only one method of getting some independent
news. He slept always as far as possible from his guard and staff, in a
shelter or, during the dry season, alone in the bush. "Your people will
never come out into the bush at night, unless they have to—they are
much too afraid of ghosts, lions, hyenas, and so on. And as for you, no
lion, however hungry, will ever attack a mosquito net. Lions simply don't
understand such things."

I took this advice, put my bed under a tree about thirty yards from
camp, and after some disappointing weeks suddenly began to have results. I was waked up about three one morning by a voice whispering
out of the dark, an urgent voice full of bitterness. I don't remember what

it said, whether a trivial complaint (one man talked half the night about a deer into which, he claimed, he had shot the first arrow and of which he had been cheated of the share due to the first arrow) or one of the really important ones, such as the revelation (by an aggrieved petty trader) that a certain chief had closed up fifty miles of the international frontier with Dahomey. Or more important still that my Political Agent was in league with this same chief, to get him special privileges.

But I did in fact, perhaps on a dozen occasions in any one year, get news. Much of it, of course, was false; all of it needed careful checking. But what was valuable was of a sort that I could not have gotten by any other method; and all of it was sufficiently important to some native to make him take the risk of hostile ghosts, as well as the ordinary terrors surrounding a dictator.

You may think that this plan, really that of the anonymous letter, should be beneath the dignity of government. I can only say that a man with real responsibility for other people's lives and happiness has no scruples about dignity. And I knew no other way to get the same results. I saw too that the Lion's Mouth of Venice, via which the Doges received anonymous denunciations, was not (as the books say) the wicked device of despots to keep their people in terror; it was an essential organ of their government, to preserve their own peace of mind. Of course it was an instrument of terror also. But that is an unavoidable factor in the whole form of government, in dictatorship itself. Dictators are always alarming.

This, then, was the first discovery of my dictatorship, that even the most elementary truths were difficult to come by. The second was that they suffer a special kind of distortion. Subordinates to any absolute power have a special irresponsibility. Over and over again intelligent men—subchiefs, headmen in charge of road or bridge construction—broke out in the stupidest fashion. They suddenly went on the spree, or having done half a job in a careful and responsible manner, abandoned or botched the rest. One of them, with a long and good record, a steady family man, suddenly robbed the pay account in so careless a way that he was at once detected and brought up for trial. I asked him what had persuaded him to such a folly, and his only explanation was that gesture, a slight horizontal movement of the hand to and fro, which means, to the Moslem, "As Allah wills," otherwise "Anything can happen."

What I think is that the fear and uncertainty that pervade every such régime, as with an atmosphere, breed fatalism. A soldier recognizes the same thing in himself during war service. You have the paradox that men in daily fear of their lives are therefor more reckless than those in safety, and that subordinates under a police state, who can be jailed or shot for a very small fault, are therefor more open to sudden corruption. The enormous corruption of the Nazis and Fascists should not amaze us, and it is easy to understand why the Communists need such frequent purges.

But a still more subtle cause of the treachery infecting every relation in absolute government is the irresistible desire, even among its loyal supporters, to keep things sweet. No one ever gives his immediate boss bad news in its bare form. I can't say how many times I was taken in by reports that seemed, even to my suspicious dictator's mind, clear and exhaustive, but proved to have left out the vital point. The most exasperating and comical was the detailed news of "damage" to a bridge that, when I arrived two days later, was found to have disappeared totally. It was too late to take another road. I had to swim the river, in flood among rocks, and the old chief whom I had brought with me had to be left behind, at the risk of wasting a long, careful negotiation, in which he was to have been the peacemaker, with certain troublesome villages about district boundaries.

I cannot be surprised that Adolf Hitler, toward the end, was fighting battles with armies that had long since ceased to exist.

This disease of absolute government extends in a lesser degree throughout all governmental hierarchies. There is a fatalism in the old bureaucrat that comes not so much from fear as the thought: "This damned setup is so unpredictable anyhow that no one knows what it will do next," and so does not trouble too much about details that probably will be misunderstood or be lost in some pigeonhole. And again there is the tendency to keeps things sweet.

I don't know the real basic reason for the Labour Government's groundnuts disaster in East Africa, but plainly it arose in the first place from bad information. I have watched at least one process by which information is regularly falsified, in what we might call the chain report. I used to report twice a year on the economic position in Borgu, suggesting possible developments. I would write something like this: "The export of shea butter would be greatly increased by simple improvements at

the river port of Leaba, such as a market building. The chief expense
would be on the Leaba Road, which for over forty miles has neither any
water nor any settlement. At least two villages with wells would be needed, and there are no local welldiggers. I could find hunters ready to settle
if wells were provided and three years' tax exemption were offered. Estimate for such a road, complete, with wells and huts for ten families, can
be put at x pounds."

In the provincial report for the half year, this would read: "The district officer at Borgu reports that a new river port and market at Leaba
would greatly increase the export of shea butter. A new road would be
required from Leaba to the capital." That is to say, the qualifications
would have been left out to save space and give an encouraging effect. If
the suggestion ever reached the Secretary of State for the Colonies, it
would be in this form: "A general development of ports on the Niger
promises excellent and immediate returns. This could be achieved with
local labor." "Local labor" to the Secretary of State in London would
mean merely African labor.

The report writer has to condense. But in the act, he tends, unless he
is careful, to leave out more of the drawbacks than the advantages. Otherwise, he runs the risk that some energetic politician on the lookout for
positive opportunities will think him a knockover, a Blimp, a stick-in-the-
mud, even a secret enemy.

Now I realize why dictators, and even democratic heads of government
—Wilson, Chamberlain, Roosevelt, Churchill—tend to have confidential
advisers, favorites, to send on private missions of inquiry, and to lean
heavily on them for information and advice. This, of course, only shifts
some power to the favorite, and surrounds him also with walls and distrust. Power does not so much corrupt the ruler as the whole world in
which he is compelled to work. It becomes for him, the moment he
reaches power, a kind of Castle of Otranto, full of uncertain noises and
vague threats, in which the very servants edge away from him as if he
had the evil eye. And his friends become favorites, and therefore his
closest friends can become his most dangerous enemies. For they, above
all, have power, the power to deceive.

Christmas in Africa

Christmas in Africa

CHRISTMAS IN West Africa comes in the dry season, the time for feasts. The ground is too hard for working—the harvest has long been gathered, and yet there are still corn and yams in store. The time of scarcity, in our summer, when old stocks are low, and the new crops are not yet ripe, when women starve themselves to keep their men fit for work, is still months away. There is nothing for the farmer to do but hunt, gossip and dance. Whole villages go hunting together with bows and spears and sometimes a few old muzzle-loading guns; the dry grass, six or eight feet high, is set on fire to drive the game and there is plenty of meat for the feast. Beer, often very strong beer, is brewed from millet or corn and so there is plenty to drink—the celebration will last all night. Christmas with the African as with us is a time of family rejoicing, but the family is a whole village, even the whole tribe. For a primitive African tribe is still essentially a family to its own idea of itself and local feeling—and the hunters' feast is a time when men and women whose lives are full of hard work take a return for it.

It was supposed to be a matter of sympathy when I, already overdue for leave, had to spend Christmas in the remote bush. But now I am glad of that unique experience. A whole week before Christmas Day my sergeant of police came to salute me "for the holiday." I gave him a sheep and beer money and leave to entertain friends in the police lines, the *"bariki"* about fifty yards behind my bungalow.

Just after sundown on Christmas Day, I took my bath in my top story as a file of women in their bold flowered prints, and in separate groups their men in their best but still dusky white gowns, streamed past the corner of the office below with that continuous babel of African talk and laughter which always seems more gay than any other in the world —and with a special kind of gaiety. A children's treat is excited, noisy, but it has not the same tone of purpose. Children do not know so well when or how they are going to celebrate, to invoke a spirit. That is to say, in spite of common talk, Africans are not children, they are shrewd and hard-working peasantry with the natural feelings and limitations of an illiterate peasantry wherever you find it. The only element of truth in the comparison is that both children and illiterates are highly dependent. That is why the ruler in Africa, white or black, is, so to speak, elected by the people themselves to a father's place, and often addressed as a father.

A friend of mine, district officer to a cannibal tribe on the Naraguta plateau, used to resent this title. He was a man of small sentiment, fonder of sport than files, and indifferent to power. He would answer the greeting of "our father" with a snort and the question, "Who have you been eating now?" He was not going to be got round by flattery.

But he kept a pack of hounds for his pagans, or, as he called them, his blackguards, and he would hold a special meet on every important festival, especially at Christmas. They would go, or some of them would go, to a mission service and then join the hunt, led by my friend in beautiful boots and a velvet cap. And the solemn dignity of this appearance was not at all impaired when he opened, as the sun grew hot, an immense carriage umbrella, in alternate red and white stripes, labeled on the white sections in red letters eight inches long, STOLEN FROM J. FINCH. A state umbrella in Nigeria is the mark of a king. Finch was the master of those cannibals and I've no doubt of the reason—both he and they loved hunting and he made the hunt for them. He stood no nonsense in the field. He would shout at some pagan stuck to his bareback pony by mere dirt, "How dare you ride over my hounds, sir? Do you want me to take them home?"

The very threat was worse to that man than seven years' imprisonment. His life would have been in danger if Jimmy had indeed taken his hounds—that is, his collection of pie-dogs, outcast mongrels, rescued from some pagan cooking pot—back to the kennel.

Not that Jimmy ever did send his beloved pagans to gaol—he did not need to. His prestige was too great, his mere indignation too much dreaded. It was under that immense prestige, the discipline of the Master of Fox Hounds, that stray tin prospectors were reasonably safe from murder, and missionaries could preach, and even the telegraph wire (much valued for bangles, anklets, etc.; every good husband was expected to provide it) was left uninterrupted for as much as three months at a time.

Finch's rule, of course, was paternalism, now so much decried. But paternal rule where it is still possible, that is, among primitive tribesmen, has two great advantages. It is flexible and its reasons can be explained. The police state with its cruelty, its indifference to the individual, bureaucratic democracy with its complications and its bylaws, defeat and discourage simple people till they rebel or simply lose the wish to live. What they want is an actual ruler to whom they can state their special case. Finch did not need to impose a liquor law. If there was too much drinking anywhere, he could say "No more hunting" and explain his displeasure. I did not need a special act to let my people in Borgu drink all night or to declare them for that night a family party and the stars their family roof—the sergeant major had leave to celebrate and that was enough.

And I on my side knew that even if regulations had forbidden such a feast in barracks, it was time to set them aside. For the mood of the people and the police (and no one can follow such moods unless he is on the spot and close to the people) was more than usually restless. They needed a break. Drums had been bursting out into exclamations for a week past, and on Christmas Day they were warming up in the town from earliest morning. There were also at least three amateurs in the barracks. Eight were playing when, half an hour after the first arrivals, the dance began in earnest. Scores of hard feet in rhythm made a sound that came to me on the other side of the house, the quiet dark side, like the steam that used to jet out of my toy engine as it worked up power—the very noise of mechanic passion.

It made the quietness still more sensible when, dressed formally in clean pajamas and mosquito boots, I sat down to dinner. I was alone in that station, Kaiama of Borgu, and I had been alone there for nearly a year. I was beginning to think and even to dream native, and in consequence, I suppose, I had a deeper sense of Europe. I read the English classics; I was, for the first time in my life, punctilious, tidy; I kept up all the ceremonies of parade, drill, and courtroom. When I sat in court, for an important case, I put on uniform, at least down to the waist (what I wore beneath the table fell, I considered, into my private domain), and I dined by candlelight.

My dinner that year consisted of the same meal that I ate at least ten times a week—soup from the tin and roast chicken with sweet potatoes. But I had pudding and I opened a bottle of champagne, brought for the celebration.

My mail had not arrived—mails to Borgu were extremely erratic and there was no wire to ask what had happened to the runner. Probably he had stopped somewhere in his five-day journey to enjoy a Christmas party.

Champagne is a wine that goes with the mood—but enlightens it. It makes a man alone more keenly aware of his aloneness, but as a vantage ground instead of an exile. As I found myself ready to enjoy the mere expectation of letters, so I began, like any of my police outside, to be glad of idleness in which to follow the music.

By this time the drumming had reached a high point of virtuosity. The symphony was so complex that one had to listen with the closest attention, as to Beethoven, only to follow the rhythms.

And they were strange rhythms, of a furious ecstasy of exhortation as well as triumph—two drums especially, in the middle register, would grumble and argue together like a couple of old warriors behind the fire, then suddenly break out in shouts of menace and warning, defying some enemy of the feast, some ghost in the dark. One could understand the note of excited challenge in Borgu, a solitary and desolate land where the very night seems to have a special quality of threat. At my first coming, I had hated it. I had left an Emirate of the North with its desert traders, its pageants of horsemen, and got in exchange this twelve thousand miles of waste. I did not mind the solitude, but I felt deprived, I had not even a wire; there was no news of the real world outside this limbo.

Now all that feeling had changed. I saw how lucky I was in an exile that made me my own master. Just because Borgu was remote and cut off, just because I had no wire, I had been given free leave to make quick decisions, in fact to do what I liked. And there was always interesting and practical work at hand, mapping, road making, bridge building, the founding of markets and towns, the training of native staff; work I preferred very much to the endless minute writing and form filling of a big station in a rich province. Besides, when most of my colleagues were living in mud huts, I had a bungalow on a hill, a house of two storys, with a broad balcony all around it.

True, it was falling into ruin, and in one of my two upper rooms most of the floor was hole. But this too was an advantage. I could see from my bath right down into the office and know at once what I was in for that morning: a visit from old chiefs anxious to get up a war on the French frontier, hunters quarreling about the correct division of a deer, one of my road gangs complaining of evil spirits who turned the edge of their tools, or a witch murder with about twenty-five witnesses, all convinced of the existence of witches and the expediency of killing them.

Another advantage of my tall house on its hill was that it gave me command from my balcony of a long stretch of that same desolate Borgu bush which had once so disgusted me. For that very desolation, the want of all romantic airs, had now become its charm.

Borgu is an ancient land whose antiquity stands over it as history broods over Europe. But in Borgu the history is not of mankind but of primeval nature, of beasts and trees in their eternal battle for life, and I had discovered the special fascination of such a scene.

And now I was not surprised by this attraction—I had asked myself why the traveler likes to find even a single valley that no one has ever seen before, what thrill he receives from being first at the Pole, a bare ice field like any other ice field. Certainly it is not the pleasure of discovery.

There is nothing to be discovered in most of the places "explored" by explorers. And well they know it. The spell is quite different. It is to look on something that no human eye has even seen before and above all on a piece of nature that has never submitted to man. And looking now outwards, over the bush stretching in the bright steel starlight up to the sky, a lazy ocean of blue-black waves, I felt again that savage indifference which was at once its attraction and its estrangement.

It was true that the people in common greeting called it my land and themselves my people, but it was only as Jimmy's cannibals saluted him as their father and their mother; I was as far from them in time as from the bush in spirit. And yet as the difference between the children and the parents brings them together, as the greater difference between the grandparents and the grandchildren gives them, often, a more immediate sympathy, so I felt joined to the unseen dancers in the barrack yard.

I was like a man in a tower. He is so high that he is cut off from the people below, he can't understand what they are saying to each other, he can barely guess at what they are thinking by their gestures and the sound of their cries.

But as he climbs, the horizon lifts about him—the higher he goes, the further it sinks him down into that vast ring of the savage earth, more foreign to him than any creature. I was cut off from the dancers by a thousand years. But now, surrounded by the untamed bush, we were brought together in a common solitude which was a fellowship—the community of travelers in time. And their dance, their drums expressed for me, as well as themselves, the needs as well as the power, the tension and the exultations of humanity, everlastingly besieged by ghosts and devils.

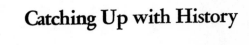

Catching Up with History

Catching Up with History

[A review of *Black Power*, by Richard Wright]

THIS IS THE REPORT of a British colony in West Africa, the Gold Coast, where Britain has lately appointed a Negro Prime Minister, Nkrumah, with large powers. As reporting, it is a first-class job and gives the best picture I've seen of an extraordinary situation.

The culture of Negro Africa is Stone Age. Nine-tenths of the people belong in mind to at least five thousand years back. And the mind, the education of a people, is what finally you have to reckon with in politics. This culture, this mind, has now been pitched into the twentieth century by no fault of Africa, or of Britain. It is the consequence simply of the speed-up of history by two great wars and the enormous technical and scientific progress of the last thirty years. Wireless alone, apart from modern economics, makes it impossible to isolate any culture from external shock, from new exciting ideas, and from the demagogue. In a series of brilliant scenes Wright shows the effects, social and political, of this violent clash.

He describes traders, black and white, each as naive as the other, and as confused by a situation which is completely new and dangerous but inevitable: juju chiefs and their households, bound still by the magic rites of the blood in service and in sacrifice; funerals where the corpse is represented in the coffin only by a cutting from nails and hair, to deceive envious spirits, the actual body being hidden in some secret place.

He describes political meetings where each family head brings his dependents, who at word of command cheer, clap, and shout for freedom. He can tell a story against himself. At a great meeting summoned by Nkrumah, he addresses the crowd on the responsibility of the Gold Coast Africans as pioneers in the fight for African freedom. The local reporters ask him for the text of his speech. He submits it to Nkrumah for approval. The Prime Minister glances over it and then stuffs it into Wright's coat pocket. The speech is censored.

Wright not only reports against himself; he writes so honestly, so directly as he feels, that he gives the material for another book contradicting his own arguments. He tells us that the chiefs are all scoundrels but also that there is more genuine religion in tribal paganism than in the bourgeois Christian church; that Africa is in desperate need of education but Britain has been wrong in educating Africans too well. We read that Britain has shattered tribal culture and also that tribal life is breaking up because the people find it a bore and rush to the towns.

This latter is, of course, the significant fact. Tribal life is inconceivably narrow and boring—a combination of totalitarian government and authoritarian church in their most oppressive forms, a system that has succeeded with the help of the climate in preventing almost all progress. But humanity cannot stand boredom. Its imagination revolts instinctively and incessantly against the blimp. It may worship and tremble, but give it the smallest chance to escape and it will fly. So the tribes break up as soon as any paramount power establishes peace, stops slave raiding, and gives protection to the individual. The consequence is an immense growth in the towns—especially any town with industry, cinemas, shops—and enormous slums, more difficult to control even than the Negro districts of Chicago or New York. I say slums, but they are slums only to the European mind; to the African escaped from the tribe they are dwelling places full of delights, above all of freedom.

Governments in Africa, whatever they are, have the choice between seeing the tribes break, the slums grow, or bringing in legislation to control the movements of the people. And repression in Africa, especially in Africa's present explosive mood, can very easily produce shooting, which means more repression. How are you going to maintain the tribe by police action? How are you going to convey tribesmen with a Stone Age mind through developments that in Europe took thousands of years, fast enough to catch up with history?

When I joined the African service forty years ago, I was instructed that our aim was to prepare Africans for self-government by the development of their own native institutions—that is, we were to attempt to give Africa the social history of all civilized nations but to speed up the process as much as possible, without destroying our means. This limitation was highly practical. I found my local judge taking bribes. But I did not sack him. I had been instructed that almost all African judges took presents; the question was whether he gave fair judgments. Also whether I could find a better judge, for men of the necessary education were very scarce.

So too among primitive pagans chiefs were kept in power but given councilors who spoke for various sections of the people—the first step toward popular representation.

This plan for West Africa brought about smooth and rapid progress: that is to say, it gave the primitive administration we found as much development in forty years as primitive Europe accomplished in a couple of centuries. Of course we had the advantage over the Dark Ages of modern techniques, a trained staff, and the telegraph.

But then there was the war, immense economic disturbance, slumps— the same political turmoil that fell upon the whole world, India, China, South America.

Nkrumah, on the Gold Coast, demands, of course, complete independence, but he has no other choice. As a nationalist and a demagogue he is obliged to do so or some other demagogue would overbid him.

Democracy, of course, is impossible in any state where 90 per cent of the people are illiterate. It exists only in literate and industrialized nations with a powerful middle class and organized unions capable of standing up to central government. All other states are dictatorships more or less disguised. Nkrumah will have to be a dictator whether he likes it or not, and the question is whether he has the kind of genius which Ataturk brought to a much less difficult problem in Turkey, with a far greater educated class to help him.

Wright himself vividly pictures this difficulty, as he does all the others which face an African national government—except one, the rising population. Yet this by itself can smash all efforts, however well organized, to raise standards of living and education.

Population in Africa is increasing fast, and the country as a whole is poor in soil, difficult in climate, full of deserts. The battle for land is already acute. Mau Mau is one consequence, and the elements of Mau Mau are present everywhere, in the breaking tribe, and in the shape of the primitive mind. For the mind is still the mind of the tribal mass and will be so long after the tribal sanctions which controlled its repressed passions and neurotic panics are no more.

Wright's own answers to these political conundrums are offered to Nkrumah in an open letter. He urges him to sacrifice a generation, and not be afraid of *militarism*, or *regimentation*.

The author has rejected the party, but his political thinking still belongs to communism. He imagines that violence, cruelty, injustice, and some clever lying can achieve a new civilization. But this is false. They can only produce new forms of oppression, new totalitarian states, which, because they are founded on oppression, face exactly the same difficulties as the ones they replace. If they do not educate, if they prevent the entrance of new ideas, new techniques, they stagnate and are finally destroyed by some outer force. If they educate, organize, develop, they generate large classes of rebels, more or less secret, who sooner or later will destroy them from within. Russia in the years since 1917 has had four or five internal revolutions, executed dozens of rebel leaders, purged thousands of their followers. And it is probably more unstable now, as a regime, than at any time before.

There are no easy answers in politics, especially nowadays. We are still groping our way, and need, above all, the facts of the new situation, facts all the harder to get because of universal propaganda, the practice learned from Communist and Fascist alike, of the big lie. That is why books like this of Wright's are so valuable—so far, that is, as they give facts, and so far as the facts can be distinguished from the bias. Wright is so honest a reporter, so vivid a writer, that this is easily done in the course of reading.

It would be a public service if he could give us a similar report on Liberia, where a Negro government has been in full independent power for more than a century.

INDEX

Abba (place): riots in, 45

Abolition of the Slave Trade, Committee for: success of, 156

Abyssinia: slavery in, 16; races in, 48; James Bruce in, 163

Accra (fort): mention of, 177; railway built to, 179; self-government in, 198

administration, local: and general staff, 83, 85; delegation of executive powers to, 83–84; duties of, 84; virtues of, 84; and small industry, 114; of law, 183

administrators, government: accomplishments of, 19

Africa, British East. SEE Kenya

—, East: races in, 48

—, French West: French colonial policy in, 17; compulsory co-operatives in, 117–118

—, German East. SEE Tanganyika

—, Southwest: occupation of, by Germany, 168

—, West: Cary in, ix, 203–209, 213–217; British ignorance of, ix–x; need for general development in, x, 196; co-operatives in, 123–124; early traders at, 141; trade on coast of, 144; explorers of, 146; neglect of, 153; nature of, 153–154, 177–178; causes for acquisition of, 162; geography of, 177–178; population of, 177–178; exports from, 177–178; economic development in, 193, 194; progress in, 196

African Company: as chartered company, 147; destruction of, 147

Africans. SEE natives; negroes

African Witch, The: by Joyce Cary, ix; theme of, xi; on exploitation of natives, xiii

"Africa Yesterday": publication history of, xii

Agent, Political. SEE Musa (Cary's political agent)

agricultural program: native assistants in, 76, 77; plan for, 77

agriculture: 76, 77; importance of, 18, 186; mechanization in, 28, 70–72; and degeneration of land, 29; nature of, 68–69

Agwarra (tribe): 44

airplane: effects of, 46

Aissa Saved: by Joyce Cary, ix

Algeria: French colonial policy in, 17; agriculture in, 18

America: first slaves taken to, 148

American Revolution: negroes in, 157

American Visitor, The: by Joyce Cary, ix

Anamabu (fort): 177

anarchists: and abolition of slavery, 156; attacks of, against Maclean, 160; influence of, 128–129

animal husbandry: under British colonial policy, 179. SEE ALSO agriculture

Arabs: slave trade by, 16, 155; in Africa, 46; health of, 74

army: recruits for, 73

Ashanti (place): securing of, by Britain, 172; French claim to, 172; mention of, 173; exports from, 177; geography of, 177; population of, 177; Indirect Rule in, 189; self-government in, 196, 198

Ashanti empire: war of, with Fanti tribes, 159; and killing of Sir Charles McCarthy, 159; British campaigns against, 159–160, 165–166, 167; claim of, on Elmina, 166

Asia: adaptation to development in, 71

Assiento Company. SEE Royal Company

Association for the Exploration of Africa: formation of, 163; explorers sent by, 163–164

Ataturk (Kemal Ataturk): 223

Austrian empire: fall of, 134

authorities, municipal: duties of, 198–199

—, native: duties of, 198–199

Catalog

If you are interested in a list of fine Paperback
books, covering a wide range of subjects
and interests, send your name and address,
requesting your free catalog, to:

McGraw-Hill Paperbacks
330 West 42nd Street
New York, New York 10036